The Case Against
Psychotherapy Registration

Richard Mowbray is a practitioner of Primal Integration, a form of human potential work, and has been in group and individual practice for the last 16 years. He is co-director, with Juliana Brown, of the Primal Integration Programme in London and has been a member of the Open Centre, one of the UK's longest established growth centres, since 1979.

The Case Against
Psychotherapy Registration

A Conservation Issue for
the Human Potential Movement

Richard Mowbray

Trans Marginal Press

First published in 1995 by
Trans Marginal Press
36 Womersley Road
Crouch End
London N8 9AN
England
United Kingdom

Cover illustration by Juliana Brown
Cover design by Tony Pinchuck
Typeset by Trans Marginal Press
Printed on recycled paper by Calvert's Press Workers' Co-operative
London E2

British Library Cataloguing in Publication Data
A catalogue record for this book is available from the British Library

Bookshops, file under: Psychotherapy/psychology/counselling
and: Law/political economy/professional regulation
and: Human potential movement/personal growth

ISBN   0-9524270-0-1

This book is dedicated to Bill Swartley who led the way,
Juliana Brown with whom I travel
and my clients, *sine qua non*.

Contents

Section II
Human Potential Work and Psychotherapy - A Suitable Case for Differentiation

Section III
No Treatment Required

Section 1V
Appendices, 'Case' Notes and Bibliography

Preface

This book started life in 1993 as an idea for a paper or booklet intended as an attempt to forestall what I then saw to be a risk of imminent legislative endorsement of UKCP, the presumptuously titled United Kingdom Council for Psychotherapy. Then, as now, my deepest concerns were with the impact this would have upon the human potential movement and its capacity to promote personal and social transformation. An 'inevitable' advance towards statutory control was widely touted at the time and in the face of this prospect, a climate of compliance and passivity, if not support, prevailed amongst practitioners. Apart from a few critical articles, there was little protest, even from the humanistic world.

As I delved into the issue, however, it became apparent that the risk of legislation was in the medium or longer term rather than an immediate prospect and this realization allowed me to reassess, broaden and internationalize the objectives of the project. Moreover, the more I discovered about the issue, the wider its ramifications and the deeper its significance appeared to be.

Consequently, although its imminent arrival had already been announced in some quarters, this project developed something of a life of its own and continued to grow into the more comprehensive study which you now hold. Even as 'vapourware' however, it seemed to have been doing some good by publicizing the fact that there actually *is* a case against psychotherapy registration - a fact that seemed to have escaped the notice of many people.

This project would have come to nought, however, were it not for the shared world-view and endless support and encouragement of Juliana Brown whom I must thank for tireless feedback, painstaking editorial, research and administrative input, and for the splendid cartoon that graces the cover. In many respects this project is as much hers as mine.

I am also very grateful to all those friends, colleagues and clients who have helped the project on its way with encouragement, with information, with feedback, with criticism of the drafts and with other support of various kinds. Particular thanks are due to Silke Ziehl, Kate Wylie, Christine and John Woodruff, Lola and Peter Wilkins, Mike Wibberley, Eric Whitton, Annie Sullivan, Mike Shackleton, Tony Pinchuck, Barbara McCrea, Murray Mahon, Betty Hughes, Guy Gladstone, Sandra Evans, Basiro Davey, Hyone and Tony Criscuolo, Wilma Brown and David Babsky.

I also owe a special debt of thanks to Daniel Hogan for his inspiring study of psychotherapy regulation and for permission to quote portions therefrom.

I am also grateful to all those others whose views on this subject I have referred to herein and to which I hope I have done justice.

I also wish to acknowledge the journal *Self and Society* which - as a "channnel of communication for the human potential movement" - has been one of the few forums where the issues addressed by this book have been actively debated.

Last but not least, my thanks for the VW Beetle of computing - the Tandy 100 (Super Rom equipped), the marvellously simple and distraction-free writing machine with which much of this book was written. It may not be fast but it gets there.

Please note that the following convention regarding emphasis in quotations has been adopted in this book: emphasis in quotations is in *italics* if present in the original and in ***bold italics*** if added by myself.

Introduction

The Emperor's Wardrobe

... a veritable Emperor's wardrobe of nonsense.
(David Wasdell, 1992:5)

During the 1990s, the practice of psychotherapy and counselling has at-
tracted a great deal of adverse publicity. Tales of sexual exploitation, false
memory implantation or other dubious activities have become so common
in the media that one could be forgiven for thinking that this is a very
hazardous activity indeed, perhaps carrying risks comparable to those that
have so often accompanied drug-based approaches to personal problems
whether 'professionally' or 'privately' prescribed.

Alongside this clamour, calls for statutory regulation to curb the 'men-
ace' posed by 'unqualified' psychotherapists and suchlike practitioners
have become more strident in the UK.

In this climate, the United Kingdom Council for Psychotherapy
(UKCP) came into being and has established a voluntary register for which
it seeks statutory endorsement. Other large organizations in the field have
also shown interest in statutory approval for their registers. Psychoanalytic bodies including the British Psycho-Analytical Society have set up
their own register under the aegis of the British Confederation of Psychotherapists (BCP). In conjunction with other counselling organizations, the
British Association of Counselling (BAC) is pursuing a register for counsellors. The British Psychological Society (BPS) has had a register since
summer 1990 which, through the system of Crown privilege, already gives
its members a form of title protection over the term 'Chartered Psychologist'. They also aspire to statutory control of the term 'psychologist'.

So far, the UK government has not been persuaded to introduce legislation to endorse any of these registers. In my opinion government would
be very ill-advised to do so. However, such is the general lack of aware-

1

ness of the arguments against such a move that governmental compliance might eventually be forthcoming. This book is an effort to forestall that situation by raising the level of awareness of the issues involved and presenting the case against such statutory validation.

In 1990, following on from a special issue of *Self and Society* on the subject of psychotherapy registration,[1] my colleague Juliana Brown and I wrote an article for *Self and Society* (see Appendix A) which expressed our misgivings about the proposed formation of a 'profession' of psychotherapy via the registration of psychotherapists as embodied in the United Kingdom Standing Conference on Psychotherapy (UKSCP, the forerunner of UKCP). We were particularly concerned about participation in this process by organizations associated with the human potential movement. We also offered alternative proposals based on empowering the public to make informed choices via 'full disclosure' provisions. We felt that these alternative proposals were more in tune with 'human potential' values than the proposed registration schemes.

The response that we received from some of those spearheading the involvement of humanistic organizations in the process of registration ignored the substance of what we had to say and the alternative proposals we had made and instead seemed to focus on the fact that we had criticisms at all![2] This reaction did not inspire us with any greater confidence that a beneficial process was under way and prompted us to look more closely at what was going on. Our resolve in this regard was strengthened by discovering that the most comprehensive exploration of the whole business of psychotherapy regulation to date had come to conclusions not far removed from our own - including a support for 'full disclosure' provisions. This four volume study undertaken at Harvard by Daniel Hogan (1979) seems to be rarely referred to despite its importance. The arguments presented in this book owe a considerable debt to Hogan's work.

In my view, proposals for the accreditation and registration of psychotherapy are most usefully addressed as part of a political process concerned with power and control and it is this perspective that informs much of this book. Insights as to the unconscious dynamics underlying this process (e.g. Wasdell, 1992) are valuable, but are of limited practical use unless those actively engaged in, or passively going along with, this process are 'ready to receive the interpretation'.

UKCP has acquired a bureaucratic momentum and a 'bandwagon' has begun to roll, driven I think more by fear and fatalism than by wisdom. Practitioners are seeking access to its register out of concern for their future right to practise or for fear that otherwise their stream of referrals may dry up. Training organizations (who form the bulk of UKCP) are climbing aboard to give their courses a 'respectable' status for fear of losing out in the competition for trainees. Would-be trainees are in a situation particularly prone to these fears as they ponder which course to invest in for their future.

In the course of writing this book, it has become clear to me that there is nothing inevitable about these proposed restrictions becoming law. In fact, the beliefs that have inspired all this fearful contemplation are largely unfounded. Neither the UK government nor the European Community/ Union institutions have expressed any intentions of making legislative changes regarding the activities of psychotherapists. Nearly all the pressure for this has come from the psychotherapists themselves or professions with an overlapping sphere of interest, aided and abetted by media 'horror' stories.

The establishment of a statutory register of psychotherapists in the UK would in my view have a significant detrimental impact on the working environment both for 'psychotherapists' and for practitioners in the human potential field. In a climate of fear and false rumours, where what registration advocates *wish* to be the case has become confused with what *is* the case, the establishment of what is merely a voluntary register by UKCP has already had a deadening effect on practice, training and innovation.

It is important to note that the practice of psychotherapy and other forms of related work, although not subject to statutory professional regulation, is not totally unregulated in the UK. Under common law there exists a right to offer such services for payment, and to call yourself a psychotherapist if you wish to do so (or spiritual healer or whatever). This right is however subject to the same laws (of contract, trade description, etc.) that regulate the provision of any other service.

Britain provides a uniquely open milieu which is in my opinion more conducive to the healthy development of personal growth work and psychotherapy than the restrictive situation which the 'therapy bureaucracies'

seek to impose. The legal framework for practice is not in need of remedial 'treatment' and moreover provides an important example for other
countries already saddled with inappropriate legislation. If legislative restrictions such as sought by UKCP et al. are to be introduced in Britain,
the onus should be upon those who favour this change to prove the neces-
sity and to substantiate their position that the restrictions they seek would
be beneficial. I am of the opinion that the case for statutory registration in
this field does not stand up to scrutiny. As I will endeavour to show, whilst
at first sight statutory registration may appear to be a sensible idea, the
balance of available evidence indicates that in all probability it would do
more harm than good.

Although this book tends to focus on UKCP and its schemes, the
arguments presented are in most cases equally relevant to the pursuit of
registers by the other organizations mentioned above and indeed registration schemes in this area generally, whether in Britain or elsewhere.

Proposals for psychotherapy regulation bring into sharp focus the relationship between the human potential movement and the worlds of psychotherapy and counselling. A major concern of this book is to present a
case for the maintenance of a clear boundary and appropriate terminological differentiation between human potential practice and psychotherapy
with a view to the conservation of a broadly based and thriving human
potential movement. I hope to raise the general level of awareness about
this issue and to challenge the involvement of humanistic organizations in
bodies promoting statutory registration.

The issues addressed in this book go beyond those of a parochial
professional squabble. They concern the interface between the spheres of
the personal and the socio-political. Insofar as some of the activities involved are intended as systems for personal growth and transformation,
the role of the state in relation to these bears comparison with issues of
artistic, religious and educational freedom.

> In 1660, John Bunyan, a tinker, was arrested for unlicensed preaching.
> He was imprisoned in Bedford jail, where he remained for twelve years
> and was subsequently to write *The Pilgrims Progress*. He died in 1688
> whilst in London to preach and was laid to rest in Bunhill Fields, the
> great London burial-ground for religious non-conformists.

Section I

Psychotherapy

A Suitable Case for Statutory Treatment?

Chapter 1

The Terminology of Regulation

Terminology in the field of licensing is confusing....
(Daniel Hogan, Vol. 1, 1979:237)

What *is* 'accreditation'? What *is* 'registration'? Some dictionary definitions will help to get us under way. According to *The Shorter Oxford English Dictionary* (3rd edn.), 'Accreditation' is: "the action of accrediting"
leading to somebody being 'accredited' or "furnished with credentials;
authoritatively sanctioned". 'Credentials' are "letters or written warrants
recommending or entitling the bearer to credit or confidence". *The Concise Oxford Dictionary* (4th edn.) defines 'accredited' as: "officially recognized (persons); generally accepted, orthodox (beliefs)".

Note that 'accreditation' has an implication of being able to take someone on trust as a result of 'official' recognition. 'Accreditation' in this area
is usually understood to refer to some form of 'official' approval to practise through having met certain standards or having fulfilled certain requirements. 'Registration' is: "the act of registering or recording" (*The
Shorter Oxford English Dictionary* , 3rd edn.) and in this context usually
refers to the process of registering those with the required credentials.

Daniel Hogan has surveyed the terminology in this area as follows:

Terminology in the field of licensing is confusing. To illustrate
the definitional problems involved, laws that forbid people from
practicing without a licence have been referred to as licensing
laws, mandatory licensing and practice acts [and in the UK, 'functional' regulation or registration (Sieghart, 1978)], while laws
that only forbid the use of titles have been termed certification
laws, permissive licenses, or title acts [and in the UK, 'title protection', 'indicative' regulation or registration (Sieghart, 1978)
or 'nominal registration']. Both types are frequently referred to

as licensing or licensure laws [and in the UK, 'statutory regulation' or 'statutory registration']. In addition, laws that do not require a practitioner to meet certain standards but do make registration mandatory are termed registration laws, and are also generally considered a form of licensure. (Hogan, Vol. 1, 1979:237)

Hogan goes on to outline how he uses the terms in his study:

> For the sake of consistency and conceptual clarity, laws that forbid the practice of a profession without a license and require meeting certain minimum standards will be termed ***practice acts***. Laws that require meeting certain minimum standards to use certain titles, but which do not restrict the right to practice will be referred to as ***title acts***. Those laws that only require registration with a state agency and do not demand the successful completion of an examination or the meeting of other minimum requirements will be referred to as registration laws [see below]. ***Licensing*** and licensure will be used interchangeably and will include both title and practice acts and registration. The term "certification" will be reserved for nongovernmental associations and their efforts to determine whether practitioners have met certain standards of competence, which may be either minimal or maximal. Accreditation will be defined as the process a governmental or nongovernmental agency undertakes to determine whether an academic or nonacademic training institution or program meets certain standards. (ibid.) [Emphasis added.][1]

Note that Hogan uses 'certification' where an organization is validating an individual practitioner and 'accreditation' when it is the training organization that is being validated. In the UK such a clear distinction is not commonplace so reference is also made to individuals being 'accredited'. Furthermore, a distinction between training 'certification' seen as a qualification to practise and 'accreditation' seen as a renewable licence to practise, has been promoted within UKCP (Young, 1990:6).

Writing in a North American context (with a Canadian focus), Trebilcock and Shaul (1982:285) maintain a distinction between 'certification' (reserved title) systems, that is title acts, and 'licensure', used only to refer to practice acts. The Association of State and Provincial Psychology Boards (ASPPB), again in a North American context, adopts a similar position:

> When both the title and practice of psychology are regulated, the law is called a licensing law; when only the title of psychologist is regulated, the law is called a certification law. [However to avoid redundancy where both are being discussed] ... the word "licensure" will be used to stand for either licensure or certification. (ASPPB, 1994b)

The use of 'certification' and 'licensure' as distinguishing terms seems to be quite common in North America. However, as in the case of ASPPB, the simultaneous use of 'licensure' to refer to both types of law can lead to misunderstanding.

In the UK, the term 'registration' has been used in the sense of a *voluntary* register, that is one without legal backing or in the sense of a *statutory* register which does have legal backing. The difference is not always made clear, in news reports for example, and this has led some people to erroneously suppose that a legally backed register for psychotherapy already exists. Both voluntary registration and statutory registration are consequential on the certification of the practitioner by some accredited body or other, but only in the case of the latter is registration equivalent to what Hogan calls a 'title act' if it applies only to title, or a 'practice act' if it controls the activity as well.

In this book, for the most part, I have tended to adopt the terms *practice act* and *title act* since I think they offer the most explanatory value. The term *licensing* will be used to cover both types of statutory control. Note that *practice act* should generally be taken to mean that titles are protected as well as practice.

In contrast with the usage in the UK, the 'registration laws' referred to by Hogan do *not* require any prior credentials for registration, and for the sake of clarity I will refer to them as *non-credentialled registration*. The issue of *indirect regulation* will be addressed mainly in Chapter 20.

Chapter 2

Some Stated Justifications for a Psychotherapy Register - and Some Refutations

The reasons put forward by Courtenay Young [Jan. 1990] and others to justify these moves towards regulation and licensing include: "protect the public", "definite status and legality", "official recognition", etc. Whatever the validity of these reasons, (little we feel) in our view the 'cure' is liable to prove worse than the 'disease'.

(Juliana Brown and Richard Mowbray, 1990:32)

... it's argued that, to stay autonomous, we have to 'put our house in order' and establish ourselves as a defined profession.... So is our house really 'out of order'? Psychotherapy in Britain proceeds in a thoroughly self-regulated fashion which throws up some anomalies, some misuse of power and certainly some inefficiency, but which may well be a much better vehicle for the activity than any central organization. It seems that the new control initiatives will seriously deform psychotherapy - in fact, they have already started to do so.

(Nick Totton, 1992:26-27)

Stated justifications for the establishment of UKCP and the registration of psychotherapists tend to be either of the sort that claim this would represent some sort of *improvement* on the existing situation for the public or practitioners, or those which claim such developments are necessary *defensive strategies* against worse situations arising for practitioners.

Arguments for psychotherapy registration which hold that it would represent an improvement are as follows:

10

Remedy the 'disorder' in the field

Justifications are sometimes couched in terms of reducing 'fragmentation', putting houses in order, clearing up messes, or standardizing hotchpotches:

> The point of accreditation, as we spelled out at the time [1980 - founding of AHPP - the Association of Humanistic Psychology Practitioners] was to put some structure into a disorganized field which had become quite messy. We felt we wanted to put our house in order, so that we could say to all and sundry that there were some decent standards of practice.... (Rowan, 1991:32)

> ... the implications of what it means to have a profession of psychotherapy, rather than the present hotchpotch of variously trained people from a great variety of backgrounds and disciplines who cannot agree on very much common ground. (Young, 1990:4)

This state of 'the field' could, from another point of view, be seen as diverse, decentralized, deregulated, 'grass roots' and fostering emergent order rather than requiring order imposed upon it. (See e.g. Horrocks, 1990:56.) Le Corbusier's plan for the redevelopment of the Right Bank in Paris comes to mind: "He proposed to replace the genial disorder of the Rue de Rivoli, les Halles and the Faubourg St. Honore with a grid of cruciform tower blocks. He argued: 'Imagine all this junk, which has until now lain spread out over the soil like a dry crust, cleaned off and carted away and replaced by immense crystals of glass' " ('Centipede', 1993). Thankfully, his wish was not granted![1]

Form a profession of psychotherapy

Hand in glove with the above concern with standardizing is the urge to establish psychotherapy as a 'profession', notwithstanding Freud having once dubbed psychoanalysis as an 'impossible' profession (Freud, 1937). Holmes and Lindley, for example, hold that:

> ... A psychotherapy profession is needed if the cacophony of one-man bands is to be harmonized for the benefit of the would-be patient. (Holmes & Lindley, 1989:217)

Since UK governments have proved consistently reluctant to legislate in such a diversified area as this one, the goal of a statutory register is both a means and an end to this process of forming a unified profession (ibid.:207).

Comparisons are made with occupations that already have statutory recognition and which psychotherapy might emulate:

> It is also worth at this point, saying what is meant by a profession. A profession, like that of an accountant, solicitor, or architect, has a definite status and legality. There is official recognition.... (Young, 1990:4)

Whilst accepting that there is great diversity in the activities of the different professions, Trebilcock holds that there are common elements as well:

> In each case we find the application of a body of knowledge that is systematic and sometimes arcane. This is a knowledge which, by its very nature, can be acquired only by long and arduous training.... the essence of a professional relationship involves the assumption of an *agency role* by the practitioner, acting on behalf of all the relevant interests involved in the decision making, i.e. the client's interest and those of third parties.... (Trebilcock, 1982:101)

Thus members of professions generally act as agents for their clients, carrying out for them tasks that they would not have the knowledge base to perform. I think that equating psychotherapy and even more so human potential practice with such professions is very misleading. Whilst the acquisition of an elaborate body of professional knowledge may be fundamental to competence in the typical profession, there is little reason to suppose that basic competence in psychotherapy or human potential work is founded on a similar basis.

Some of those who favour the establishment of a psychotherapy pro-

fession acknowledge this difference - and the difficulty this poses for that
goal:

> One hallmark of a profession is that its practitioners have techni-
> cal knowledge and skill that do not exist, or exist only in rudi-
> mentary form, outside the profession. This creates a problem for
> psychotherapists whose skills, being to do with people rather
> than things, and with people as people, rather than people as
> things, can be hard to specify as compared, for example, with
> those of an architect or chiropodist.... (Holmes & Lindley,
> 1989:210)

For some, the way this activity should be socially organized, that is, whether
it should be regarded as a profession or otherwise, is a matter crucially
related to the goals of the activity itself. Nick Totton sees the matter as
follows:

> This central fact [that any value in psychotherapy resides in the
> quality of the meeting between two individuals] reveals psycho-
> therapy to be quite a different activity from the professions with
> which it is now being compared. It starts to explain the radical
> thrust therapy so often shows in practice: How to move people
> away from social norms and conformity. It suggests strongly that
> the best therapists may *not* be those with top-notch academic
> backgrounds. Psychotherapy is founded above all on *authentic-
> ity*, a quality which throws into question many of the ways soci-
> ety is currently organized. (Totton, 1992:27)

In our article "Whither the Human Potential Movement?" Juliana
Brown and I argued that:

> In our view, the current moves towards regulation and licensing
> derive from an implicit association with the medical model and
> with the medical professions as a model for professionalization.
> Members of the medical professions (as well as professions such
> as those cited by Courtenay Young - accountants, solicitors and

architects) are by and large persons who give advice or carry out actions on behalf of their clients. Their professional status assures the client of their authority and competence to act *without the client being fully involved* - not something we would hope is typical of humanistic practitioners! (Brown & Mowbray, 1990)[2]

These views reveal a crucial aspect of the 'professionalization debate': that different and conflicting aims are envisaged by activities that all refer to what they do as 'psychotherapy'. For example, a perspective that envisages psychotherapy as a treatment and cure business focusing on the illness or problem to be alleviated (i.e. a 'medical model' activity) conflicts with a view of it as something primarily concerned with individual authenticity and uniqueness.

Whether or not one regards psychotherapy as a medical model activity in itself, the structures and procedures being established by UKCP do seem to me to be highly reminiscent of those of the medical profession. They do seem to me to be following the example of the medical profession as a model for professionalization as did the Foster and Sieghart reports that UKCP is heir to (see Chapter 5).

It is worth pointing out that there is in fact nothing legally dubious about the status of psychotherapy as things stand at present. The question of whether the creation of a statutory profession in this area would be a 'good thing' is of course a major concern of this book.

Protect the public from dangers and abuses

This is the standard justification put forward by professions seeking legal protection, and dangers and abuses are what seem to most preoccupy the media (a frequent lament is that 'anybody' can practise as a psychotherapist, which is true, but then would you go to just 'anybody'?). 'Safeguard the public' is the standard stimulus for the standard reflex response 'registration'. The Foster and Sieghart reports regard this as the primary objective of statutory control (see Chapter 5) and UKCP cites protection of the public as a main justification for its existence (see Chapter 6). However such justifications originating from within the humanistic psychology movement are noticeably infrequent.

What is usually absent from statements about this issue is evidence of the scale and severity of the risk to the public and of the reduction of risk that can be expected to ensue from statutory registration. Later chapters will explore these matters in depth.

Arguments for some form of psychotherapy registration as a necessary defensive strategy for practitioners are as follows:

Inevitability

An air of fatalism about statutory regulation has pervaded discussions amongst practitioners. It has often been talked about as though it was *inevitable*. What is an outcome desired by some has been assiduously 'talked up' as though it will be an inevitable achievement. Those who are unenthusiastic about the prospect of a statutory profession are counselled to go along with the process of its formation and thereby gain what little influence they can over it. From this stance there is little point in opposing it or questioning its wisdom.

Petrūska Clarkson assures us that whereas: "Previously, anybody could set up as a psychotherapist: that is, prior to the formation of UKCP.... The voluntary Register which appeared in May 1993, will [*sic*] form the foundation of a Statutory Register of psychotherapists ..." (Clarkson, 1994:12).

Shirley Wade, writing about the involvement of humanistic psychology holds that: "We do not have the power to stop this tide of movement towards professionalism, and I see no fun in playing at being Canute ..." (Wade, 1990:53).

Courtenay Young proclaims forthrightly: "... Let me state it very clearly that psychotherapy (which includes psychoanalysis, humanistic psychology (as it is practised), clinical psychology, behavioural psychotherapy, NLP, family therapy, hypnotherapy and possibly psychodrama and many other psychotherapies) is almost certain to become more organised and regulated - *whether we like it or not*. This is a sign of the times. It is happening. There will be a register of accredited psychotherapists (almost certainly). This will have some form of government approval (eventually). It is becoming a (recognized) profession ..." (Young, 1991:54).

The Association of Humanistic Psychology Practitioners (AHPP) pronounced confidently in 1991 that: "... The UK Government is expected to legislate in about four years time (1995) to protect either the title 'psychotherapist' or the title 'registered psychotherapist'" (AHPP, 1991a:37) and in 1992 Martin Jelfs, as chair of AHPP, extolled the latter's major influence on: "the inevitable and unstoppable professionalization of psychotherapy" (Jelfs, 1992a:17).

The assumption of 'inevitability' is heavily dependent upon the arguments that follow. As we shall see there is nothing inevitable about statutory professionalization.

Restrictions may be forthcoming from the government and it is better that we pre-empt them

Maybe, but it seems to be much more the case that far from providing a better alternative to less congenial legislative initiatives emanating from the government, UKCP is itself *a*, if not *the*, main source of pressure on a reluctant government.

In the course of compiling an issue of *Self and Society* on the topic of the registration of psychotherapists, the editor David Jones, having sounded out a "government source" on what the government had in mind for the registration of psychotherapists, concluded that: "I am not an experienced government-watcher and I make no claim as a prophet, but I would judge that the likelihood that government takes the initiative and introduces laws to change the basis on which psychotherapy is practised is about zero" (Jones, 1990:1).

According to Courtenay Young:

> ... the government have effectively said that they are not interested in legislation unless we (the UKSCP or the profession) want it.... (Young, 1990:5)

So, the government does not seem to be very interested in legislation - certainly not unless UKCP courts it, and UKCP *is* courting. UKCP representatives began to hold meetings with Members of Parliament and the Department of Health in 1990, launched its register in a room at the House of Lords in May 1993 and considered the need to hire a professional public relations officer to handle publicity: "in this crucial stage when we are working towards statutory registration" (UKCP, 1993i).

However the object of UKCP's attention has yet to warm to the idea of a statutory register. Dr. Glenys Parry, from the Mental Health Policy Unit, Department of Health, implied that: "the possibility of a statutory register was not a 'hot issue' at the Department of Health, and was not likely to happen in the near future." (*Self & Society*, 1994). The British Confederation of Psychotherapists states that: "we understand that the government has no intention of introducing statutory legislation in the fore-seeable future" (Richards, 1994). Enquiries by 'The Psychotherapy Cen-tre' have revealed that: "In the foreseeable future, according to the Department of Health, the idea of a statutory register of psychotherapists is a dead duck" (The Psychotherapy Centre, 1992). Finally, in his speech at the launch of the UKCP register, Tim Yeo, the then Parliamentary Un-der Secretary of State for Health, was explicit that: "the Government is most reluctant to contemplate legislation" (Yeo, 1993). This is a stance that has been consistently adopted by UK governments since the question of statutory control was first mooted by the Foster report in 1971.

Restrictions may be sponsored by other professional groups such as the medical profession or the academic and clinical psychologists. It's better that we 'get in on the act' so that we don't get left out.

This is always a risk. Laws in this area are nearly always initiated either by the occupation itself *or* by a rival group, as Hogan's researches have re-vealed:

> Licensure laws can be divided into two categories, depending on whether the law was initiated by the occupation or profession itself ("friendly" licensure) or by a group antagonistic to the group being licensed ("hostile" licensure).... Examples of the latter in-clude many of the licensure laws applicable to the allied health professions.... Typically with hostile laws it is either a superior or rival professional group that initiates the law to curtail the development of the rival profession. This usually happens in an occupation that has hazy limits [such as psychotherapy] or which

overlaps with other related occupations [ditto].

In most cases, however, the profession itself is the one to seek legislation. Rarely if ever does a legislature license an occupation as a result of complaints raised by the public or specific consumers of the occupation's services.... Since few organized groups exist that might be opposed to licensing, it is not difficult for a profession to have itself licensed. Only when another professional group is threatened is there likely to be a legislative fight.... (Hogan, Vol. 1, 1979:243)

It has been argued that because UKCP includes representatives of the Royal College of Psychiatrists and the British Psychological Society, there is less risk of such bodies doing their own deal with the government with respect to psychotherapy (Young, 1990:8).

Maybe, but the government has not shown any interest in legislation (see above) and the psychiatric establishment was, it seems, opposed to the only actual legislative initiative to introduce statutory control of psychotherapy (Graham Bright's Private Member's Bill, 1981), since it feared that it: "would expose many of their members who were, alongside their NHS appointments, in private practice as psychotherapists without any proper training whatsoever" (Heron, 1990:18).

Furthermore, the government actually scuppered that bill by ensuring there was no time available for it to be taken up by parliament on account of there being: "too much dissension in the field to warrant statutory intervention" (ibid.).

Certainly, organizations such as the British Psychological Society and the British Association for Counselling have shown interest in some sort of statutory control, but the disparity of the field (amongst other things) has so far disinclined government to comply. It is UKCP's efforts to 'unify' the field that increase the chance of legislation.

The British Psychological Society (BPS) has been a Chartered Body since incorporation by Royal Charter in 1965, and has been authorised to maintain a Register of Chartered Psychologists since amendments to its Royal Charter in 1987. This also gave the Society a measure of title protection in the form of 'Chartered Psychologist' (BPS, 1993b). Because a Royal Charter is granted by Royal prerogative, the Society achieved this by Privy Council approval without legislation having to go through the House of Commons in the usual way. At its 1993 annual conference the BPS voted to pursue a statutory register of 'psychologists' and called for title protection of the term 'psychologist' (Hall, C., 1993; *Independent*, 1993). However, I do not believe that this could be achieved via the Royal Charter route.

From one perspective psychotherapy could be regarded as a form of 'psychological practice' and in some countries (e.g. Australia, Canada and the USA - see Chapters 8 and 12 and Appendices B and C) the practice of psychotherapy has been subjected to laws drafted to regulate the practice of psychology (though medical practitioners are usually exempt). This could conceivably happen here if BPS achieved its ambition to obtain title protection over the term 'psychologist', depending on how 'psychologist' was defined - if it was defined at all. It would be as well to be vigilant and to oppose any moves to allow such a licence, but one does not have to have a UKCP to prevent it happening.

European pressure

Developments in Europe, particularly the establishment of the European single market, have been cited as major justifications for the need for registration schemes here. These arguments deserve a chapter of their own.

Chapter 3

The European Bogeyman

1992 is the year of increased political union between the 12 [now
15] countries of the European Community. We can expect new laws
to come into force within the next few years standardizing the regulations for psychotherapy in all member countries.

(David Boadella, 1991:33)

We feel that '1992 and all that' has become the 'bogeyman' frightening this [human potential] movement into becoming a "profession" and "getting its house in order" whereas actually the main
impetus seems to have been coming from a rather small nucleus of
people within the movement (many with a vested interest in training) rather than from actual threats of regulation from outside. Ironically it may transpire that the resulting system of internal regulation
will be what precipitates legislation by making it easy for government to legislate through the *apparently* representative bodies.

(Juliana Brown and Richard Mowbray, 1990:32)

During the run-up to the establishment of the European internal market in
1992, UKCP gained a higher profile as the issue of psychotherapy registration was discussed in terms of preparation for, or protection from, this
closer union with Europe. Fears of the 'coming European laws' did much
to boost support for UKCP from training organizations and practitioners.

It was argued that UKCP should be recognized as the only competent
authority in the UK which can speak for all psychotherapists: "... hopefully thus preventing the atrocious oppression which has taken place in
most countries of Europe, where only such psychotherapy as is approved
and controlled by the psychiatric establishment is allowed to take place.
Those countries where strict control is also exercised by the psychological
establishment are regarded on the continent as liberal ..." (Rowan, 1991:33).

There are three related issues concerning the right to practise that are
involved here: (a) the right of a national of another European Community/

Union[1] country to practise psychotherapy in the UK; (b) the right of UK nationals to practise psychotherapy in other European Community/Union countries; and (c) the right of a UK citizen to practise psychotherapy in the UK. Regarding rights (a) and (b), Courtenay Young has stated that:

> ... 1992 is the date that a free labour market is created in the European Community, which means that, if you are qualified or registered to work in one country, you have the right to work in any other EC country.... However, in practice this means that within psychotherapy, as no one is registered to work in this country, no-one in Britain can claim this right, but all the Dutch psychologists and psychiatrists can claim the right to work in Britain - where there aren't any restrictions anyway. So, behind the initial sighs of relief, there is quite considerable pressure to form a register of psychotherapists.... those people on the register will be able to identify themselves in some way and can thus claim the right - in stroppy countries like Holland and Spain - to work as a registered psychotherapist. (Young, 1990:5-6)

A statutory register in the UK would restrict other European Community/ Union nationals in the same way as UK citizens and thus presumably stem any 'flood' of would-be but 'unqualified' continental psychotherapists heading for Britain and taking work from us 'Brits'. However, statutory registration in the UK would not affect the right of UK citizens to practise in another Member State *unless* that country also has such official recognition of a profession of psychotherapy.

As of February 1995, it appears that Member States which have statutory recognition of psychotherapy as a distinct profession are in a minority (see Chapter 8). Arguments for a statutory register in the UK that concern rights (a) and (b) are not very strong unless you are keen to practise in one of these countries (such as Italy or Austria) or are eager to prevent the residents of other Member States from practising here.

Most fear has, I think, been generated by the spectre of changes in the European Community/Union affecting (c), the right of a British national to practise psychotherapy *in Britain*. However, developments regarding the European internal market do not affect this right:

... The EEC Directive [The Mutual Recognition Directive 89/ 48EEC], to be implemented in 1991, not 1992, will not affect the right of complementary and alternative practitioners to practise privately under common law in the country....

The Directive contains nothing specific to individual professions or occupations. It will not affect existing systems of internal regulation and the text of the Directive makes this clear. In the UK therefore, where there is no registration or qualification required in order to practise, the Directive makes no difference to the existing pattern of alternative therapy practice. Similarly, nationals of other Member States will be free to practise in the UK on the same terms. Where other Member States prevent alternative professions from practising or require supervision by medically trained practitioners this too will remain unchanged. ('A Government Source', 1990:3)

In 1990 David Jones informed us that: "And what, I hear you ask, has the EEC and 1992 (well 1991 actually) got to do with this? The EEC has no plans to legislate for psychotherapy so the answer is it provides an occasion not a cause for people to see if their house is in order" (Jones, 1990:2).

However in 1991 he reported that: "The Dutch government, prompted by its professionalized psychotherapists, are taking the lead in proposing that EC countries register psychotherapists and that it be a profession limited to those at postgraduate level. The British government looked into this and consulted the established bodies in the mental health area such as the British Psychological Society, social work organizations, psychiatrists etc. - about two dozen bodies altogether. They wanted a view of, among other things, the standing of the United Kingdom Standing Conference on Psychotherapy (UKSCP which emerged from the Rugby conference). Government seems to be persuaded that UKSCP is competent but comprehension seems to be seriously hindered by the assumption on government's part of a medical model of treatment" (Jones, 1991a:51). Moreover: "... The Department of Health is centrally concerned with this issue although in some ways the Department of Trade and Industry is more involved with the actual regulations. Both departments, indeed the whole civil service, assume that psychotherapy means either psychiatry or psychoanalysis ..." (ibid.).

In June 1991, David Boadella, referring to: "the coming Euro-laws", maintained that: "There exists a professional watchdog of the EEC called SETLIP. It has the power to issue sectoral directives regulating the practice of psychotherapy. These are compulsory restrictions binding on all member countries. SETLIP can be asked to issue such a sectoral directive when the professional associations of any seven member countries unite to ask for this. At the moment [June 1991], the Dutch Psychology Association (NVP) has begun a process of contacting six other national psychology associations in Europe to request SETLIP to issue a sectoral directive ordering that the title 'psychotherapist' could be legally used only by doctors and psychologists ..." (Boadella, 1991:33). He went on to present UKSCP as a bulwark against the threats posed by SETLIP, the EEC, and the: "faceless men of Brussels" and as an organization seeking to: "directly protect the rights and freedoms of both responsible therapists and of the public" (ibid.: 34).

When I made enquiries about SETLIP with the London Information Unit of the European Commission and the pertinent department in Brussels neither had ever heard of any such organization and I was told that the above description of the powers attributed to SETLIP (whatever that organization is, perhaps SEPLIS?[2]) was: "completely false". Only the Commission itself has the power to issue sectoral directives (under very restricted circumstances) and it has abandoned the policy of doing so in favour of Directive 89/48/EEC (see below). If all this leaves you uncertain as to whether SETLIP actually exists, well so am I.

The European legislation applicable in this area is to be found in Articles 48-58 of the Treaty of Rome which provide for the free circulation of wage earners and allow others to work in another Member State, either permanently (right of establishment) or by supplying services across frontiers, along with the directives that derive therefrom.[3] These provisions were intended to foster economic integration by creating a "common market in manpower" on the basis of non-discrimination on the ground of nationality (Cuthbert, 1994:70).

In 1987 the Single European Act came into force, supplementing the Treaty. It gave the Community the means to establish, by the end of 1992, a large European internal market - an area with no frontiers between the Member States. To that end, barriers to the free movement of persons, goods, services and capital needed to be eliminated. Among those barriers are differing conditions for the exercising of many professions. These conditions infringe upon the right under the Treaty itself for the self-employed to establish themselves in any member country, under the same conditions pertaining to nationals of the host country (*European File,* 1989).[4]

The response of the Community to this problem of differing requirements between Member States was the adoption of various specific or 'sectoral' directives applied to particular professions starting in 1976 with medical practitioners. These directives were based on a process of harmonizing the conditions under which professions could be exercised and particularly, coordination of training (ibid.). However, this process was found to be so difficult and slow, because of the need for consensus between all Member States, that from 1985 it was abandoned in favour of a broader approach in line with the subsidiarity principle of the Maastricht Treaty[5] (European Commission, DG 15/E/2, 1995). This new approach is based on a general system for the mutual recognition of diplomas incorporated in the Mutual Recognition Directive 89/48/EEC. This states the basic rule that Member States who themselves require a 'diploma' as a condition of practising a *regulated profession* must accept a 'diploma' issued in another Member State, provided it conforms to the following conditions:

It must be awarded by a competent authority in a Member State (i.e. one designated in accordance with its own laws or regulations) after successful completion of a course lasting at least three years at a university or similar establishment and of professional training required in addition where appropriate. The diploma must fulfil the professional qualifications required for the taking up or pursuit of a *regulated* profession in that Member State. Qualifications obtained via non-standard routes (e.g. part-time study or correspondence courses) are also covered, provided they are equivalent to those obtained by the conventional route *and* give the same rights of access to the profession in that state (*Official Journal of the European Communities*, 1989).

A professional activity is "regulated" in the sense of the Directive if its pursuit is restricted to the holders of a "diploma". The

24

Directive gives two particular examples of "regulation": Regulation by means of protection of title, i.e. by restricting the use of a professional title to persons with a with a particular diploma, and regulation by virtue of the fact that social security arrangements only allow the remuneration of professionals holding a diploma (often the case with professions in the health field). (Commission of the European Communities document, 3.90)[6]

In a telephone conversation, the head of the European Commission department concerned with the recognition of professional qualifications emphasized that the Commission is *only* concerned with facilitating migration *between* Member States. The Commission is *only* concerned with the mutual recognition of diplomas between Member States *in which a profession is already regulated*. The Commission is not involved with altering the situation *within* a Member State such as with promoting the registration of a profession in a particular Member State where it is not already subject to statutory regulation (European Commission, DG 15/E/2, 1993).

So, the Commission is not seeking to harmonize the regulation or training of *any* profession. Regarding 'psychotherapy' in particular, the term is regarded as vague and the Commission is aware that this activity is quite different between Member States - in some it is a regulated profession, in some it is not and in some it is difficult to distinguish psychotherapists from psychologists (European Commission, DG 15/E/2, 1995). "The possibility to have an evolution [in this profession] is quite little, quite small" (ibid.).[7]

The Commission still has the power to pursue a specific, sectoral directive for psychotherapy, but this would involve a reversal of policy by the Commission and in any case such a specific directive would only be possible if the following three conditions were met: (1) there is a consensus amongst Member States; (2) there is a consensus amongst all the organizations that represent the profession and (3) the Commission thinks that a such a directive is needed to improve the free movement of members of the profession (ibid.). So, the possibility is indeed "quite small".

To summarize, the position in the European Community/Union regarding the regulation of psychotherapy (as of February 1995) is that *there is no pressure from the Community institutions to introduce statutory regulation of psychotherapy in Member States*: "The Commission does not plan to make specific proposals for psychotherapists regarding their activities in general or their access to social security systems in particular" (European Parliament, 1993:2).

The more I have looked into this matter, the less has it seemed the case that the much vaunted 'pressure from Europe' has been anything to do with the Community/Union institutions or has really been something that would affect the right to practise psychotherapy *in the UK*. This view is confirmed by the British Confederation of Psychotherapists: "... It seems very unlikely that this government will introduce statutory legislation at any stage in its lifetime or that standards will be imposed from Europe" (BCP, 1994). It seems more likely that the supposed 'European pressure' has been a stalking horse for pressure from interested parties within the UK in cahoots with interested parties in other European countries. Certainly '1992' proved to be a non-event in this regard. There seems to have been a great deal of misinformation put about and reliable information has been hard to come by. Whatever pressure there has been from outside the UK seems to have had its source in continental professional groups rather than The European Community/Union institutions as such.

Increasingly this appears to me to be a classic case of a purported 'external threat' used to bolster domestic political objectives by harnessing the fear so engendered. If everyone is led to believe that 'Euro laws' requiring regulation of psychotherapy are inevitably coming our way, it becomes easier to invent the domestic version.[8]

The conclusion that there is no impending European regulation of psychotherapy was confirmed in June 1994 by Dr. Alfred Pritz, Chief Executive of the European Association for Psychotherapy (EAP)[9] who, in his address to the EAP sponsored conference 'A Peaceful Revolution for Health Care in Europe', described the future of psychotherapy in Europe as being not about one regulation for all countries but rather about recognition of quality standards between various countries (Collis, 1994b:2).

Even if the threat of pan-European regulation were to prove real and substantial, a UKCP register is not the only response that could be made. The arguments in this book are very much concerned with the drawbacks of conventional systems of professional regulation and the barriers to entry to an area of economic activity that they represent. I favour the deregulation of professions except where a really solid case can be made for the protectionism their establishment represents. The principles behind these arguments are therefore quite compatible with the principles of an open market that lie behind the European legislation - although applied from a different perspective. Removing unnecessary barriers to entry to occupations would actually foster the European internal market if it were done on a Community wide basis.[10]

There are in fact trends in Europe moving in favour of deregulation and the elimination of restrictive practices. For example Roland Berger, German management 'guru', has described Germany's service sector as suffering from excessive protection and regulation which has inhibited its efficiency and growth (Eisenhammer, 1993) and in Britain the monopolies of traditional professions have come under attack from government.

Furthermore, the legal situation for the field of psychotherapy in Germany has undergone a dramatic liberalization as a consequence of a court case in January 1993 (Bundesverwaltungsgericht, 1993). This case challenged some of the previous requirements of the 'heilpraktiker' system on the grounds that they were in contravention of free market legislation, since they were irrelevant to the practice of psychotherapy. The resulting judgement found that the freedom to exercise a profession had been unacceptably restricted. According to Silke Ziehl (1994a), as a consequence, there has been an enormous loosening of the system of regulation, allowing for a much broader access to the occupation.[11]

Given a greater understanding of the issues involved, the UK government, favouring deregulation as it does, might be encouraged to support these trends, to lobby for more deregulation in this field in the rest of the Europe and to resist any pressure to go over to a *more* regulated way of doing things here. The government obviously has no idea what growth models and humanistic psychology are all about (Jones, 1991a:51), perhaps through having taken its counsel largely from the medical profession and psychoanalytic lobbies in the past. The government could be educated more about the variety in the field of 'psychotherapy' and the lack of basic agreement as to models, goals and means - revealing the 'disorder' - rather than hiding this under the cloak of an apparently representative body which invites, nay yearns for, legislation and makes it easier to enact.[12]

27

Chapter 4

The Hidden Agenda of Professions

It is my opinion that the professional's role in a free society should be limited to contributing technical information men need to make their own decisions on the basis of their own values. When he preempts the authority to direct, even constrain men's decisions on the basis of his own values, the professional is no longer an expert but rather a member of a new privileged class disguised as expert.

(Eliot Freidson, 1972:382)

... vested interests masquerading as the public interest....

(Kenneth D. Benne, 1979)

... [Dr. Sandy Macara, chairman of the British Medical Association (BMA)] is also part of what, until recently, was the most successful interest group in politics. Dr. Macara, after all, is nothing more than a trade union leader, defending, with a revenue of £40m a year, the interests of 90,000 highly-paid workers. Other unions have tried to give the appearance of transcending sectional interest ... but only the BMA really brings it off. "Patients will suffer unless doctors get more" is the medical correspondent's joke....

(Jack O'Sullivan, 1994)

Why should a 'profession' be regarded differently from other occupational groups and allowed special privileges, such as protected titles and practices and yet be exempt from the application of monopoly laws and, more often than not, retain effective control of the systems intended to regulate it? It is clearly not just a question of doing a 'professional' job of something as this description could be applied to any occupation. As discussed in Chapter 2, professions tend to occupy an 'agency' role, doing things for their clients on the basis of an elaborated body of knowledge that their clients would not have the time, capacity or inclination to master. However the same might also be said of an electrician or plumber.[1] The professional's knowledge base tends to be highly theoretical and academic and access to it is usually on the basis of a university degree. Professions with a less academic background tend to have a lower status - and income potential - and may be supplementary to, or under the aegis of, another profession as for example nursing is to medicine. The increased lifetime's earning capacity that often results from becoming a member of a recognized profession is usually far in excess of the cost of the education and training involved, notwithstanding that the cost of such training is likely to be directly or indirectly subsidized by government. There are also overtones of social class about professions. Professions such as medicine or the law have come to occupy the upper reaches of the occupational class system in terms of perceived status.

It is usually supposed that one of the distinguishing features of the professions is that, compared with other occupations, their members are motivated less by profit-maximization and more by altruistic considerations of public welfare as evidenced by their codes of professional ethics. For this reason, amongst others, professions tend to have high prestige. However Talcott Parsons (1968) argues that it is more in keeping with the facts that the professional has much the same motivation as the business person. In addition to whatever altruism there may be (a human trait not confined to the professions), there is also a more self-serving side to professions. Slovenko maintains that:

> According to theory, in return for a monopolistic right of practice, there is a reciprocal commitment to admit only individuals of proven competence, to insist on the observance of an ethical code of conduct, and to protect the public against bungling and extortion. In virtually every profession, however, disciplinary enforcement is virtually nonexistent. The little enforcement that is applied, does not act as a deterrent and is often done to protect the reputation or economic interest of the group rather than protect the public from harm. (Slovenko, 1979)

Take the case of the medical profession for example, which is often supposed to be amongst the most altruistic of professions. The British regulatory authority for the medical profession, the General Medical Council, was given its monopoly over the medical register when it was set up in the nineteenth century. Meg Stacey, Emeritus Professor of Sociology at Warwick University served as a lay member on the General Medical Council in the eighties and has made it the subject of detailed research. Commenting on the establishment and operation of the Council, she said that: "They really made a pact with the state to say we will regulate ourselves so that patients who come to us can trust us to treat them in a proper manner. We'll do that, if you give us certain privileges ..." (BBC Radio 4, 1994b). However she had to conclude that in practice: "... the pressures from the profession always made them [the members of the Council] lean somewhat to the profession rather than to the public" (ibid.). (For more on the General Medical Council see Chapter 9.) One view on the BMA has been quoted at the beginning of this chapter. Rayack's study of the American Medical Association (AMA) came to the conclusion that:

> Our analysis of the policies and practices of the American Medical Association since the turn of the century demonstrates beyond question that the critics of the AMA are fundamentally correct.... Society has delegated considerable power to organized medicine, and the AMA and its constituent societies have all too frequently used that power in a socially undesirable manner. Furthermore, our brief look into prospective developments in the medical market indicates that organized medicine will often be in the position where it can continue to use its power to protect the economic interests of its members at a very real cost to society. (Rayack, 1967:287)

More recently, the US medical/pharmaceutical/health insurance lobby has been described as the most powerful lobby group in the world and one that has waged virulent campaigns against any other systems that could be held up as better and cheaper alternatives (such as the UK's NHS or the Canadian health care system): "Anything that comes forward as a plausible alternative will be subject to violent attack" (BBC Radio 4, 1993a).

So, however altruistic the individual medical practitioner may be, it would seem that on the collective level medical practitioners cannot be relied upon to act any more altruistically than your average corporation.[2]

According to the analysis of Lippitt and his associates, historically, professions have had:

> ... a tendency to confuse credentials with competence. They have tended to define credentials more and more in terms of external badges of schooling and degrees, which are only obtainable through a rigid educational route. They have acted at times solely to protect the vested economic interests of their members, including resisting expansion of membership. Professions have also tended to resist the development and use of paraprofessionals [and self-help], and have been tardy in recruiting and training volunteers. They have tended to cultivate in the public the myth that the profession is all-knowing and all-powerful, rather than educating the public as to the profession's strengths and weaknesses. Finally, the professions have tended to coalesce with and be responsive to established institutions, rather than those lacking power. (Lippitt et al., 1975)

Defining a 'profession' is problematic. Goode concluded that the two most important characteristics cited in common definitions of a 'profession' are a : "prolonged specialized training in a body of abstract knowledge, and a collectivity or service orientation" (Goode 1960:903). In addition, Goode argues that as occupations become more professionalized they tend to possess more and more of the following highly specific traits:

1.   The profession determines its own standards of education and training.
2.   The student professional goes through a more far-reaching adult socialization experience than the learner in other occupations.
3.   Professional practice is often legally recognized by some form of licensure.

31

4.   Licensing and admission boards are made up of members of the profession.

5.   Most legislation concerned with the profession is shaped by the profession.

6.   The occupation gains in income, power, and prestige ranking, and can demand higher calibre students.

7.   The practitioner is relatively free of lay evaluation and control.

8.   The norms of practice enforced by the profession are more stringent than legal controls.

9.   Members are more strongly identified and affiliated with the profession than are members of other occupations with theirs.

10.   The profession is more likely to be a terminal occupation. Members do not care to leave it, and a higher proportion assert that if they had to do it over again, they would again choose that type of work. (ibid.)

Some who support the establishment of psychotherapy as a profession actively encourage the 'socialization process' referred to above:

> Professional training, if it truly succeeds, leads to a psychologic amalgamation of the person with the function that he is to perform. We speak then not of having a job, but of being a member of a profession. Professional people are strongly identified with what they do, they derive pleasure and pride from the status which their function affords them in their community, and they find it difficult to think in terms of change even if greater economic security is offered, because their deepest satisfactions stem from carrying on their profession which has become part of their life. This sense of professional identity is an essential attribute in a profession such as psychotherapy, and its acquisition must be considered as one of the important training goals. (Ekstein & Wallerstein, 1958:66)

Responding to this, Masson tersely concludes that: "In short, one is learning to become a loyal member of a select group" (Masson, 1988:294). In fact the term 'profession' derives from the vow taken by novitiates entering a religious order (Holmes & Lindley, 1989:209).

The adoption of a specialist language that is both a vehicle for the profession's particular area of knowledge and a means whereby that knowledge remains less accessible to lay understanding is often part of this 'socialization process'.

The rise of the professional model as a form of social organization in this century has been compared by many political scientists to a return to the guild society of the Middle Ages (e.g. Lieberman, 1970). This has occurred in parallel with a shift from capital to knowledge as a basis for power in society. Hogan outlines the nature of the guilds as follows:

> The basic element of the early guilds consisted first and foremost of the requirement of compulsory membership. This ensured that all practitioners would be subject to the guild's mandate and effectively established a monopoly.... The guilds fit perfectly into medieval conceptions of society, which included a belief in a hierarchical organization of authority, *the importance of status versus contract*, and a fusion of governmental authority with non-governmental bodies. (Hogan, Vol. 1, 1979:223-224)

The guilds had a debilitating effect on economic growth through their monopoly power and through the irrelevant membership requirements that maintained it. When they eventually disintegrated - most of them shortly after the fifteenth century - this was considered a:

> Welcome release from what had become an unreasonable interference with the free play of economic forces, and their demise generally is accounted one of the principal elements in our vaunted advance from 'status' to 'contract'. (Grant, 1942:303)

Professions seek a monopoly over an area of economic activity supposedly to protect the public from incompetent practitioners ('non-malfeasance'), but they have in practice tended to become perpetually over-concerned with the establishment of, the protection of, and the enhancement of their own social status and economic position. In view of this well documented hidden agenda, the statements of professional bodies should not be taken on trust but rather regarded with appropriate circumspection. Sound evidence should be demanded to justify any legal restrictions in their favour. Such evidence is sadly lacking in the Foster and Sieghart reports that set the psychotherapy registration ball rolling in the UK and to which I now turn.

Chapter 5

Precursors of the Current Proposals for the Statutory Registration of Psychotherapy in the UK

Scientology did not become a matter of major concern for the Press again until the summer of 1966, when one of the national daily newspapers reported extensively on "The Case of the Processed Woman".

(Foster, 1971:1)

... When Scientology was investigated (Foster, 1971), their practices of 'auditing' and 'processing' were seen to be so dangerous that statutory regulation of psychotherapy was called for....

(Mark Aveline [UKCP Board member 1993], 1990:325)

Following twelve years of deliberations, UKCP is now launching a national register of psychotherapists, as recommended by the Sieghart Report of 1978.

(UKCP, 1993b)

UKCP presents itself as the natural outcome of the Foster and Sieghart Reports and refers back to them for validity. A look at what these weighty sounding reports actually are and the context of their production is instructive since the case for statutory control is in part based a presumption of the soundness of their conclusions. Despite their relevance to the current debate, the Foster Report is out of print and the Sieghart Report is difficult to get hold of.

The 'Foster Report' (Foster, 1971) was produced by Sir John Foster KBE, QC, MP as the outcome of his inquiry into Scientology which was instigated by the government in response to: "public outcry about the 'abduction and corruption' of vulnerable young people by L. Ron Hubbard's Church of Scientology" (Holmes & Lindley, 1989:209). Margaret Percy gives a different slant on the background: "... the British popular press began a witch hunt of Scientologists and their founder and by 1968, in an extraordinarily uncharacteristic move, the government slapped an Aliens Order on Scientology, a ban which was only lifted three years later ..." (Percy, 1987).

The Sci-fi jargon and computer-speak such as 'Preclear', 'Thetan', 'Engram', and 'Processing' that is endemic in Scientology must indeed have sounded very strange as readers perused their *News of the World* on a Sunday morning. One could forgive them for concluding that 'aliens' had indeed landed!

Foster did in fact condemn the government's use of an Aliens Order as "wrong in principle" on the grounds that it was discriminatory to exclude foreign nationals simply because they were Scientologists, when there was no legal impediment to the practice of Scientology by UK citizens, and all the more so, when there was no right of appeal against an 'Aliens Order' as was the case at the time (Foster, 1971:158).

The Foster Report comprises 193 pages, most of which is taken up with extracts from Scientology publications and documents. Foster's inquiry was held "in private" and he did not hear any witnesses or advocates: "... In consequence, I have treated myself as being disabled from passing any adverse or favourable judgement of Scientology, its practitioners or practices ..." (ibid.:v). Nor did Foster seek any direct evidence or testimonials as to the harm or otherwise that Scientology might be causing in the UK. As "background", he cites reports from elsewhere, notably Australia, where a similar story concerning reactions to Scientology underlies the history of Australian psychology legislation (see Appendix B).

In 1963 a Board of Inquiry was set up in the state of Victoria under the leadership of Mr. Kevin Victor Anderson QC and produced a "wholly unfavourable" report on Scientology in 1965 - six years before Foster (ibid.:5). This 'Anderson Report' came to the lurid conclusion that:

> Scientology is evil; its techniques evil; its practice a serious threat to the community, medically, morally, socially; and its adherents sadly deluded and often mentally ill. (Anderson Report, 1965:1)

Note the blanket condemnation. In fact the Anderson Report also states that: "The Board has been unable to find any worthwhile redeeming feature in Scientology" (ibid.:2).

More soberly, in 1970 the Report of the Committee on the Healing Arts in Ontario, Canada concluded:

> We had already adopted the position ... that there was a point beyond which we would not go in restricting the rights of mentally competent individuals to seek treatment from health practitioners of their own choice, unless we found evidence that the practice might be harmful.... We did not believe that the compilation of further evidence pertaining to Scientology would be likely to cause us to recommend the prohibition of its practice in Ontario.... (Quoted in Foster, 1971:11)

Amongst the features of Scientology which gave rise to public anxiety in various countries at the time were promotional and recruitment methods that would put some double-glazing firms in the shade. As Foster said: "Some people may also find it novel to discover a religion which recruits new members by the methods of salesmanship and a 'free personality test' ..." (Foster, 1971:58). Moreover this was a church that offered processing and training courses for considerable fees. The notorious 'free personality tests' were studied by a working party of the British Psychological Society who concluded that there was: "an extremely strong case for assuming it to be a device of no worth" and that: "The prime aim of the procedure seems to be to convince ... people of their need for the corrective courses run by the Scientology organization" (ibid.:76-7). However, apparently there are now doubts about the validity of *any* personality tests. Occupational psychologist Steve Blinkhorn for example regards personality testing as: "inaccurate 90 to 99 per cent of the time", a view which is attracting growing support (Palmer, 1994).

Also giving rise to public concern were those Scientology activities that were held responsible for contributing to family estrangements. The practice of 'disconnection' involved inducing trainee Scientologists to disconnect from close relatives who were considered to be acting as 'Suppressive Persons'. This activity was part of Scientology's strict disciplinary arrangements which were administered by an executive agency call 'Ethics' that operated by holding 'Ethics Courts' with the sanction of the assignment of a 'Lower Condition' on the accused - including a 'Suppressive Person' order. There was also concern about the 'auditing' of minors albeit with their parents' consent and about the pressurizing of former members of the organization. The above might be described as amongst the more 'cultish' aspects of the organization.

Of more immediate concern to the subject of this book are the Scientologists' 'processing' or 'auditing' techniques which Foster regarded as the principal practice of Scientology and which he concluded constituted the practice of a form of psychotherapy, a view which Hubbard himself had shared at one stage. In fact, Foster concluded, largely on the basis of their own literature, that the Scientologists were practising both psychology - the offering of 'personality tests', and psychotherapy - the 'processing' or 'auditing' procedures (Foster, 1971:176).

Foster showed distinct signs of an allegiance to the medical model in this area and referred to psychotherapy as "psychological medicine":

> ... Psychiatrists [*sic*] broadly speaking, practise two distinct kinds of therapy: 'physical' medicine, which seeks to affect our minds through our bodies by material interventions such as electric shocks or drugs; and 'psychological' medicine, which seeks to affect our minds directly and without any material intervention. For this last technique I propose to use the expression 'psychotherapy' regardless of the particular school or discipline - such as 'psychoanalysis' or 'analytical psychology' - which the therapist happens to follow.... (Foster, 1971:176)

Foster went on to conclude that there was a strong case for legislation to control the practice of psychotherapy or 'psychological medicine' in the UK:

> ... psychotherapy (in the general sense of the treatment, for fee or reward, of illnesses, complaints or problems by psychological means) should be organized as a restricted profession open only to those who undergo an appropriate training and are will-

ing to adhere to a proper code of ethics, and that the necessary
legislation should be drafted and presented to parliament as soon
as possible. (Foster, 1971:v)

Given that Foster, because of the form and scope of his inquiry, did not see
himself as being in a position to judge the practices of Scientology, whether
of psychotherapy or otherwise, it is hard to see how he arrived at this
conclusion on the basis of the content in the body of his report. The report
is largely uncluttered by any supporting evidence regarding such things as
the scale of problems concerning the unregulated practice of psychotherapy
in the UK (by Scientologists or anyone else) or the efficacy of statutory
regulation as a solution.

In fact Foster cites only one particular example of where harm was
supposed to have resulted from the application of Scientology 'processing' techniques as such and that was in Australia. This concerned a person
whose 'auditing' session actually formed the basis of a demonstration for
the Anderson Board, who reported on it as follows:

> The particular session demonstrated what was called 'listen style
> auditing'. It was said that this was one of the simpler processes,
> quite a low grade process, and was designed to help people to
> talk about their worries and problems and get them 'off their
> chests', on the basis that people found relief when there was
> someone ready and willing to listen to them. It enabled the per-
> son with problems and worries to talk about them and the 'audi-
> tor' [i.e. the practitioner], on this occasion being very literally
> one who listened, merely started the 'preclear' [i.e. the client]
> talking and then sat silent, providing a receptive ear.
>
> The demonstration session was of about thirty minutes du-
> ration....
>
> ... Nine days [*sic*] after the demonstration session this
> 'preclear' was admitted as a patient to the care of the Mental
> Health Authority.
>
> The Board is appalled at the realization that it witnessed
> this unfortunate woman being processed into insanity. At that
> early stage of the Inquiry the Board had not been informed of the

potentially dangerous nature of this apparently simple and easy 'listen style auditing'. Subsequently a psychiatrist witness who read the transcript of this woman's demonstration session gave evidence that her behaviour in the session indicated clearly that she was in a state of mania rather than ecstasy, which would have been readily apparent to a psychiatrist [Is an exploration of ecstasy part of a psychiatrist's training?]....

The kind of treatment given to this unfortunate woman was the very kind which precipitated her breakdown. The Board heard expert psychiatric evidence to the effect that it was one of the well known traps in handling depressives to believe that by encouraging them to talk and 'get things off their chest' one was doing some good. In dealing with a person showing signs of depression, psychiatrists have to exercise great care and judgement in determining whether it is advisable to allow the person to talk about himself or not.... In order to determine whether a patient should be allowed to talk about himself, the psychiatrist must be a highly trained physician, with insight of many branches of medicine....

There was further expert psychiatric evidence that such techniques as 'listen style auditing' encourage a trust and dependency by the patient on the 'auditor', and tend to mobilize guilt and bring up emotions and anxiety in the 'preclear'. Such anxiety tends to provoke more symptoms, more anxiety and perhaps more depression, leading to a worse situation.... (Anderson Report, 1965:134-5)

The response of the Scientology organization to the above account from the Anderson Report is of interest:

Out of thousands of persons who had been helped by increasing their knowledge about themselves and life generally, Anderson could only find one person whom he could allege had been harmed by Scientology. He deals with her case at length in the Report. Even then he was way off!

He announces to the world that one woman was processed

into mental derangement in his presence. He does not state that he knew that this person had a long history of mental illness; she had been in and out of psychiatric wards.... Her husband and relatives were violently against Scientology. After she went home [from the demonstration], she had a very troubled time from some members of her family. Her husband threatened her and continuously insulted her and threatened to injure her daughter. This caused a heavy strain. Her grandmother told her all the time how bad she was; she had no one to turn to. The doctors were against Scientology, which, at that time, was under heavy governmental attack. Thus nine weeks [*sic*] later, in order to get away from these persons who were literally driving her mad, she signed in as a voluntary patient in one of Dr. Cunningham Dax's institutions. Anderson was so delighted about this case, that he refused to hear any evidence of the contributory causes of this woman's relapse.... (Church of Scientology, 1967:23)

Such 'evidence' of harm as this is hardly a sound basis for a proposal for statutory regulation. So how did Foster arrive at the apparent *non sequitur* of his recommendations?

A partial explanation is offered by Foster thus: "That it is the phenomenon of Scientology which has pointed out this need in the existing law is a matter on which, if it is the leadership's sincere desire to help humanity, they will have cause to congratulate themselves. Without coming to any conclusion on whether they in fact exploit their followers for their own profit, or whether it is desirable for auditors who may have had only a few weeks training since they came to Scientology with problems of their own, to be encouraged to practise psychotherapeutic techniques on those who, *ex hypothesi*, are sitting targets for exploitation, the mere fact that such a situation could easily be abused at the present time with impunity demonstrates the urgent need for reform" (Foster, 1971:179-180). Thus, being careful not to actually judge the practices of Scientology because he regarded himself as being disabled from doing so by the nature of his inquiry, Foster nevertheless makes clear his opinion of those practices and in effect says there isn't a law, there could be abuse, therefore there should be a law as there is elsewhere.

Looking a bit deeper, it seems that Foster: "... knew very little about psychotherapy, and therefore took advice from the psychoanalytic lobby. Following this advice, he condemned the Scientologists on the grounds that they were exploiting emotionally vulnerable people *and abusing the dynamics of the transference*. And he recommended the statutory registration of psychotherapists in private practice in order to protect the public from this kind of abuse" (Heron, 1990:17). This makes sense of the analytic bias in his final chapter where he makes his recommendations. For example he refers to the 'transference effect' as the: "principle technique in the armoury of modern psychological medicine" (Foster, 1971:177).

Foster explicitly cited established professions such as lawyers, doctors, architects and nurses as analogies for the statutory profession he proposed: "all put at their clients service, for reward, intricate skills of which the clients are ignorant and which they must largely take on trust" and showed enthusiasm for: "the traditional method ... to protect the weak from the exploitation which such a dependence makes possible ... [the creation of] a controlled 'profession' ... [which has] worked excellently in the past ..." (ibid.:178).

Foster's enthusiasm for statutory professionalization as a form of social regulation should not be particularly surprising given the era in which he was writing and that he was himself an eminent member of the legal profession, a profession whose own restrictive practices had yet to come under much in the way of public scrutiny.

Foster's recommendation that psychotherapy should be regulated by statute received the support of the British Medical Association and the Royal College of Psychiatrists.

In 1974 the British Psycho-Analytical Society initiated a meeting between the Department of Health and Social Security and itself, along with six other practitioner organizations, in order to discuss the recommendations of the Foster Report. In response to this meeting the DHSS indicated in a letter dated 22 January 1975 that: "it could not hold out any hope of any government legislation in the foreseeable future" (Sieghart, 1978:1). The DHSS suggested that the organizations present might like to establish a joint working party to develop their proposals in more detail - hence the 'Sieghart Report': "Statutory Registration of Psychotherapists: The Report of a Profession's Joint Working Party." Chairman Paul Sieghart, 1978.

The Sieghart Report is an altogether much slimmer work than Foster's, consisting of a pamphlet of about 40 pages (10 of them devoted to extracts from Foster's report). The Sieghart Report introduced the terms 'Functional Registration' (practice act) and 'Indicative Registration' (title act) and favoured the latter for psychotherapy registration on the grounds that there was no way of defining the practice of psychotherapy with enough certainty to allow a court to decide whether someone was practising it or not. Titles to be protected were 'psychotherapist', 'psycho-analyst' and similar titles, "together with (as is customary in such cases) any other description which might lead people to believe that the user was on the statutory register" (Sieghart, 1978:vii).

Foster had not been specific about which type of registration he proposed but he appeared to have in mind a practice act (ibid.:6).

Sieghart proposed the setting up of a Psychotherapy Council and: "... As in the case of other professions, the Council must therefore be composed of experienced and responsible members of the profession which it will regulate..." (ibid.:ix).

This turns out to be largely nominees of the bodies who constituted the working party along with a few elected places for registered psychotherapists not already represented by those bodies and a "lay" membership of approximately a quarter of the Council. "Lay" here means people who are not themselves psychotherapists. What they had in mind were doctors, lawyers, nurses, social workers etc. and: "... Ideally, there should be someone who can represent the interests of the profession's patients, but we have not been able to suggest how such a representative could easily be identified" (ibid.:x).

Like the Foster Report, the Sieghart Report leans heavily towards the medical model and the profession of medicine as the model for a profession of psychotherapy and refers to 'psychotherapy' as: "this field of medicine" (ibid.:1).

Like the Foster report, the Sieghart report has great faith in the: "well tried method of creating a statutory register of practitioners" as the best way to protect the public (ibid.:5).

A 'grandfather clause' was recommended as is common in these cases of profession formation, not least because it forestalls possible opposition from already established members of the occupation.

The Sieghart Report does not cite much in the way of empirical evidence to support its recommendations and largely relies on Foster for this who, as we have seen, does not cite much evidence either. However, it does cite a memorandum submitted by the Royal College of Psychiatrists in response to a request from the DHSS for comments on the recommendations of the Foster Report for legislation to control psychotherapy. This memorandum claimed that:

> There is ample clinical evidence that psychological procedures can cause harm if carried out by unqualified practitioners. The very procedures of psychotherapy which in competent hands can produce major beneficial effects are more likely in unqualified hands to have harmful effects.... The danger of harm would be reduced if there were sufficient statutory control.... (Royal College of Psychiatrists, 1972)

Sieghart also cites with approval a similar memorandum by the British Medical Association and concludes: "We have no hesitation in subscribing to all these views. We agree with Sir John Foster's conclusion that there is a strong case for legislation in the UK to control the practice of psychotherapy ..." (Sieghart, 1978:5).

However these views are refuted in the "Note of Dissent" by the British Association for Behavioural Psychotherapy at the end of the Sieghart report which states that:

> ... the [Sieghart] report cites opinion by the Royal College of Psychiatrists and by the British Medical Association that psychological procedures cause harm if carried out by unqualified practitioners. In fact evidence is lacking that harm occurs to members of the public through psychotherapy being given by unqualified as opposed to qualified practitioners at the present time.... (ibid.:17)

This is a state of affairs that, as far as I am aware, is still the case.

The Sieghart Report is not the report of a government sponsored body nor an independent inquiry but rather is essentially a discussion paper representing the views of the analytic lobby (Freudian and Jungian) at that time, along with those of the psychiatrists, and in the separate note, the dissenting views of the behaviour therapists. The latter argued that since there was no clear evidence of the efficacy of psychotherapy it should not be given the honour of statutory recognition. According to John Heron, who as Assistant Director of the British Postgraduate Medical Foundation was *au fait* with these matters at the time, their opinion was more vociferous in private: "[The behaviour therapists] also said, in more radical tone, that psychoanalysts in particular were hypocritical in wanting to protect the public from transference abuse, when their own therapy was riddled with this very phenomenon.... What the psychoanalysts really wanted, said my behaviour therapy sources, was to manoeuvre the government into protecting their lucrative monopoly on transference abuse. Strong stuff indeed but with an important grain of truth, in my judgement and experience ..." (Heron, 1990:17).

Various other bodies (including the newly formed British Association for Counselling) were also invited to comment on a draft of the report, but there is no indication in the report as to what comments were made by them nor to what extent their views were incorporated into the final version.

In 1981, on the basis of the Sieghart Report, MP. Graham Bright introduced his Private Member's Bill to regulate the practice and profession of psychotherapy and related disciplines. This bill failed at the second reading because the government had been advised that there was too much dissension in the field to warrant statutory intervention and consequently ensured that there was no time for the bill to be taken up (ibid.:18).The failure of the Bright Bill was part of the inspiration for the 'Rugby Conferences' out of which UKCP was eventually to come forth.

It seems ironic to me that the path to the proposed statutory registration of psychotherapy in the UK had its first step with an inquiry into the activities of a group which does not now use the term 'psychotherapy' and is organized as a religion and therefore unlikely to be much affected by any legislative restrictions that may arise.

In fact, Hubbard set up the Church of Scientology in the early 1950s specifically to be free to explore the world of the mind without being subject to licensure and to defend his 'Dianetics: the modern science of men-

tal health' (Hubbard, 1950) from the hostility of the American Medical
Association which, in secret alliance with other members of the US establishment, was seeking to destroy the movement:

> ... the American Medical Association was not amused. When
> newspapers quoted Hubbard as saying that Dianetics could cure
> all manner of ills from asthma to sex deviation the AMA ac-
> cused Hubbard of quackery and of encouraging unqualified per-
> sons to dabble in psychoanalysis armed with no more than a
> diploma in Dianetics. When Hubbard publicly denounced prac-
> tices such as electroconvulsive shock therapy and lobotomy as
> crude assaults on the brain, the psychiatric establishment was
> outraged. A surreptitious war began. Closed meetings were held
> with Hubbard's name on the agenda. The assistance of govern-
> ment agencies was enlisted - the Food and Drug Administration,
> the FBI and even the Attorney-General of the United States. So
> much trouble over the activities of a quack.... (Percy, 1987)

In 1963 the American establishment's campaign against Hubbard and Scientology came out into the open. The FDA raided the movement's head-
quarters in Washington and books were seized along with Hubbard's
'E-Meters' ('electro-psychometers') which were designated as 'quack
devices' (Percy, 1987). The FDA applied to the District Court for permission to destroy the seized material: "on the grounds that the E-meters were
'devices' with accompanying 'false and misleading labelling' and lacking
'adequate instructions for use', contrary to the Food Drug and Cosmetics
Act 1964" (Foster, 1971:59).

For anyone who is familiar with the persecution of Wilhelm Reich's
Orgonomy by the FDA and US medical organizations during the same
Cold War period of American history, this story will have a familiar ring.

In the light of what we now know about the nature of American institutions at the time, for example the FBI under Hoover and the excesses of
the US psychiatric profession in the fifties, this would seem to be at best a
case of 'the pot calling the kettle black'.

Since the late 1950s Hubbard had been running Scientology from
England where he had felt safer from attack than in his homeland. How-

ever by 1966 questions were being asked about Scientology in the House of Commons, to be followed by the press campaign and the Aliens Order already mentioned - and Foster's inquiry.

Whilst the Scientology organization was undoubtedly authoritarian in form, one wonders to what extent the exaggerated response to Scientology in the UK was 'seeded' by the hostile American establishment and also to what extent both the more 'cultish' developments in the Church of Scientology and the development of Hubbard's own 'paranoia' (as in the case of Reich) were actually 'fostered' by the vilification that they received. As Hubbard himself said: "Society tolerates far worse than we are" (Hubbard, 1966).

It bears repeating that these two reports, Foster and Sieghart, are the supposed historical underpinnings for the current proposals for statutory regulation embodied in UKCP. In the next chapter I will explore the nature of this 'organization of organizations'.

Chapter 6

The Nature of UKCP

By a sort of creeping putsch, the UK Council for Psychotherapy has established itself and its register at the centre of the therapy world in this country. This is against the will of a number of practitioners....

(Nick Totton, 1994a:47)

As with the parallel debates going on during this period [1970s to date] concerning the registration of psychologists, effected [for chartered psychologists] in 1987, those arguing for the need for regulation [of psychotherapy] emphasized the protection of the public and underplayed the issue of professional self-interest (protectionism, kudos, status, salary improvements etc.). Such is the way of professionalization exemplified in the maturer professions like law and medicine, that public interest not self-interest tends to be the hallmark of official statements and rhetoric....

(Pilgrim, 1990:13)

When in 1990 I first attempted to find out something about the nature of UKSCP directly, by writing (privately) for information, the response that I got informed me that UKSCP "is an organization of organizations and cannot at present answer queries from individuals" (UKSCP, 1990). Rather more information is now available directly to members of the public. One can send off for a brief descriptive leaflet and a directory of member organizations. A list of registered practitioners is also now available. Since July 1993 a newsletter has been available to members of the organization and is published twice a year.

Status

UKCP is a registered charity, having achieved that status (as UKSCP) in 1989. The major advantages of becoming a charity are largely financial. Being a charity brings tax advantages, rate relief, and an enhanced capacity for fund raising through public appeals, donations and, more importantly, access to grants (Phillips, 1979:2). One might suppose that a professional organization seeking a statutory monopoly would be rather too political to become a charity and accrue these financial advantages, given that: "... a body which has an object to change the law in some way, will not be registered as a charity. Further, regardless of its objects, if the main weight of a charity's activity is directed to changing the law it is acting outside charitable limits" (ibid.:46).

However, although clearly a main aim, acquiring statutory privilege is not one of UKCP's explicit objectives in its constitution (see below).

The issue of political activity by charitable bodies is something of a grey area. According to the Charity Commissioners (1994), the Courts have held that seeking to change the law or government policy are certainly political activities rather than charitable ones. Nevertheless, a charity may engage in such political activity but its freedom to do so is quite restricted. Any political activity undertaken by a charity must be in furtherance of *and* ancillary to the objects stated in its governing document. 'Ancillary' means that political activity must serve and be subordinate to those objects and not the main aim of the organization: "... They cannot, therefore, be undertaken as an end in themselves and must not be allowed to dominate the activities which the charity undertakes to carry out its charitable purposes directly ..." (ibid.:6).

There is an onus on the charity to show that its political activities are likely to further its charitable objects: "... The trustees must be able to show that there is a reasonable expectation that the activities will further the purpose of the charity effectively and so benefit the beneficiaries" (ibid.). "... It is not sufficient for the trustees simply to *believe* that their activities will effectively further the purposes of the charity; there must be a *reasonable expectation* that this is so ..." (ibid.:16).

Consequently, whilst a charity *may* seek to influence public opinion or promote a change in government policy it must not do so on the basis of "... slanted and inaccurate data. This is particularly important where material which arouses emotion is used" (ibid.:10). "A charity must not issue information which is biased" (ibid.:13). Regarding the publication of research by a charity: "... Where solutions requiring political action are advocated, they must arise from a proper analysis of the research findings ..." (ibid.:13). Thus charities are supposed to present balanced information in support of their political activities, not propaganda.

In sum, it seems that, as a charity, for UKCP to legitimately pursue statutory registration this must be a subsidiary activity not its primary objective and there is an onus upon it to present a well-founded case that statutory registration would, in truth, further its charitable objectives as set out in the 'objects clause' of its constitution and benefit the public. This case would, in the interests of the unbiased presentation of evidence that behoves a charity, also need to address the arguments and evidence presented in this book and elsewhere which indicate that there are by no means grounds for a "reasonable expectation" that such a change in the law in the case of psychotherapy would in fact benefit and protect the public rather than simply serve the economic and professional interests of the practitioners and trainers of which UKCP is largely composed.

History

UKSCP, the UK Standing Conference for Psychotherapy finally sat down and became the UKCP, the UK Council for Psychotherapy, in early 1993. UKSCP came into being in 1989, growing out of an annual conference known as the 'Rugby Psychotherapy Conference' that was first organized by the British Association for Counselling in 1982. In the previous year, MP Graham Bright's Private Member's Bill (based on the recommendations of the Sieghart Report), had failed at the second reading (Heron, 1990; UKCP 1993b). According to Derek Gale:

> In the 1980s, prompted by the scare over Scientology, which had precipitated very narrow and unconsidered legislation in Australia, and the subsequent Sieghart report in this country, many psychotherapists feared Government interference and the imposition of controls on psychotherapists. The Sieghart Report was

heavily slanted in the direction of psychoanalysis and other psychotherapists feared that their views would not be considered[1].

Out of this fear emerged the Rugby Conference, which was
organized by the British Association for Counselling, as a neutral body acceptable to all those attending. This became an annual meeting. (Gale, 1989:102)

The BAC has since bowed out of this particular arena (although it remains
a "Friend of the Council") and in conjunction with other counselling organizations is pursuing a separate register for counsellors.

Aims (see also - "UKCP aspirations" below)

After seven preparatory years of 'Rugby' Conferences, the United
Kingdom Standing Conference for Psychotherapy (UKSCP) was
formally established in 1989, with the intention of becoming the
national Council for the profession of psychotherapy. *Having as
its primary aim the protection of the public from unqualified
practitioners* .... (UKSCP, 1992)

UKCP's "Aims and Objectives" as set out in its constitution (which are
therefore its 'charitable objects' as accepted by the Charity Commissioners) are as follows:

(i) To promote or assist in the promotion of the preservation and
protection of public health by encouraging high standards of training and practice in psychotherapy and the wider provision of
psychotherapy for the public.
(ii) To promote for public benefit research and education in psychotherapy and to disseminate the useful results of any such research.

In furtherance of the above objectives but no further or otherwise the Council shall have the following powers:
a) To encourage the exchange and understanding of the different
theories and practices within psychotherapy.
b) To represent the organizations whose members engage in psy-

chotherapy to other professions, institutions and to the Government.

c) To do all other things as shall further the above objectives. (UKCP, 1993a:1)

As mentioned in Chapter 2, safeguarding the public from harm by weeding out the unqualified is the standard argument put forward by groups seeking the legal privileges of a statutory profession. In newspaper articles coinciding with the launch of the UKCP register, those who are regarded by UKCP as unqualified have been referred to by the pejorative label 'charlatans' ("imposter in medicine, quack" - *Concise Oxford Dictionary*, 4th edn.), a smear tactic borrowed from the allopathic medical profession where this term has been frequently used to discredit alternative practitioners. (See e.g. Illman, 1993; Pepinster, 1993.)[2]

The validity of this claim to be safeguarding the public will be explored in depth in later chapters, but let me just note here that the historical run-up to UKCP is, from the practitioners' position, characterized more by fear, competition and rivalry than by altruism.

It is also noteworthy that UKCP has established itself without apparently offering a public definition of 'psychotherapy', the activity which it seeks to oversee. The nearest thing to a definition that I could find in available UKCP documents was:

> All psychotherapists are expected to approach their work with the aim of alleviating suffering and promoting the well being of their clients.... (UKCP, 1993d & e)

John Rowan seems to regard this sort vagueness as a virtue: "... The reason why this has been possible [the holding together of UKSCP] is that it is not agreement on theory which is being attempted, but agreement on staying together so that the UKSCP can be recognised as the only competent authority in the UK which can speak for all psychotherapists ..." (Rowan, 1991:33).

This lack of definition may be good for the acquisition of power, but it is not exactly a point in favour of the legitimacy of the authority to which

UKCP aspires. By avoiding the tricky but fundamental issue of defining psychotherapy, the dissension in the field mentioned above (which inhibited governmental support for legislation last time), is glossed over in the interest of acquiring statutory privilege. Thus the boundaries of this activity which is UKCP's concern have not yet been drawn.

In countries where some form of statutory registration in this sort of area has been introduced (such as Australia and the USA), it is not unusual for a clear definition of the occupation to be omitted from the legislation other than to define it in a circular fashion such as: 'a psychologist is someone who is on the psychologists register' or to do so in so broad a fashion as to make it difficult to know what might *not* be covered. Such legislation leaves tremendous discretionary power in the hands of the registration board. (See also Chapter 12, Appendix B and Hogan, Vol. 2, 1979.)

However UKCP is now coming under pressure from The Lead Body for Advice Guidance and Counselling and from the BAC in regard to this issue of specifying the boundaries of psychotherapy (see Chapter 19).

This question of the definition and delimitation of the field regarded by UKCP as psychotherapy is important. In particular it impinges upon the right of human potential practitioners (and others who do not regard themselves as psychotherapists) to practise outside the UKCP structure if UKCP were to gain title protection and eventually attempt to go beyond title protection to a control of practice as well (see Chapter 24).

Structure

UKCP regards itself as having a 'federal' structure (UKCP, 1993b). Similar kinds of psychotherapy are grouped together in sections. There are currently eight of these: The Analytical Psychology Section, the Behavioural and Cognitive Psychotherapy Section, the Experiential Constructivist Therapies Section, the Family, Marital, Sexual Therapy Section, the Humanistic and Integrative Psychotherapy Section, the Hypnotherapy Section, the Psychoanalytic and Psychodynamic Psychotherapy Section, and the Psychoanalytically-based Therapy with Children Section (ibid.). Most member organizations associated with humanistic psychology are part of the Humanistic and Integrative Psychotherapy Section known as 'HIPS'.

Sections have a duty to meet at least twice a year, to organize themselves as they judge appropriate, to consider applications for membership in conjunction with the Governing Board, to approve the Codes of Ethics and Practice of member organizations and to process complaints and appeals (UKCP, 1993a).

In addition there are categories of Special Membership, Institutional Membership and non-voting categories of Associate Membership and Friends of the Council. The Special Members of UKCP are the British Psychological Society and the Royal College of Psychiatrists. Special members are Full Members of the Council and each has a seat on both the Governing Board and the Registration Board. The Institutional Members of UKCP are the Association of University Teachers of Psychiatry and the Tavistock Clinic. Institutional Members are Full Members of the Council and have two seats on the Governing Board and one seat on the Registration Board (ibid.). These latter two are apparently to be joined by a new Institutional Member, the University Psychotherapy Association, which will provide a direct route onto the register for graduates of university courses in psychotherapy (UKCP, 1993i). The BAC is a Friend of the Council, not a Full Member, and therefore has no voting rights (UKCP, 1993f). Associate Membership is a category for organizations which are not eligible for, or not wanting, Full Membership (UKCP, 1993a).

Membership

Membership of UKCP is only available to organizations and not directly to individuals. In addition to the Special, Institutional and Associate Members listed above, there are currently 68 member organizations in the Sections (Pokorny, 1994:517). Prospective organizations must:

> 1. Possess an accountable administrative structure, such as a constitution, compatible with that of UKCP (UKCP, 1993a:3).
> 2. Be the: "largest composite body, relevant to psychotherapy, of immediately related organizational units, and not a branch or sub-unit of a larger body eligible to join in its own right;
> 3. ... possess a membership, of any standing, of no fewer than fifty persons;
> 4. ... have been in existence for at least three years" (ibid.).

In making an application for membership: "Organizations mainly concerned with practice or teaching will describe their practice and their selection and training procedures, including length and frequency of training, requirements for personal therapy if any, and methods and standards used to evaluate trainees. Other organizations must show that they contribute to the development of psychology or psychotherapeutic work, either by accreditation, or by the promotion or maintenance of high standards of practice or teaching, or other promotional activities" (ibid.:5).

However, any organization that declared an interest in UKSCP and attended at least one 'Rugby Conference' prior to the inauguration of the Standing Conference in 1989 was allowed to become a Full Member without having to meet the above criteria (ibid.:7).

Membership of UKCP is subject to a 'sunset clause' under which the grounds for membership of each member organization are reviewed every five years (ibid.:8). I presume that this is unlikely to affect the Special and Institutional Members.

A quick survey of the 1993 membership of the eight Sections of UKCP reveals that they are virtually all practitioner organizations and that approximately 90 per cent of them are training and/or accrediting organizations.

Training organizations have a particular vested interest in participating in registration schemes like UKCP's, especially when a bandwagon has begun to roll. In a climate of uncertainty about the future right to practise and misinformation about the actual risks, prospective trainees may avoid organizations which are not 'approved'. Thus both training organizations and prospective trainees are under pressure to board the bandwagon whatever its merits. Through the support it gives to an organization like UKCP, such an 'insurance' mentality actually increases the risk of a restriction on title and/or practice that it is intended to indemnify. Moreover, whereas "interested organizations" - original participants in the 'Rugby Conferences' - are exempt (until their 'sunset' review) organizations who join subsequently must fulfil the above criteria of a minimum of three years establishment and a minimum membership of fifty. As Michael Wibberley has pointed out to me (1994a), the more established UKCP becomes and the more it is perceived as presaging some form of statutory control, the harder it may become to start up a new training organization, since potential trainees cannot be guaranteed eventual access to the register unless the organization is a UKCP member and the organization cannot become a member unless it has been running long enough and has enough graduates or trainees. This vicious circle for new organizations could effectively 'freeze' training in the hands of the established members and thereby stifle innovation.

The boards

There are twö boards in UKCP, the Governing Board and the Registration Board. The Governing Board is the central authority of the organization and is responsible for carrying out the decisions and policies of the Council, for convening the AGM and other meetings, for vetting applications to join the Council, for appointing sub-committees and for all forms of public representation (UKCP, 1993a; Pokorny, 1994)

The Governing Board is composed of a delegate from each of the eight sections; a delegate from each of the two Special Members; two delegates from each of the two Institutional Members; five officers and four ordinary members elected at the UKCP AGM from amongst the delegates (ibid.). These elections are on the basis of a two-thirds majority vote, as are other decisions at the AGM (ibid.). The Chairs of the Registration Board and the Training Standards Committee are also due to become Officers of the Governing Board since the existing structure has proved to be unworkable (UKCP, 1994).

The Governing Board is *entirely* composed of delegates of Member organizations: "No person shall be an officer or member of the Governing Board unless he or she is a representative of an organization that is itself a Full Member, Special Member or Institutional Member organization of the Council" (UKCP, 1993a:2).

The Registration Board set up in January 1993 administers the register according to regulations determined by the Governing Board, monitors complaints received by member organizations and: "reviews the registration of any psychotherapists if grounds for doing so are put before it" (ibid.).

The Registration Board is composed of a delegate from each of the Special and Institutional Members and: "delegates from the Sections in the ratio of one delegate for every ten or part thereof accredited training or recognized accrediting organizations in that Section. Only delegates of accredited training organizations, or recognized accrediting organizations may serve on the Registration Board ..." (ibid.).

Thus, like the Governing Board, the Registration Board is *entirely* composed of delegates of member organizations and in this case, apart from the Specials and Institutionals, *entirely composed of training or accrediting organizations*. The Registration Board is neither answerable to the Governing Board nor to the Council as a whole in the AGM (Pokorny, 1992:26; 1994:517). There is no appeal against it (Collis, 1994b:8).

Power and representation

UKCP is essentially an exclusive club for psychotherapy trainers - a political lobby for the psychotherapy training business.

There is no representation of the public interest on the Boards of UKCP. There are no votes for consumer groups with an interest in this area (though apparently there is some sort of liaison with MIND (UKCP, 1993i). Clients/patients (past, present or future) do not have any representation. Students/trainees on psychotherapy training courses do not have an independent voice in UKCP. Graduates of training organizations are only represented via the organization where they trained unless a separate graduate organization has been established and admitted to UKCP (as in the case of graduates of the Westminster Pastoral Foundation) or there is some other option in their section (such as is provided by AHPP in the Humanistic and Integrative Psychotherapy Section). The non-training practitioner is barely represented in UKCP. For example as we have seen, the Registration Board is the exclusive province of training and accrediting bodies.

In sum, there is little involvement of the public interest, the consumer interest, the client interest, the trainee interest or the non-training practitioner interest in the core institutions of UKCP. Compare the above composition of UKCP Boards with what Hogan has to say about the make-up of regulatory bodies:

> The design and administration of regulatory policies and programs should not be dominated by professionals, but should be

controlled by a balanced representation of appropriate constitu-
encies ... normally including the public, professionals, government officials, clients and other affected parties. No group should
have the power to dominate, unless it is to be members of the
public. This is in recognition of the fact that regulation is primarily designed to protect the public. It also recognizes the historical fact that the professions may not act in the best interests of
the public when their economic position is threatened. (Hogan
Vol. 1, 1979:365)

Even the Foster Report argued that the governing body of a psychotherapy
profession should include: "a number of radically-minded laymen who
will act as leaven" (Foster, 1971) and as described in Chapter 5, the Sieghart
Report, following Foster's recommendation, called for a substantial 'lay'
membership of the order of one quarter of the Council. Granted UKCP is
not a statutory body, but the current arrangements hardly bode well should
it become one.[3]

Criteria for the acceptance of training organizations:

The agreed baseline criteria for acceptance of training organizations into
the Council are:

Graduate level entry, M. A. equivalent content, supervised treatment of clients, and training in the appropriate management of
the trainee's own involvement in the therapy process .... (Pokorny,
1992:25)

Apparently "graduate level entry and M. A. equivalent content" does not
necessarily mean that you have to have a degree to train, but rather that the
content of the training should be at a postgraduate level. This sounds rather
ambiguous to me. The rationale seems to be directed at elevating the academic content and status of the courses. One organization is known to
have rejected applicants who have a degree, but not one in psychology, on
the grounds that their right to practise in the future cannot be assured without a degree in psychology.

Criteria for those who actually do the training, as contrasted with the requirements of their courses, do not appear to be specified. In fact, the criteria for the Humanistic and Integrative Section actually stipulate: "... We are not necessarily concerned with the credentials and intentions of the organization's founders or present directors ..." (UKCP, 1993j). Thus the amount of experience someone should have before beginning to train others is not referred to. It is not uncommon for people who have quite limited experience, having completed their own training a year or so before, to be training the new intake of their Alma Mater or setting up their own training organizations (see also Appendix F).

As we have seen, UKCP is an organization of organizations and overwhelmingly an organization composed of training organizations. Practitioners gain access to UKCP and its register via membership of a constituent organization. In most cases, this will be the organization with which they trained. In addition, as currently structured, the complaints procedures [see below] operate in the first instance through the member organizations, that is in most cases through the organization with which the practitioner trained. A consequence of all this seems to be that practitioners never really sever the 'umbilical cord' between themselves and those who trained them - if they want to stay on the register. This would appear to leave a great deal of power in the hands of the trainers. Given that training organizations are the ones largely responsible for setting up the whole UKCP edifice, I suppose that's not very surprising (see also Chapter 18). The vast majority of the training organizations involved, including those in the Humanistic and Integrative Section, train people to practise individual psychotherapy rather than group work - a very different skill. Will a separate register for group leaders be proposed?

Training standards

The UKCP Training Standards Committee was established in January 1993 to: "advise the Governing Board from time to time as to what regulations are appropriate for the registration of psychotherapists by the Council and other matters of training" (UKCP,1993a:5). The constitution is rather ambiguous on this point, but the composition of the committee appears to parallel the 'in-house' pattern of the other core institutions of UKCP. The

Committee is appointed by the Governing Board, with half the member-ship nominated by the Registration Board (ibid.). The Training Standards Committee seeks to raise the standard of the minimum requirement that any training will have to meet, including: "UKSCP requires member or-ganisations to ensure that training as a psychotherapist includes the acqui-sition and maintenance of a level of competence in self-awareness regarding conscious or unconscious processes, demonstrably appropriate to the type of therapy practised" (Pokorny, 1992:26) [How pray?].

David Wasdell has convincingly suggested that the processes of pro-fessionalization and accreditation that concern UKCP serve the uncon-scious societal task of defence maintenance and are forms of collusional countertransference (Wasdell, 1992:13). If so, those involved in UKCP are caught in a fundamental 'Catch 22': If they are so unaware as to en-gage in such a process they have failed to demonstrate the necessary com-petence cited above and are *ipso facto* too incompetent to be part of the profession they aspire to, since they do not meet their own standards!

The trend in training requirements sponsored by UKCP seems to be towards longer training courses (four or five years), increased academic content, more uniform standards of training to stay in line with the par-ticular UKCP section, and for what were recommended prerequisites and aspects of content to become requirements.

> There is strong support at the conference for everyone on the register having to do a 'mental health' placement and those or-ganizations which are recognized by the UK Conference as train-ing organizations have until 1994 to implement this requirement. There is a strong feeling that this should lead to training pro-grammes of four years duration. There is also a strong feeling that only graduates should be taken on as trainees. (AHPP, 1991a)

> For some time there has been a significant shift towards a more uniform standard of training by a subtle kind of upgrading that has gone on almost unnoticed. In order to stay in line within their own section, member organizations have been adjusting their training requirements. Two examples: one organization in the Analytic Psychotherapy Section used to recommend that its

trainees have own therapy, now they demand it. One of the Jung trainings used to require twice-weekly analysis, now it requires thrice. We have kept a steady pressure on the sections to produce criteria that are distinctive and satisfactory. (Pokorny, 1992:25)

UKCP 'standardization', if given the statutory 'seal of approval', could stymie alternative forms of training such as apprenticeship (see Chapter 18).

As mentioned above, the vast majority of organizations accredited by UKCP do not offer courses that train people to do group work.

Codes of ethics and practice:

Psychotherapists on the UKCP register are required to adhere to the Codes of Ethics and Practice of their own member organization which must be consistent with UKCP Ethical Guidelines and approved by the appropriate UKCP section. As guidelines, some of these would not be quibbled with by any person of integrity and would be inherent in an honest relationship. In effect they amount to: be 'upfront' and honest about your background and terms; respect your clients; put their interests first; don't exploit them.

The guideline concerning contact with professional third parties holds that: "Psychotherapists should consider the client's best interest when making appropriate contact with the client's GP, relevant psychiatric services, or other relevant professionals. Psychotherapists should be aware of their own limitations" (UKCP, 1993e).

This represents a significant liberalisation of the earlier version which assumed a closer working relationship with the medical profession: "It is normally desirable that psychotherapists should notify the client's General Practitioner that the client is in treatment ..." (UKCP, 1993d).

Other guidelines represent requirements that are more problematic. For instance: "Psychotherapists are required to ensure that their professional work is adequately covered by appropriate indemnity insurance" (UKCP, 1993e). This begs quite a lot of questions about 'standards'. Note that professional indemnity insurance is *required* rather than say 'encouraged' as in the BAC (see Chapter 21).

Furthermore, UKCP psychotherapists: "are required to refrain from any behaviour that may be detrimental to the profession, to colleagues or to trainees." (ibid.) and UKCP psychotherapists: "are required to take appropriate action in accordance with Clause 4.8 with regard to the behaviour of a colleague which may be detrimental to the profession, to colleagues or to trainees" (ibid.).

These two are standard clauses used by professions to protect the reputation and public image of the profession. Who decides what is detrimental? The profession, of course.

Complaints and disciplinary procedures

Each UKCP member organization is required to have a Complaints Procedure approved by the appropriate UKCP Section. A client wishing to make a complaint against a psychotherapist initiates the procedure of the relevant member organization. "After the completion of the Complaints Procedure within an organization, an appeal may be made to the Section *on the grounds of improper procedure*" (UKCP, 1993g:4). Appeals (on the grounds of improper procedure) not resolved by the Section are referred to the Governing Board which has the power to appoint an Appeals Committee: "as need arises" - i.e. on an ad hoc basis (UKCP, 1993a:5). The composition of the Appeals Committee is agreed amongst the parties where possible, but if not, the Governing Board decides. The views of this Committee are to be taken into account by the Registration Board but are not binding on it (ibid.).

If someone is sufficiently *compos mentis* to negotiate this complaints process, I imagine they also could cope with anything a dodgy therapist might throw at them.

However, although currently: "... Registration is through the Sections and the organizations and is not done on an individual basis. That is because the Register is voluntary. A statutory register would be managed quite differently and on an individual basis; any complaints would go to the disciplinary committee of the register" (Pokorny, 1994:517). This would result in a much more centralized system.

If UKCP's register were to become statutory, its complaints and disciplinary procedure could become a quasi-judicial process in itself, although set apart from the main body of the justice system with the latter's checks, balances and rules of evidence, standards of proof and investigation, and open courts. Yet it could have the power to remove someone's livelihood, including for things judged by the profession to be detrimental to the profession. Whether this process would constitute a 'palace of justice' or a 'kangaroo court' is a moot point.

The register

UKCP's 'National Register of Psychotherapists' is even more presumptuously titled than the organization itself, reflecting aspirations rather than current reality. The register comprised some 2600 practitioners when launched in May 1993. It was presented to Tim Yeo, who was then Parliamentary Under Secretary of State for Health before being forced to resign from the government in the midst of the 'family values' policy débâcle. In his speech to mark the event, Yeo cited sexual misconduct amongst psychiatrists and psychologists as giving rise to public concern (Yeo, 1993).

The launch of the register was celebrated by about ninety people in the 'Moses' Room of the House of Lords (not the Commons let us note) at the invitation of Lord Clinton-Davis (UKCP, 1993h). The event received considerable press coverage and a cursory reading of these press accounts might lead one to believe it had become law, however it is important to realise that the register was *not* passed into law but merely *celebrated* in the House of Lords. Good PR though.

> But any hopes that statutory recognition of the register would follow in the near future were dashed by Mr. Yeo who said that the Government, although strongly supportive of the efforts being made to regulate the profession, was reluctant to contemplate legislation to make the register a statutory one. *(Ham & High,* 1993)

Tim Yeo also made it clear at the launch that government would only negotiate about registration with a unified psychotherapy profession (UKCP, 1993i).

Those of us who are not keen on the idea of a 'united profession', may take heart from the fact that in addition to all those opponents of statutory registration that the government has yet to become aware of, a group of psychoanalytic organizations have broken away from UKCP to form their own 'umbrella' (Pepinster, 1993; *Ham & High,* 1993) and take exception to UKCP's claim to be: "now firmly established as the national umbrella organization for the entire psychotherapy profession" (BCP, 1994) (see also Chapter 7).

The UKCP register currently totals 2800 practitioners (UKCP, 1994). Since its inception, UKCP is in a position to derive a significant new income from the fees that practitioners must pay to go on the register. Some of that income will no doubt be used to fund continued political lobbying for a change in the law (see also Chapter 2).[4]

UKCP aspirations: title protection

The UKCP register of psychotherapists is currently a voluntary one without any legal backing. The organization clearly intends to try to make its register a statutory one involving restriction of the use of the term 'psychotherapy' to those on its register, a move which would obviously require government backing:

> We want statutory control but we are not getting it. So the only option is to have voluntary control. It will help, but there will still be nothing easier than for a charlatan to set up shop and get clients. They will be beyond our control. (Emmy van Deurzen-Smith, UKCP chairwoman, 1993)

> ... the register is voluntary and in itself will not bar the untrained and the unscrupulous. They will be free to practise as before. The UK Council wants the use of certain titles such as "psychotherapist" to be restricted by law to members of the register. This would put psychotherapists on a similar footing to doctors. (It is a criminal offence for anyone to claim to be a registered medical practitioner without a primary medical qualification.) (Illman, 1993)

It is worth noting as an indicator of the power of statutory registration of title alone, that in the UK, unlike say the Dental Register where a practice act applies, the Medical Register actually only distinguishes between qualified and unqualified practitioners (i.e. represents a title act). With certain exceptions anyone may practice medicine with impunity (as long as they do not call themselves a 'Doctor', 'Registered Medical Practitioner', 'General Practitioner', or 'Surgeon'). And yet, thanks to the influence of the NHS over fee payment and public reluctance to employ the 'unqualified', very few unregistered allopaths exist. Moral: Do not underestimate the power of labels!

UKCP's register seeks to protect the public from the 'unqualified'. If it becomes statutory and a title act is thereby invoked, it is likely to draw upon this public reflex of equating 'qualified', 'registered' practitioner with competence even though in this field, as we shall see, the equation does not hold. Even if the health system moves further in the direction of private health insurance, similar factors are likely to apply (see also Chapter 20).

In addition to seeking to convert the term 'psychotherapist' into a protected title, UKCP is also planning to reach agreement within itself upon the labels, by which the different modalities practised by its psychotherapists are to be known (Pokorny, 1992:27). Thus, there may be an effort to legally restrict the use of other labels (besides 'psychotherapy') to those on its register.

Furthermore, as previously mentioned, the British Psychological Society, which is one of the institutional members of UKCP, is simultaneously pursuing a statutory register of 'psychologists' (see also Chapters 2 and 7).

UKCP aspirations: beyond title protection?

Writing in 1992, David Jones, editor of *Self and Society*, had the following to say:

> In three to ten years time UKSCP will have got its procedures in place and will press for formal recognition by the British Government. If that happens, as it probably will, only people registered with UKSCP will be able to call themselves psychotherapists and practise as psychotherapists in Britain. And of course

any EC citizen may register, if they fulfil the requirements, and they too may then practise in this country.

If the law changes so that you must be registered with UK-SCP in order to call yourself a psychotherapist then what happens if you practise something which other people say is psychotherapy but you do not call it that yourself? You might for example say you are a Gestalt therapist. Under Common Law in Britain you may do this providing your clients consent and you do not claim to cure anyone of anything [I believe this is true for cancer and some other conditions such as venereal disease but that it is not generally the case]. I do not know whether the EC will try to regulate practice in such a way that you would be prevented from this loop hole - is it a loop hole? *Self and Society* has been told that in some EC countries, Germany for example, you are liable to prosecution if you are deemed to be practising anything for which you must register even if you call it something else. Does UKSCP intend to push for that arrangement in Britain or is it only the name psychotherapist rather than the activity which they want subject to legal control? (Jones, 1992:1)

Clearly UKCP is promoting a 'licensing' system, specifically a 'title act', perhaps eventually a 'practice act' and that therefore the full weight of the arguments that follow regarding licensing would apply to the statutory arrangements that UKCP seeks.

Chapter 7

UKCP in Perspective - Other Register Builders

... it is the nature of psychotherapy that none of the existing professions can legitimately claim a monopoly on it....

(Jeremy Holmes and Richard Lindley, 1989:214)

... Because of its ambiguous epistemological status (is it a psychological practice or medical treatment?) as far as ownership is concerned, psychotherapy has been at the centre of important boundary disputes and conflicts between professional groups inside the mental health services over the past twenty years....

(David Pilgrim, 1990:12)

In 1990 counselling obtained official recognition as a treatment in the UK when the then Minister of State at the Department of Health agreed that family health service authorities could offer GP's between 70 and 100 per cent reimbursement of the costs of hiring counsellors and other ancillary workers to work in their practices. From then on their numbers were calculated to grow in the NHS and, many counsellors hope, within five years an official register of counsellors will confer legal privileges on the profession.

(Myles Harris, 1994:9)

About 40,000 people are officially estimated to work full time in the area of 'advice guidance and counselling' (Harris, 1994:11). As mentioned in the previous chapter, UKCP comprises 67 member organizations plus one 'friend' (UKCP, 1993g) and currently has 2800 psychotherapists registered (UKCP, 1994). Other organizations with an interest in register building are:

The British Association for Counselling (BAC)

BAC was formed in 1977, only one year before the Sieghart Report was published and has expanded rapidly since then, growing by approximately 300 members per month in 1993 (Harris, 1994). BAC allows both individual and organizational membership and had a total membership of 10,700 individuals in 1993 (ibid.). Of these, 640 have so far gone beyond full membership to the long and involved process of becoming BAC accredited (ibid.).

BAC estimates that there are about 600 counselling courses in the UK (ibid.) and has approximately 550 organizations listed in its 1993 'Resources Directory'.

BAC is one of the members of a Steering Group for a United Kingdom Register for Counselling which it hopes will eventually lead to a statutory register (Baron, 1994:14). Like UKCP, BAC is a registered charity and therefore subject to the same limitations on its freedom to engage in political activity.

BAC does not consider that it is really possible to distinguish counselling and psychotherapy: "It is not possible to make a generally accepted distinction between counselling and psychotherapy. There are well founded traditions which use the terms interchangeably and others which distinguish them ..." (BAC, 1992). BAC has also promoted a label of 'therapeutic counselling'. (See also Chapters 12, 19 and 26.)

The British Confederation of Psychotherapists (BCP)

BCP was inaugurated on 13th September 1993 as an umbrella organization for psychoanalytic psychotherapists, independent of UKCP.

Its register of approximately 1200 practitioners was published in January 1994. It consists of ten organizational members, five of whom including the British Psycho-Analytical Society (approximately 530 practitioners) were formerly members of UKCP but broke away to establish BCP. It was felt that the structure and constitution of UKCP did not allow "appropriate differentiations" within the field of psychoanalytic psychotherapy and that: "the diversity of standards and trainings and the size of what was then called the Analytical Psychotherapy Section (over 30 organizations) posed insuperable problems to the establishment of appropriately rigorous standards for training and practice within this field" (Richards, 1994). Four BCP members have retained membership of UKCP and therefore have a foot in both camps.

BCP claims to be a complementary rather than rivalrous umbrella to that of UKCP and has taken UKCP to task for suggesting that BCP become incorporated within UKCP and for assuming that a single umbrella is necessarily essential - or preferable. (BCP, 1994)

The medical profession has a strong presence in BCP (and in psychoanalysis generally) in that a significant proportion of its practitioners are medically qualified. In the case of some constituent organizations such as the British Psycho-Analytical Society, more than fifty per cent are medically qualified and most of these are psychiatrists. As discussed in Chapter 5, The British Psycho-Analytical Society, along with other analytic bodies, was a main mover behind the working party that produced the Sieghart Report.

The British Psychological Society (BPS)

As both a registered charity and a body holding a Royal Charter, BPS is under a double legal obligation to conduct its affairs in the public interest.

BPS has a Register of Chartered Psychologists with 7000 practitioners entered (BPS, 1993b). As discussed in Chapter 2, the designation 'Chartered Psychologist' already gives a form of title protection. However BPS now aspires to title protection of the term 'psychologist' and not for the first time - BPS had hoped to sponsor a parliamentary bill with that end in view in 1984 (BPS, 1984). As things turned out they had to put that particular ambition on the back burner.

The Foster Report actually gave the thumbs down to the statutory control of the practice of psychology, designated by Foster as the study of intellectual ability as opposed to the alleviation of emotional illness (psychotherapy) (Foster, 1971:176).

BPS is: "university and cognitive science oriented and tends to adopt a medical model of suffering - diagnosis, treatment by an expert and prognosis" (*Self & Society,* 1991:28). BPS uses the term 'psychological therapy' to describe one of the functions of clinical psychologists (BPS, 1990, 1995). This is a term which perhaps 'fits' better with notions of psychologists being the ones who should do the 'therapy'. Besides, in the context of NHS history, the label 'psychotherapy' has usually been associated with medical posts (Kosviner, 1994:287). However, BPS also promotes 'counselling psychology' as one of the services offered by its members (BPS, 1995). Counselling psychologists work with people to help them: "improve their sense of well-being, alleviate their distress, resolve their crises and increase their ability to solve problems and make decisions" and to help them: "cope more effectively with normal life cycle developmental issues, such as relationship breakdown, career change, redundancy, loss and bereavement, and illness" (ibid.). BPS has a 'counselling psychology' special group that is seeking to differentiate 'counselling psychology' from other sections of psychology and from other sections of counselling (Baron, 1994:14). This may prove difficult.

According to Holmes and Lindley (1989:213-5) clinical psychologists are amongst those most opposed to the establishment of 'psychotherapy' as a separate profession and BPS has argued that registration is necessary only for the private sector and that NHS funded therapists should all be members of existing professions such as psychology or social work.

BPS and the clinical (and other) psychologists it represents have little historical claim to legitimate authority in the field of psychotherapy generally. It was only in the 1980s that British clinical psychology began to boast the advantages of eclecticism including verbal psychotherapy (Pilgrim, 1990:7). Clinical psychology only emerged as a new profession in Britain in the early 1950s. It was not characterized by any sort of therapy until the late 1950s, when it began to champion 'behaviour therapy' (and later 'cognitive-behaviour therapy') in the course of its 'status war' with psychiatry and challenge to the medical profession's monopoly of therapeutic authority in the health service (ibid.:7-12). Peace was largely declared after the 1977 Trethowan Report into the role of psychologists in the NHS (ibid.) and more recently, BPS and the Royal College of Psychiatrists have issued a joint statement proposing cooperation in the development of a coordinated psychotherapy service in the NHS (Kosviner, 1994:288). Kosviner claims that the largely behavioural bias that has previously characterized clinical psychology is being balanced out and that all major psychotherapeutic approaches (including humanistic) are now covered in the core curriculum for clinical psychology training (ibid.:299).

Apparently, it is: "the ability to combine or change psychological approaches as appropriate, while remaining rigorous in their application" (ibid.:289) that is supposed to distinguish clinical psychologists from "other practitioners of formal psychological therapies" (ibid.).

The Royal College of Psychiatrists (RCP)

The Royal College of Psychiatrists, into which the old Royal Medico-Psychological Association transformed in 1971, is amongst other things the political lobby for the psychiatrists. It has in the past been concerned to maintain medical dominance inside the state mental health services and in 1975 advised the DHSS of the importance of medical management of NHS psychotherapy services (Pilgrim, 1990:12). RCP has shown an interest in a statutory register of psychotherapists provided it has a central role in establishing and policing the register (ibid.:13). RCP is a Special Member of UKCP. As indicated above, the Royal College has signalled a willingness to cooperate with the other 'core profession' currently involved with the provision of psychotherapy in the NHS (clinical psychology) in order to develop a coordinated service.

Curiously, it seems that there is no publicly accessible register of psychiatrists as such. The Royal College regards itself as a members' organization and does not give out information about its members to the general public (RCP, 1995). The statutory Medical Register does not require more than basic medical qualifications to be lodged. (See also Chapters 24, 25 and Appendix E for more on psychiatry.)

All these organizations monitor and are to some extent involved with the activities of each other. BPS, a Special Member of UKCP, is also an organizational member of BAC. BAC is a 'Friend' of UKCP, has organizational members in common with UKCP and has many individual members who are also on the UKCP register. BCP also has member organizations in common with UKCP. RCP is a Special Member of UKCP and a significant number of BCP members are also members of RCP.

Chapter 8

Comparisons with Other Countries

Seemingly few groups are not licensed in one state or another [of the USA]. The following sampling [of licensed occupations] from a Department of Labour study ... illustrates the wide range: aerial horsehunters, athletic exhibition agents, alligator hunters, astrologers, bedding cleaners, quail breeders, ice cream buyers, cactus plant agents, antifreeze dealers, junk dealers, dog training area operators, fortune-tellers, clairvoyants, palmists, handlers of frozen desserts, installment paper purchasers, moving picture operators, photographers, rainmakers, cemetery sales people, toy salespeople, tattoo artists, tree experts, weatherpeople and wildlife exhibit managers.

(Daniel Hogan, Vol. 1, 1979:242)

Would a statutory UKCP register be very different from other licensing systems elsewhere? A leading proponent of the involvement of humanistic organizations in UKCP has argued that what has been happening in this country is: "something quite unique and exciting" (Young, 1990:5). This is in comparison with various European countries where: "... it has been successfully argued that psychotherapy is an activity that should only be practised by other professionals such as psychiatrists, psychologists and nurses ..." (ibid.:4), or the US model where to be: "... a *licensed* psychotherapist you effectively need an M.A. or Ph.D. or to be a psychiatrist. Otherwise you are condemned to practise psychotherapy as a 'therapist'. You cannot call yourself a psychotherapist ..." (ibid.:5).

Because of the ambiguous nature of psychotherapy, the assessment of relevant legislation in other countries is an extremely complicated business, not least the question of determining what the relevant legislation is. Often 'psychotherapy' is a territory claimed by various rival occupational groups which may have obtained some sort of licensing legislation in their favour. Without a country by country study of the actual statutes (which I have only undertaken in the case of Australia, Canada, the UK and some of the US states), false impressions can easily arise. I have had to rely on secondary sources for much of my information. Regarding these, Hogan's massive study of the legal framework in the USA (Hogan, Vol. 2, 1979) seems very thorough though it only takes matters up to 1979.

The situation in Europe is particularly hard to elucidate. There are not only inter-country differences but provincial ones also. In Switzerland, for example, the status of psychotherapy is a cantonal matter rather than a federal one (Swiss Embassy, 1995). There are twenty-six cantons.[1]

Regarding the European Community/Union, even the central institutions have not yet been able to obtain definitive information for all Member States. On the basis of the information acquired so far, as of 1995 it seems that a majority of the fifteen Member States of the European Community/ Union do not have statutory recognition of psychotherapy as a distinct profession.[2] Indirect regulation by limiting access to health insurance reimbursement is as, or more, prevalent than direct forms of regulation in the European Community.[3] (See also Chapters 3 and 20.)[4]

In the USA, the relevant legislation is on a state by state basis. All fifty states and the District of Columbia prohibit unlicensed practice of medicine and most medical practice acts include psychotherapy within their definition of practice, whether directly or indirectly (Hogan, Vol. 2, 1979:71). In addition all states now have some form of psychology licensing laws, all of which have been introduced since 1945. Under this legislation in some states you could practise within the law as a "therapist" as Young has stated. According to the Association of State and Provincial Psychology Boards, as of 1994 only nine out of the fifty states plus DC have psychology legislation limited to the control of title usage, that is certification laws (title acts) (ASPPB, 1994a). The rest are regarded by ASPPB as having some form of licensure law (practice act). Therefore in many states it appears that you would be practising outside the law if, given suitable definitions in the relevant act, the licensing authority chose to regard what you were doing as practising psychotherapy, whatever *you* chose to call it. For example, since the human potential movement got under way in the sixties, various US psychology licensing boards have ruled that encounter groups are already within the realm of their particular field of regulation (Hogan, Vol. 2, 1979 and Hogan, Vol. 1, 1979:248). This has presumably been a factor affecting how the human potential movement has developed, or not, in the USA.

Hogan cautions that the legal situation regarding the right to practise psychology in the US is even more complex than it seems at first sight since, even though many state psychology laws are worded so as to restrict the right to practise, their effect may only be to prevent title usage:

> ... The American Psychology Association has apparently overlooked this point, since it believes that "the vast majority of the fifty [state] laws control *the practice* of psychology and are licensure laws" (APA Off. of Prof. Affairs, 1976) (emphasis added). If one looks at the actual effect of the laws, only twenty-seven make it illegal to practise psychology without a license. The other ten merely restrict practice in conjunction with representation, the effect of which is no different from state laws that only restrict the use of certain titles. (Hogan, Vol. 2, 1979:33)

No doubt by now the APA has read Hogan (unlike perhaps many of the unlicensed practitioners and their clients who will be affected) and is taking 'appropriate steps', which brings us to the next matter.

There has been an incremental process of amending existing state legislation to make it more restrictive or widen its scope - title acts have been converted into practice acts and definitions of applicable areas extended. As an illustration with a novel twist at the end, Kate Wylie informs me that, at the instigation of the APA, Vermont recently amended its psychology law so as to make it a criminal offence to practise psychotherapy without a licence (Wylie, 1993). However, thanks to a rearguard action by practitioners 'outlawed' by the new law, awareness of the issues was raised and a reamendment was subsequently passed allowing for a roster of "non-licensed and non-certified psychotherapists" that would confer a right to practise (Wylie, 1994).

Furthermore, minimum academic requirements for licensing in the USA have gradually inflated. Where a master's degree in psychology once sufficed now a doctorate is likely to be required. Virtually all US states now require a doctorate for full licensing as a psychologist (ASPPB, 1994a).

In addition to medical practice acts and psychology acts, the would-be therapist in the USA may fall foul of statutes concerned with 'healing arts', 'drugless healing', 'massage practice', 'social work' and, increasingly, 'counseling'. By 1993 over half the states had introduced legislated regulation of counseling at the behest of local counseling associations and the American Counseling Association (ACA) (Alberding et al., 1993:33). The ACA apparently favours licensure (practice acts) (ibid.:36).

The situation in Canada is covered in Appendix C.

In Australia, there is no registration of psychotherapy as such, but nearly all states have psychologist registration boards, some of which have claimed that psychotherapy is a form of 'psychological practice' over which they have jurisdiction. Australia provides some useful lessons for us in Britain, given the close relationship of its legal system to our own (see Appendix B).

In countries where licensing legislation is in place, there are also issues relating to how stringently it is applied. As discussed in the following chapter, whether or not these laws are assiduously applied may depend upon whether the occupation protected thereby feels itself to be under immediate economic threat from unlicensed practitioners. Thus a 'black market' in practice may or may not flourish depending on the economic situation of the 'official' occupation, including the availability of third party funds and the degree to which access to them is monopolized by licensed practitioners (see Chapter 20).

It is certainly the case that the composition of UKCP includes a broad range of psychotherapy organizations so that if it does become the "overseeing" organization it aspires to be, one would not necessarily have to be a member of some other profession first in order to practise as a psychotherapist or have some other profession 'in charge' - unlike in, say, the USA or *some* of Europe. UKCP does not for instance involve having the psychiatrists 'on top'. (Although this could still happen if the whole matter is referred to a Royal Commission where apparently the psychiatrists could wield more influence). Compared with *some* countries then, this is quite a liberal position and those involved can be congratulated on their system being *relatively* free from irrelevant prerequisites - compared to *some* systems of regulation abroad.

Compared with the *existing* situation in the UK however, it represents a marked deterioration. The UK situation is *already* more like the system that Hogan and others who have studied the matter recommend as being preferable to conventional licensing systems. In many important respects a statutory UKCP system would be all too much like the systems of licensing prevailing elsewhere.

If psychotherapy regulation is introduced in the UK in conjunction with the rest of the European Community/Union, there are consequences arising from differences between the British and other European legal systems that need to be considered. Many continental European countries have legal systems derived from the Napoleonic code.[5] Under these systems you, in effect, require legal permission to engage in a remunerative activity: "... The question about the legality of any particular mode of employment is therefore, 'Has this been legally endorsed as a remunerable activity within the public sphere?' If not, it is illegal ..." (Wasdell, 1992:7). In the UK, thanks no doubt to Wellington et al., it is generally speaking the other way around. We have the right to offer a service for reward unless the law specifically forbids or restricts it. So far, it does not in this area.

According to a legal commentator interviewed on the BBC, in countries with legal systems based on the Napoleonic code there tend to be lots of rules which are not however applied very assiduously, whereas under the British common law system there tend to be fewer rules but those that do exist are taken much more seriously. So, if European law is applied in a British way it tends to be enforced more rigorously than would be usual on the continent resulting in an *over*-regulated situation that is more restrictive than elsewhere (BBC Radio 4, 1993b). For example, the application by the UK government of EC Directives concerning food production has been judged as overzealous by continental standards and consequently many small scale UK food producers are in danger of being put out of business by the cost of conformity (ibid.).[6] By contrast in Germany, where legislation to control alternative therapists has been in place for quite a while, I understand that there is also widespread 'underground' practice.

Compared with other countries it is the open milieu currently provided by the existing situation under British common law that is the *really* 'unique and exciting' thing! This needs to be safeguarded and enhanced - and promoted as a model for other countries to follow. In fact, the unfettered situation pertaining in Britain provides a rare 'control' for comparative international studies of the *impact* of licensing systems, a subject which I will address in the following chapters.

Chapter 9

Licensing and the Public Interest - the Purported Benefits

> ... The legal basis for licensure lies in the right of a jurisdiction to enact legislation to protect its citizens. *Caveat emptor* or 'buyer beware' is considered an unsound maxim when the 'buyer' of services cannot be sufficiently well informed to beware, and hence jurisdictions have established regulatory boards to license qualified practitioners. A professional board is a state or provincial agency acting to protect the public, not to serve the profession. However, by ensuring high standards for those who practise independently, the Board is simultaneously serving the best interests of both public and profession....
>
> *(Association of State and Provincial Psychology Boards, 1994b)*

As we have seen, although the register operated by UKCP is currently without statutory endorsement, this is only regarded as a first stage. Like other bodies in this area, UKCP aspires to what is in fact a licensing system involving legal restriction on the use of title, if not eventually practice as well. In either case a new kind of crime would be created and it would be wise to carefully assess the consequences:

> In seeking regulation, counselors [or any other occupational group] are asking society for the privilege of legal sanction. This legal sanction involves the creation of a new kind of crime and the control of certain titles, skills, and knowledge. Any attempt to control the use of skills or knowledge, especially when accompanied by a criminal penalty, may be of serious social concern. Therefore, it behooves professionals, as well as the public at large, to be well informed of the potential consequences of the legislated regulation of a profession. The gravity of the request and the consequences of the privilege cannot be minimized by

the profession without calling into question its commitment to public service and professional ethics. (Alberding et al., 1993:33)

The claim that a licensing system will enhance the protection of the public is the argument most commonly employed by professional bodies to persuade a legislature to grant that privilege. This chapter explores the means whereby licensing systems in general are supposed to protect the public and explains why all too frequently this does not prove to have been the case: "... much can be said about regulation protecting consumers, but this has not been a proven consequence of these laws (Gross, 1978; Hogan, 1979; Koocher, 1979) ..." (Alberding et al., 1993:34).

Many studies of the efficacy of licensing systems have focused on the situation in the USA where the right to pursue a vast range of occupations, from junk dealers to psychotherapists, has been restricted by a plethora of licensing laws. It may be argued that studies of US licensing systems are not applicable here. However the US context, where licensing is rampant, is ideal for studying what the effects of licensing actually *are* - unlike the situation in the UK where it is relatively untried in this sort of field. Indeed, so prevalent are licensing systems in psychological fields in the US that Hogan, recognizing the political inertia of this, has one set of recommendations focused on ameliorating rather than replacing these systems - despite their detrimental effects (Hogan, Vol. 1, 1979:372-80).

According to Hogan, licensing systems are generally supposed to benefit the public through performing the following functions: "(1) they establish entry requirements that must be met before a person enters the field; (2) they make provisions for disciplining wayward licentiates; and (3) they empower appropriate authorities to prevent unlicensed practice or title usage" (ibid.:238).

Restricting entry - excluding the incompetent practitioner

The establishment of entry requirements represents a form of what is known in economics as the 'input regulation' of a market for goods or services. It is intended to 'weed out' the incompetent supplier, thereby protecting the public from the social costs of their incompetence. This form of regulation is particularly prevalent in professional markets, where it is felt that the costs of incompetent supply for the consumer or third parties are particularly high and that there are also high costs for the consumer in terms of the knowledge base required to be able to make an informed purchase decision - because the body of knowledge involved is systematic, sometimes arcane, and can be acquired only by long and arduous training (Trebilcock, 1982). Thus restrictive entry requirements are supposed to protect the public from the incompetent practice of occupations which involve a considerable potential for harm and yet about which the consumer cannot reasonably be expected to know enough to make an informed choice as to who is competent.

As discussed in Chapter 2 (and further addressed in Chapter 17), I do not think it is appropriate to conceive of psychotherapy, counselling or personal growth work as 'professions' characterized by an elaborate body of knowledge inaccessible to their clients nor as activities in which the practitioners act as 'agents' in the sense of doing things *for* their clients which the clients are not capable of doing for themselves. Nor are they appropriately equated with professions where practitioners act as trusted agents for the state such as when a doctor signs a certificate for death, compulsory admission to mental hospital, or a 'sick note'. If psychotherapy, counselling or personal growth work are not professions in this sense, the argument for restrictive entry requirements is correspondingly weaker.

'Input regulation' *may* be beneficial *if* the entry requirements to the market show a strong positive correlation with competence. If not, they will simply distort the market and have a negative impact:

> In attempting to redress the informational deficiencies in a market, certification systems [title protection] carry a potential of their own for introducing misinformation into the market *if inappropriate criteria are chosen for differentiating the quality of the various providers in the market*.... Moreover, certification schemes necessarily tell a consumer nothing about the quality of service to be expected from, or risks entailed in dealing with, an uncertified provider. To the extent that certification is generally taken to imply a marked quality differential between certified and uncertified providers, at the margin this is almost certainly bound to be misleading. (Trebilcock, 1982:94)

The rationales used to justify statutory regulation (e.g. specialist knowl-edge) also usually ensure that the regulatory mechanism is largely under the influence of the profession in question. Hence, as discussed in Chapter 4, a prevalent tendency is for entry requirements to be distorted in favour of the profession rather than in the interests of the public as a whole:

> To the extent that professional interests control or influence both the setting and enforcing of licensing standards, there is a risk that the standards will be set too high in order to restrict entry unduly and drive up the incomes of existing practitioners (thus shielding them from the competition of new entrants). The em-phasis placed by most professional cultures on technical excel-lence over other issues of service quality and over issues of cost and access is likely to increase this risk. (Trebilcock, 1982:98-9)

Subsequent chapters include a detailed exploration of the entry require-ments that have been established and proposed for psychotherapy regis-tration and the relationship of these to the the competence of practitioners.

Disciplinary action - restraining the delinquent practitioner

In addition to screening out the incompetent at the entry stage, licensing systems are intended to provide means of deterring subsequent 'unprofes-sional conduct' by practitioners. To this end, codes of ethics and practice may be promulgated and complaints and disciplinary procedures estab-lished. Grounds for revocation or suspension of a practitioner's licence ('struck off' or suspended from the register) vary but usually include, in addition to professional misconduct, conviction for a criminal offence and unfitness to practise due to physical or mental illness, alcoholism or drug addiction.

Interestingly, in the case of the medical profession in the UK, the disciplinary processes of the General Medical Council do not operate in relation to an explicitly elaborated code of professional ethics but rather two broad categories: conviction for a criminal offence and 'serious pro-fessional misconduct' - which means: "... serious misconduct judged ac-cording to the rules, written or unwritten, governing the profession"

(General Medical Council, 1991). When serious professional misconduct is deemed to be the result of illness, for example alcoholism, the General Medical Council's confidential 'health procedures' apply and the doctor stays on the register but is not supposed to practise (BBC Radio 4, 1994b). Issues of medical negligence such as those concerned with errors of diagnosis and treatment are not generally thought to be a subject for disciplinary procedures (ibid.).

> ... here it has been generally felt that the patient's proper remedy is to sue the doctor for damages for his negligence, and that it is only if his conduct shows a total abandonment of his responsibilities, either towards several patients or over a period of time, that disciplinary measures are justified. (Taylor, 1976:18)

I would have thought that errors of diagnosis and treatment are perhaps the very things patients most want protection from or remedy for. After all, patients can readily notice if the doctor is drunk, read in the newspaper that he's been convicted of a crime and can charge him with sexual assault if he molests them, however areas such as diagnosis, surgical procedures or the prescription of drugs are just the sort of thing that do require the vast knowledge base acquired over many years that justifies the doctor acting on the patient's behalf. Rather than concerning themselves with aspects of medical practice where the patient is at such a huge informational disadvantage, the disciplinary proceedings of the medical profession seem to be more concerned with things that affect the public image of the profession and public 'blind' trust. However, some amelioration of this situation may result from new 'performance procedures' proposed by the General Medical Council to address cases where a doctor's 'pattern' of performance falls below an 'acceptable' level. These procedures, which would require further legislation, would however be subject to the same confidentiality as the 'health procedures' (BBC Radio 4, 1994b).

Studies of disciplinary enforcement in professions in the USA have revealed that *disciplinary action is extremely ineffective as a means of protecting the public*: "... Jervey [1961] ... concludes that between 2 and 10 percent of all physicians are involved in unscrupulous, unethical, delinquent, or incompetent activity. This is certainly nowhere near the number of those disciplined. In the mental health professions, data from the field of psychology support the proposition that board discipline is virtually non-existent" (Hogan, Vol. 1, 1979:260).

Moreover, in the case of physicians, the most common ground for action was for narcotics: "... which accounted for 50 percent of all disciplinary actions. Most of these violations were also actionable under existing criminal law, making board action somewhat redundant" (ibid.:259). The reasons for this inadequacy seem to stem from the basic nature of the system itself rather than being something amenable to tinkering. Firstly it is very expensive to operate such a system efficiently. The appeal of licensing systems to governments is the opportunity to devolve to the profession the business of policing the profession - and the cost of doing so - while offering the public an impression of 'doing something'. Hence adequate funds to operate the disciplinary procedures are unlikely to be forthcoming from government sources since this would negate half the appeal. Secondly, the profession typically dominates the system since it will usually be assumed that its members are those who have the expert knowledge necessary to be able to pass judgement on their peers. Of the 102 members of the General Medical Council only 13 are lay members (BBC Radio 4, 1994b). This ensures that when the system does work, it tends to do so more for the profession's benefit than that of the public.

The problems highlighted by a study of the US legal profession by Jerome Carlin are considered by Hogan to be: "... probably typical of all licensing boards, including those regulating psychology, social work, and medicine. Carlin attempted to establish why some ethical violations led to more severe sanctions than others and why many apparent violations never met with any action ..." (Hogan, Vol. 1, 1979:260). Carlin came up with an 'Index of Visibility' which: "... turned out to be more important in determining disbarment than the ethical salience of the charge" (ibid.). This 'Index of Visibility' included as a major factor the extent to which the violation received publicity or notoriety. Carlin concluded that:

> The organized bar through the operation of its formal disciplinary measures seems to be less concerned with scrutinizing the moral integrity of the profession than with forestalling public criticism and control....

> Further evidence that the organized bar is responding pri-
> marily to a concern for preserving its public image is the consid-
> erable importance of the visibility of the offence to the general
> community.... It is consistent ... with a desire to avoid lay inter-
> ference and control that the most widely publicised violations
> would be the most severely and publicly sanctioned. Failure to
> punish visible violations might result in public criticism of the
> bar, and the visibility itself offers the profession an opportunity
> to demonstrate to the public that it can discipline its own mem-
> bers.... (Carlin, 1966:161-2)

I have not had access to any studies that would indicate that statutory
regulation in the British context is any more efficient and which would
support the enthusiasm of the Foster and Sieghart Reports for this "well
tried method" (Sieghart, 1978:5), which has "worked excellently in the
past" (Foster, 1971:178). On the contrary, a recent investigation of the
General Medical Council indicates that low levels of disciplinary enforcement are also the case in the UK. Of the 1600 complaints made to the
General Medical Council in 1993 ten per cent made it through the initial
screening process to the Preliminary Proceedings Committee, three and a
half per cent were referred on to the Professional Conduct Committee and
only six doctors were struck off the register (BBC Radio 4, 1994b). Of
course this might reflect the outstanding integrity of British doctors.

No doubt high on the 'Index of Visibility' these days would be the
issue of sexual misconduct. Of the 145,000 doctors in Britain in 1991,
only two (i.e. 0.0014 per cent) were found guilty of 'serious professional
misconduct' by the General Medical Council on such grounds: "... Either
the pressure of work is having a disastrous effect on the British medic's
libido or there is some 'under-reporting' going on" (Gwyther, 1992:70).
(See also Chapter 13.)

It follows from Carlin's 'Index of Visibility' that, however much they
may have cultivated media coverage of malpractice prior to licensing, once
established, professions are unlikely to take steps to actively expose it in
their midst. Activating disciplinary procedures is likely to generate publicity and court adverse public attention. Hence unless a case is already
receiving adverse publicity, the temptation will be to 'let sleeping dogs

lie'. Moreover active disciplinary monitoring is costly and time consuming. The profession's tendency will be to give priority to maintaining an impression that, because of the rigorous entry requirements, malpractice is a rarity rather than a position such as: 'well yes, it does happen a fair bit but we deal with it.' The latter is a second best policy in terms of the profession's image, status and degree of public confidence. This follows from professional control of, or dominant influence upon, the disciplinary process. If the disciplinary process were to be independent and well funded these arguments would not necessarily apply, but it rarely is. The specialized and elaborate knowledge base that typifies a recognized profession also provides the basis for the contention that only the professionals can really be in a position to judge their peers.

UKCP's disciplinary system is based on explicit codes of ethics and practice which are promulgated for each member organization. Disciplinary procedures currently operate at the level of the member organization through which the practitioner is registered (usually the one where they trained), with appeal to the section on the grounds of 'improper procedure'. Apparently, if the register were statutory, complaints would go directly to a disciplinary committee of the register, leading to a much more centralized system (see Chapter 6). Given the poor track record of systems based on professional codes of ethics and conduct and self-disciplinary action as a means of protecting the public, what reason do we have to be confident that such a system, given statutory approval, would be any more effective in producing its purported benefits for the public? Why should we not believe that it will largely function as window dressing disguising professional self-interest as has so often been the case?

Preventing unlicensed practice or title usage - curbing the charlatan

> In terms of enforcement it does seem that licensing agencies are more zealous in prosecuting unlicensed practitioners than disciplining those with a licence.... (Hogan, Vol. 1, 1979:263)

However, according to Rayack (1975) this enforcement is generally in response to complaints from those with a licence, i.e. practitioners rather than consumers, and these complaints increase when the economic situation has deteriorated: "... When enforcement does occur, it is frequently aimed at curbing economic competition, not dangerous practices ..." (Hogan, Summer 1979:2). This is hardly in the public interest.

Enforcement of legislative powers with regard to unlicensed title usage or practice is expensive and consequently such powers may lie idle on the statute book until such time as the profession feels itself to be under sufficient economic threat to warrant the cost and trouble to enforce them. (See for example the situation in Australia described in Appendix B.)

In the light of all this, the conclusions of Jeffrey Pfeffer regarding the efficacy of statutory regulation should come as no surprise:

> It must be concluded that the outcomes of regulation and licensing are frequently not in the interests of the consumers or the general public. It is difficult to find a single empirical study of regulatory effects that does not arrive at essentially this conclusion....
>
> In a review of the outcome of regulation and licensing, we have found that the effect is almost always to enhance the position of the industry or licensed occupation at the expense of the public at large....
>
> In view of these empirical results, accumulated in a series of studies covering both different time periods and different industries, the role of administrative regulation in the solution of social problems must be called into question. There is evidence that administrative regulation and licensing has actually operated against the public interest; and that rather than protecting the public from the industry, regulation has frequently operated to protect and economically enhance the industry or occupation.... Even if quality differences are observed, the question remains as to whether they are worth the cost. (Pfeffer, 1974:474,478)

The discussion in this chapter has set aside the issue of whether or not a sound case can be made for the public actually needing special protection from the occupation in question. This issue regarding psychotherapy will be addressed in later chapters.

Chapter 10

Licensing and the Public Interest - the Harmful Side-effects

> ... With respect to input regulations, a general licensure regime [for mental health services] seems highly undesirable. Social costs in terms of higher fees for services, reduced innovation, and undue interference with freedom of choice in highly subjective areas of personal values, are likely to be substantial....
>
> *(Michael J. Trebilcock and Jeffrey Shaul, 1982:289)*

Hogan (Vol. 1, 1979) concludes that systems of licensing have various negative side-effects that need to be offset against any possible benefits such systems may bring and that: "... *the harmful side-effects of licensing laws usually outweigh their supposed benefits* ..." (ibid.:238). He cites licensing laws as a significant factor in:

> (1) unnecessarily restricting the supply of practitioners [by introducing monopolistic factors into the market];
> (2) decreasing their geographic mobility;
> (3) inflating the cost of services;
> (4) making it difficult for paraprofessionals to perform effectively;
> (5) stifling innovations in the education and training of practitioners and in the organization and utilization of services; and
> (6) discriminating against minorities, women, the poor, and the aged [by raising entry requirements in terms of time, cost and academic prerequisites]. (ibid.:238-9)

Hogan clarifies how these negative side-effects operate as follows:

> In addition to not protecting the public, licensing tends to have negative side-effects. First, higher than necessary and irrelevant

entry requirements restrict the number of persons able to enter the professions, exacerbating shortages in the supply of personnel. Second, through making it unnecessarily difficult for professionals licensed in one state to be licensed in another, licensing aggravates problems in the geographical distribution of practitioners. Third, broad definitions of practice, overly restrictive regulation of paraprofessionals, and the absence of alternative routes to licensure have decreased the overall supply of services unnecessarily. These three problems produce a fourth, which is a significant increase in the cost of professional services. Fifth, licensing inhibits important innovations in professional practice, training, education, and the organization of services. It does so through disciplinary provisions and ethical standards that create difficulties in advertising services and restricting how services may be delivered, through reliance on accreditation agencies whose criteria are not based on whether schools or programs produce competent practitioners and through defining quality in terms of what is currently acceptable by the majority of practitioners, not empirical evidence of effectiveness. Finally, reliance on academic degrees or other irrelevant or unnecessary entrance requirements, results in serious discrimination against minorities, women, the aged, and the poor. (Hogan, Summer 1979:2)

Furthermore:

> ... licensing laws, as currently conceived, tend to promote unnecessary and harmful consumer dependence, since their implicit philosophy is that the public is incapable of making use of information to decide on practitioner competence. (Hogan, Vol. 1, 1979:239)

Writing in 1993, Alberding et al. indicate that these conclusions have not been superseded by later studies or changes in the pattern of licensing:

> Some counseling professionals view legislated regulation with a wary eye and are concerned that it will result in unintended and

undesirable consequences for both the profession and the public. In addition, economists, sociologists, and political scientists have long observed that there are costs inherent in occupational regulation. These potential liabilities include (a) increased consumer vulnerability, because regulation does not, in fact, protect the public as it promises to do (Gross, 1978); Hogan, 1979); (b) discrimination against some competent practitioners (Hogan, 1980); increased costs of services (Collins, 1979; Meltzer, 1975; Rottenberg, 1980); (d) loss of public power and control (Reiff, 1974); and (e) professional stagnation (Danish & Smyer, 1981; Rogers, 1973)....

... that costs increase following legislated regulation is an economic fact (Collins, 1979; Rottenberg, 1980).... In addition, the problems of discrimination, public loss of power and control, and the lulling of consumers into an unwary and vulnerable state are facts of life to political scientists, economists, and sociologists.... (Alberding et al., 1993:34-37)

The negative side-effects of licensing, which can be seen as the outcome of policies pursued by professional organizations who have control of the accreditation process (Hogan, Vol. 1, 1979:330), must be offset against the purported benefits of licensing, which are invariably argued for by those same organizations in terms of protecting the public from harm, although as discussed in the last chapter that has not been a proven consequence of such laws:

While it is true that the public needs protection from quacks, it also needs protection from the harmful side-effects of licensing.... *the preferred policy is to protect the public from harm in general*, whether or not incurred by a practitioner. Such a policy requires an examination and weighing of the unintended and potentially deleterious side-effects of licensing. (Hogan, Vol. 1, 1979:239)

This is a very 'holistic' position that takes into account the *overall balance of risk and benefit to the public rather than focusing on particular issues of risk in isolation.*

Chapter 11

Licensing and the Public Interest - Pre-conditions for Licensing

... It is important to underscore at the outset the obvious but often neglected truth that even following the identification of imperfections or failures that would be likely to persist or develop in a market, if unregulated, the decision as to whether to regulate at all, and if so, in what way, presents special difficulties because all of the available regulatory instruments are also imperfect. Thus, the policy maker is faced by a daunting calculus that involves comparing the outcome from a flawed market with the outcome of flawed regulatory instruments. One imperfect state of the world must be compared with another....

(Michael J. Trebilcock, 1982:83)

These weaknesses of an occupational licensing system are formidable and suggest that licensure should be reserved for professional markets characterized by high costs of error by providers, high information costs faced by consumers, and/or substantial and widespread negative third party effects not fully compensable in damages, and for situations where there is a reasonably high correlation between prescribed training inputs and desired service outputs.

(ibid.:99)

Hogan comes to the conclusion that laws that restrict a person's right to pursue an occupation, whether by control of title or restriction of the right to practise should *not* be enacted unless the following *pre-conditions for licensing* are met:

(a) The profession or occupation being regulated must be mature and well established.

> The fact that a profession is dominated by one professional asso-
> ciation and has highly uniform standards of practice is not nec-
> essarily a sign that such a profession is mature. ***The critical factor
> is whether agreement on uniform standards of practice is war-
> ranted by the empirical research***. (Hogan, Vol. 1, 1979:366)

*(b) The profession being regulated must have a clearly defined field of
practice adequately differentiated from other professions.*

(c) The profession must have a significant degree of public impact.

*(d) The benefits of licensing must outweigh the negative side effects cited
above.* (That is, increased cost of services, lack of availability of professional help, inhibitory effect on the organization of services and discriminatory impact.)

*(e) Simpler and less restrictive methods that would accomplish the same
purposes must be unavailable* (for example existing laws).

*(f) The potential for significant harm from incompetent or unethical prac-
titioners must exist and must be extremely well documented.*

> ... Until recently, legislatures have been more than willing to pass
> licensing laws, as long as some possibility of harm could be dem-
> onstrated. Since virtually all occupations involve some danger,
> this does not provide a very good guideline.
> Since it is generally the profession that is seeking licen-
> sure, and since there is a good reason to believe that economic
> self-interest may be involved, it should be incumbent upon the
> profession to demonstrate that licensure is actually necessary.
> This means that the dangers involved without licensure should
> be easily recognizable and not based on tenuous or remote argu-
> ment. It means that both the magnitude and the probability of
> harm should be reasonably large. Isolated instances of severe
> harm should not constitute sufficient grounds for licensure....
> (Hogan, Vol. 1, 1979:367)

(g) Practitioner incompetence must be shown to be the source of harm.

> A reasonable consensus must exist as to what causes harm and
> the causes of harm must be related to professional functioning....
> If no consensus exists as to what causes harm then it is unlikely
> that licensure laws will mitigate the dangers involved. If the
> causes of harm are related to environmental or client factors,
> then professional regulation will likewise have little impact....
> (Hogan, Vol. 1, 1979:367)

(h) The purpose of licensing laws must be the prevention of harm.

> Where licensing laws require certain standards to be met, these
> standards must be related to the prevention of harm.... It is not
> meant to ensure high quality professional practice. The efforts
> by various professional associations to require high standards of
> practice should be restricted because of the negative side effects
> inevitably engendered. (Hogan, Vol. 1, 1979:367)

*(i) Adequate enforcement mechanisms for disciplining those who violate
the law must exist.*

*(j) Adequate financial resources must be committed to ensure proper ad-
ministration and enforcement of the licensing laws.*

> ... If a legislature truly believes that licensing is necessary to
> protect the public, then it should budget an adequate amount of
> funds to do the job properly. (Hogan, Vol. 1, 1979:368)

Even when these pre-conditions are met, the type of licensing advocated
by Hogan is, as we shall see, not one of the types that commonly prevail.
    In the following chapters I will offer an assessment of 'psychotherapy'
in the light of these pre-conditions, focusing on the most important issues
raised.

Chapter 12

Licensing and Psychotherapy - Definitions and Boundaries

[Psychotherapy] is an unidentified technique applied to unspecified problems with unpredictable outcomes. For this technique we recommend rigorous training.

(V. C. Raimy, 1950:93)

The earliest use of the term psychotherapy was by J. C. Reil in 1803 in an article entitled "Rhapsodies in the Application of Psychic Methods in the Treatment of Mental Disturbances". Since then the term psychotherapy has become a lexicographer's nightmare. Definitions abound, though few have much in common with each other and many are antithetical.

(Daniel Hogan, Vol. 1, 1979:12)

... psychotherapy ranges from its conventional and established centre to obscure and quasi-religious fringes. Despite aspirations to acceptance and respectability, psychotherapy as a whole does not yet present the public with the unity and ideological coherence that are the hallmarks of a profession.

(Jeremy Holmes and Richard Lindley, 1989:204)

... Trouble is, psychotherapy is probably a whole bunch of different things that don't fit under any one obvious umbrella....

(David Kalisch, 1990:26)

This chapter addresses preconditions for licensing *(a) the profession or occupation being regulated must be mature and well established* and *(b) the profession being regulated must have a clearly defined area of practice adequately differentiated from other professions.*

Psychotherapy does not meet these preconditions. It is not 'mature' and does not have a clearly defined area of practice which is capable of legal definition. Some see it as a medical matter, others see it as an educational process, others as something more akin to a spiritual developmental process. Is one suffering from mental illness if one is a candidate for psychotherapy or is one developing one's potential? Is one restoring normal functioning, "transforming ... hysterical misery into common unhappiness" (Freud, 1893-5:393), or actualizing potential? What degree of developed potential constitutes normality? Is it about helping people to adjust to the prevailing notion of what is 'normal' or helping people to actualize themselves even if that means they become less 'normal'? (See Section II.)

Is psychotherapy a form of medical therapy - a treatment? Is it 'the talking cure'? The Foster and Sieghart Reports lean in that direction, the former seeing it as: "the practice of psychological medicine" and the latter as: "this field of medicine" (see Chapter 5) and the contents of some UKCP documents indicate that 'medicalized' language and thinking is alive and well in that organization (see Chapter 23). Some of those involved in UKCP, even in the Humanistic and Integrative Psychotherapy Section, are explicit about the appropriateness of a medical model of psychotherapy. Petrūska Clarkson, for example, regards psychotherapy as an activity which is best seen as focusing on 'revolutionary change', that is, diagnosis of pathology and a destructuring and restructuring of the personality:

> Psychotherapy, on the other hand [compared with a focus on evolutionary change in counselling], focuses on discontinuous, revolutionary change. The justification for psychotherapy often needs to be that such an expensive and time consuming intervention is necessitated because, unless discontinuous change is implemented, serious tragedy may result. In this case the medical model may be appropriate in terms of diagnosis (or at least assessment) leading to treatment implementing or seeking for a 'cure'. A medical model may be more effective when there is actual structural damage to the organism which has to be reversed before the organism can start reconnecting with its own innate healing process. Psychotherapy, whether psychodynamic, behavioural or humanistic/existential, concerns the destructuring and restructuring of the personality, whether it is conceived of as

belief-and-behaviour systems, ego states, or super-ego and self structures. (Clarkson, 1994:10)

The term 'psychotherapy' is itself medical model terminology (see Chapter 24). Psychotherapy and the medical profession have a long historical association, the more so in North America where, in the first half of the century at least, psychoanalysis was the epitome of psychotherapy and US psychoanalytic organizations were opposed to the training of 'lay' analysts - those without medical qualifications. In the post-war era, other models besides a medical one have established themselves in 'psychotherapy' however the medical model still rubs shoulders with them, and it has big shoulders! (See Chapter 25.)[1]

How is psychotherapy different from counselling? What are the boundaries? What are the distinctions? 'Counselling' used to be a perfectly serviceable word referring to the act of giving advice or guidance. Nowadays, many counsellors are more likely to eschew the act of giving counsel and regard this as a common misapprehension of their nature of their job (Bennett, C., 1994). According to Feltham and Dryden: "[The term 'counselling'] has a variety of meanings (and many of them are problematic)...." and: "... In the opinion of most mainstream personal counsellors, such usage [as 'debt counsellor', 'beauty counsellor' etc.] is incorrect and/or unfortunate ..." (Feltham & Dryden, 1993:40-2).

This 'counselling', shorn of any advisory connotations, has its roots in the USA with Carl Rogers and, before him, the radical social activist Frank Parsons (Bond, 1993:17). Brammer and Shostrum (1982) have attempted to identify the characteristics that distinguish 'counselling' from 'psychotherapy' in an American context. According to their study of the American literature, counselling is seen as being an educational process of relatively short duration concerned with solving problems that arise primarily from situational pressures rather than from severe or persistent emotional difficulties. The focus is on present time and conscious awareness. Psychotherapy, by contrast, is seen as an analytic and reconstructive process of longer duration that is more concerned with issues arising from within the personality than from the person's situation and one which works with 'neurotics' or those with severe or persistent emotional problems. The focus is more on preconscious and unconscious processes and events in the patient's past than is the case with counselling (Bond, 1993:25).

In an effort to define the differences from a UK perspective, Tantam and Rickard compared counselling and psychotherapy in relation to twelve possible distinguishing criteria and could find no obvious and clear distinctions except perhaps that psychotherapy is more associated with the treatment of mental illness or personality disorder and has perhaps a higher status due to a historical association with medicine, and that counsellors tend to have more eclectic backgrounds than psychotherapists. They suggested that the relationship between general practice and psychiatry might provide a model for how to draw a boundary between the two. However, they commenced their article with the statement that: "Neither counselling nor psychotherapy are clearly defined activities. Distinguishing between them is therefore particularly difficult. Indeed there are many counsellors who consider that they cannot be distinguished in practice, although the fact is that they continue to call their work 'counselling' rather than 'psychotherapy' ..." (Tantam & Rickard, 1992).

As mentioned above, Clarkson (1994:9-11) thinks counselling and psychotherapy are best distinguished by highlighting what she sees as their polar opposites - a focus on evolutionary or revolutionary change respectively, rather than trying to make a boundary where clearly there is at least a considerable degree of overlap. However, that will not do for legal purposes unless the 'circularity' gambit is applied (see below).

Rowan (1983:9) argues that an important distinction between counselling and psychotherapy in practice is the length of the training. Although training programmes in both cases are tending to get longer and longer it does often seem to be the case that those organizations which offer training in both counselling and psychotherapy are liable to require a longer training for the latter and to regard its status as 'higher'. However, length of training does not appear to relate to basic competence in this sort of field (see Chapter 16) and therefore even if this does constitute a general difference it does not necessarily constitute a functional distinction.

In the case of the term 'counselling' we have a word that once meant something fairly clear but which has become yet another ambiguous generic overlapping the ambiguous use of the term 'psychotherapy'. As we have seen in Chapter 7, the British Association of Counselling does not believe that a generally accepted distinction between counselling and psychotherapy can be made. According to Judith Baron, general manager of the BAC: "It's increasingly difficult to define where the boundary line is, even if there *is* one" (Bennett, C., 1994). Brian Thorne concurs and suggests that the quest for the difference between the two is illogical and invalid (Thorne, 1992). Tim Bond suspects that the differences may have more to do with status and money than with anything more substantial: "... I am frequently told that in private practice the label 'psychotherapy' attracts higher fees from clients than 'counsellor' ..." (Bond, 1993:26). (For further discussion of 'counselling' see Chapter 26.)[2]

Is psychotherapy a form of 'psychological practice' and therefore a psychotherapist a type of psychologist? This is often taken to be the case in other countries where the practice of psychotherapy is often regulated by psychology boards (see Appendices B and C). The British Psychological Society has referred to psychotherapy as 'psychological therapy' and is also designing a qualification in 'counselling psychology' (see Chapter 7 and Feltham & Dryden, 1993:42). Then there is the question of 'psychological counselling' not to mention 'therapeutic counselling' ... !

Is the term 'therapist' a shorthand for 'psychotherapist' or does it mean something different? Some people imply it is a lowlier title (e.g. Young, 1990 quoted in Chapter 8). The Association for Humanistic Psychology Practitioners 'category guide' to humanistic psychology practice (AHPP, 1993) refers to both 'psychotherapists' and 'therapists' of various types and appears to indicate that AHPP regard 'psychotherapists' as more competent to work with: "people with complex problems over a long period of time" (ibid.).

It is often suggested that psychotherapists are more *au fait* with transference and countertransference than mere 'therapists' or 'counsellors'.

What distinguishes a psychotherapist from, say, a spiritual teacher? Can psychotherapy be a compulsory treatment e.g. for involuntary mental hospital patients or for sex offenders in prison or can it, by its very nature, only be a voluntary endeavour? Is it an art, a craft or a science?

As Parloff says: "Psychotherapy cannot be defined either by evidence of its unique effects or by its professionally specialized and restricted techniques" (Parloff, 1970:295). Psychotherapy is *not* a unified field. There is not a consensus as to values, goals and means amongst the activities that are referred to by this label. There are instead different underlying models, with differing goals and values, vying for predominance. (See Section II.)

The agreement amongst those in UKCP does not so much reflect the evolution of a coherent profession but rather an agreement to stick together in the pursuit of power. It is a political alliance.

Statements commenting on the impossibility of defining the term 'psychotherapy', *especially for legal purposes*, are legion:

> No problem in licensing has proven to be a greater bone of contention than the matter of psychotherapy. Although everyone has his [or her] own private opinion of what psychotherapy is, no one has yet come forward with a definition of psychotherapy sufficiently precise to stand in a court of law. (Combs, 1953:562)

> It is also evident that the profession of psychotherapy cannot yet be adequately defined and has not yet differentiated itself sufficiently from other professions. Whether defined by goals, methods, structure, or theoretical base, psychotherapy is impossible to clearly delimit, *except through arbitrary determinations*. A committee of the American Medical Association (Gerty, Holloway, & MacKay, 1952), for instance, concluded that "after a great deal of discussion ... psychotherapy could not be defined satisfactorily, at least for legal purposes, though persons and groups, both medical and non-medical, often put forward definitions which suit their own purposes....
>
> The problems involved in defining psychotherapy and their implications for regulation were recognized by organizations such as the American Psychological Association when it originally began to seek legislation. The passage of time, however, has seen the APA and others ignore these implications. It has become apparent that political considerations of power and control have outstripped concerns about the value and quality of regulation.... (Hogan, Vol. 1, 1979:368-9)

> How can a professional group regulate an activity it is unable to define ... ? The answer, obviously is that it cannot. (Leifer, 1969:155)

But of course that won't stop them trying. As mentioned in Chapter 6, an approach that has been employed where a professional group has suc- ceeded in getting psychotherapy subject to some form of statutory regula- tion is not to define 'psychotherapy' (or 'psychology') in the legislation in any functional terms at all and to leave wide discretionary power with the registration board which it can then exercise during times of economic recession or whenever suits the profession. Associated with this, a legal definition can be achieved by a circular means. A 'psychotherapist' or a 'psychologist' can be defined *as someone who is on the register*. So, once the register is established and power has been achieved, the problem of meaningful definition and functional boundaries can be avoided altogether. Clarkson (1994) has raised this as a possibility for UKCP:

> ... There is no agreement on the exact boundaries of psycho- therapy. One result of this is that the political definition of psy- chotherapy has given rise to great arguments and considerable tensions in the profession.... It is possible to define psychotherapy as all those therapies that are recognized by the UKCP. That is a simple way of reaching some sort of agreement. The trouble is that there are always some who claim that some psychotherapy is excluded from the Council. This is merely another way of hav- ing the argument of what is, and what is not, psychotherapy. On the other hand we can recognize that other professions also have ill-defined borders [which?], and we can stop worrying so much about our general definition or our political solution by recog- nizing that the borders of psychotherapy are not fixed. (ibid.:4)

Such a solution would be very convenient for UKCP and might alleviate worries for those within that organization but would be unlikely to be beneficial for the stress levels of those outside it.

Another approach is to define the area of practice in as broad a fash- ion as possible, a 'catch all' definition as lampooned by Raimy in the quote at the beginning of this chapter. As Hogan says, many of these defi- nitions are: "so broad that it is difficult to know what is not within their purview" (Hogan, Vol. 1, 1979:248). When the Ontario Psychological Association proposed the establishment of a practice act in that Canadian province, a major public controversy ensued given that the proposed field of psychology was defined so broadly that objectors felt it covered functions performed by almost every citizen at some time or another as well as overlapping such areas as teaching, business, personal development, art, religion, etc. It was argued that it would be dangerous to allow the Ontario Psychological Association a monopoly on what values could be permitted in society. In the province of British Columbia however, similar legislation was passed before objectors (including the BC Civil Liberties Association) were sufficiently aware of it to organize opposition (Trebilcock & Shaul, 1982:286-8). (For details of subsequent legislation in Ontario and British Columbia see Appendix C.)

UKCP has yet to offer a definition of psychotherapy in its publications. However, the activities of the Lead Body for Advice Guidance and Counselling, including its 'functional analysis' of psychotherapy, along with competition from the BAC's notion of 'therapeutic counselling' indicate that this silence on the matter is unlikely to last. (See Chapter 19.)

Thus 'psychotherapy' is a term that is difficult to define in a meaningful way that covers all the activities for which it has been used. Psychotherapy, psychology, counselling, human potential practice are all things that are concerned in some way or other with something as close to home as it gets - with our experience of ourselves and the world, with our subjectivity. Trying to define such a thing 'objectively' for legal purposes is deeply problematic. Discussions such as whether 'psychotherapy' should be a regulated profession (and this discussion is no exception) are stymied by the difficulty of knowing quite what is being referred to by the term and the tendency to try to fit disparate activities under one generic umbrella - a tendency driven more by political considerations than functional ones. In Section II, I will attempt to make some functional distinctions between types of work in this area on the basis both of the question 'what?' and the question 'for whom?' since in this area in particular 'for whom?' feeds back and changes the nature of 'what?' A differentiation on the basis of the values and intentions of the people concerned and on the basis of the type of person receiving the service and *their* status is, I think, helpful and clarifying - whatever the label by which those forms of work may be currently referred to.

Chapter 13

Licensing and Psychotherapy - Protecting the Public from Harm

In a human relationship, just when is a person harmed? How can you prove it? These are difficult questions to answer for the plain fact of the matter is that people are helped by the damnedest things. Almost anything may help people to behave more effectively or to feel happier given the right circumstances. Who is to say that a particular idea taught to a client was an act of quackery, especially if the client swears it was helpful? Much of the business of human relations is carried on through no more than what one person says to another. It is doubtful if we shall ever seriously want to control such intercourse in a free, democratic society. The cure could well prove more fatal than the disease.

(Combs, 1953:558)

This chapter addresses preconditions for licensing *(f) the potential for significant harm from incompetent or unethical practitioners must exist and must be extremely well documented, (g) practitioner incompetence must be shown to be the source of harm* and *(e) simpler and less restrictive methods that would accomplish the same purposes must be unavailable.*

Safeguarding the public from harm is the key argument upon which any claim for the legitimacy of a licensing system must rest. It is the most cited rationale for such a system and, as we have seen, UKCP is amongst those organizations that have claimed protection of the public as a main aim. As Daniel Hogan puts the matter:

Central to the problem of regulating psychotherapists is the degree of risk and danger involved in the psychotherapeutic process. The demand for regulation rests largely on this alleged danger, and the constitutionality of many licensing laws hinges on an adequate demonstration of significant risk. (Hogan, Vol. 1, 1979:25)

What then is the scale of the problem? To give perspective during the course of this discussion, it is useful to bear in mind the dangers of addiction and other side-effects which have frequently accompanied the application of "chemical solutions to personal problems" (Pilgrim, 1990:6). Despite both drug and medical licensing systems, there is usually little hope of redress for such damaging effects in this country other than through the courts on a collective basis (see Appendix E).

> Determining the degree of danger is more complex than first appears. The seemingly simple task of defining what constitutes an adverse result is in fact very difficult. Determining whether psychotherapy is responsible for precipitating suicide or severe emotional distress is not an easy matter. Subtler still is the question of the duration of emotional injury since negative effects may only be transitory. ***Often ignored is the necessity of comparing the level of danger in psychotherapy with that in other activities for which no demand for regulation exists....*** (Hogan, Vol. 1, 1979:25)

Various aspects of this issue can be outlined. What constitutes harm? (and what simply relapse ?) What evidence is there of a significant risk of harm, and for whom? What evidence is there that, where a significant risk can be demonstrated, it is a consequence of practitioner incompetence? How does the risk of harm compare with activities for which no demand is made for regulation? (After all, few worthwhile activities in life do not involve *some* element of risk.) How does the degree of harm which may occur compare with the harm deriving from the institution of a licensing system intended to ameliorate it? Can simpler and less restrictive methods such as the application of existing laws accomplish the same purpose?

Thus there are rather considerable conceptual difficulties here that parallel those concerning the definition of psychotherapy. What constitutes recovery or improvement - and what constitutes deterioration - depends on how psychotherapy is conceived. For example, in discussing the proposition that all therapies aim to make the client feel better, Kline has this to say:

> This argument makes several assumptions about the nature of psychotherapy and of human life itself (the latter topic almost certainly out of bounds in respectable academic psychology!). Thus I see no necessary reason why a client should be happy. As Freud (1923) put it, the aim of psychoanalytic therapy is to make neurotic unhappiness into normal unhappiness. It seems to me a quite respectable argument, as Smail (1984) has eloquently shown, to admit that the lives of many people are unhappy and that to assert otherwise or to attempt to persuade clients that there is something wrong with them because they are unhappy, is distasteful and ultimately propping up a society that is better changed. With such a view, the aim of psychotherapy becomes one of helping clients to accept their feelings. In fact political rather than psychological change is implied in such a viewpoint.
>
> It is not my intention here to support or attack any of these notions concerning the nature of psychotherapy, psychoanalytic, behavioural or, for want of a better term, political. My point is simply that implicit within the aims of psychotherapy and consequent outcome measures lie such fundamental viewpoints or values. The problem, from the standpoint of research into psychotherapy, is that research results are unlikely to be relevant to all these views.... (Kline, 1992:74)

According to Stanislav Grof:

> Since the criteria of mental health are unclear, psychiatric labels are problematic , and since there is no agreement as to what constitutes effective treatment, one should not expect much clarity in assessing therapeutic results. In everyday clinical practice, the measure of the patient's condition is the nature and intensity of the presenting symptoms. Intensification of symptoms is referred to as a worsening of the clinical condition, and alleviation is called improvement.... (Grof, 1985:330)

Such a perspective is at variance with Grof's own view that the intensity of what are regarded as symptoms under the medical model is actually an indication that a healing and transformative process is at work:

... The therapeutic philosophy based primarily on evaluation of symptoms is also in sharp conflict with the view presented in this book [*Beyond the Brain*], according to which an intensity of symptoms indicates the activity of the healing process, and symptoms represent an opportunity as much as they are a problem. (ibid.)

Moreover, culture-bound, 'social adjustment' criteria may also be used as a basis for assessing therapeutic results in addition to, or as part of, the assessment of symptomatology. For example the diagnostic criteria for 'personality disorders' in DSM-IV (see Chapter 20) specify that such 'disorders' are: "An enduring pattern of inner experience and behaviour that deviates markedly from the expectations of the individual's culture" (American Psychiatric Association, 1994:275). From other perspectives, such a 'deviation' *may* indicate a heightened personal integrity, 'resistance to being rubricized' and above average 'sanity' (Hampden-Turner, 1970; Maslow, 1968).

In practice, most outcome studies of psychotherapy do seem to assume a medical model involving the diagnosis and treatment of psychopathology (or at the very least a problem-solving model).[1] Presumably without making this sort of assumption it would be rather difficult to even begin to do such research. (Have there been any 'outcome' studies of spiritual disciplines or religions? Which religions are the most efficacious?)

According to Isla Lonie: "... Morstyn [1989] has listed the assumptions which he believes underpin much of the current thinking in psychotherapy research: (a) That everything has a defined nature. (b) That events are fully predictable and determined. (c) That an event can be considered separately from the agent of that event ..." (Lonie, 1991b:552). Lonie adds a further concept: "... (d) That in a discipline which emphasizes the importance of the unique experience of the individual, it is possible to understand events in terms of statistical probabilities" (ibid.). These are essentially Newtonian-Cartesian paradigm assumptions applied to human beings -

and ones which imply an image of them as part of a 'clockwork universe' running according to pre-established 'Laws of Nature'. Despite having been transcended by advances in our understanding of physics, the Newtonian-Cartesian paradigm still has useful applications in some areas of the physical sciences, offering reliable predictions - yes, that apple will fall on your head. However, its applicability becomes progressively less appropriate as one proceeds from the physical, through the biological to the personal and spiritual spheres, and such a deterministic view does not really fit very well at all with, say, a personal growth view of psychotherapy.

Kline (1992:65) argues that in addition to such issues of assumptive definition and meaning, the study of outcome in psychotherapy is plagued by numerous methodological problems that few if any studies have been able to overcome. For example well known psychological tests (such as the MMPI[2]) which are often used to measure recovery (or deterioration) are of dubious validity. Bearing all these strictures in mind, I will explore the empirical research available, such as it is.

In a 1988 survey of research into hurtful psychotherapy, Striano cites Bergin's well known studies of the 'deterioration effect' which appear to show that ten per cent of clients in psychotherapy (with licensed practitioners presumably, since this is US research) deteriorate, which is five per cent more than for his control group who received no psychotherapy. So, on the basis of this study five per cent of the clients were worse off than if they had received no therapy - which seems to be about average for the studies surveyed (Striano, 1988:121).

Turning now to the area of humanistic psychology practice, in the 1960s and 1970s the burgeoning of encounter and similar groups lead to numerous anecdotal reports of dangers and subsequent empirical studies. Regarding anecdotal reports of the risks of harm involved in encounter groups, Hogan reports that:

> ... The number of cases described in the encounter field is sufficiently large, and enough of these are thoroughly documented, to warrant the conclusion that encounter groups can and do cause harm in certain instances. The frequency with which harm occurs, however, remains open to question. Unfortunately the ten-

dency has been to use anecdotal reports as proof that encounter groups are so dangerous that rigid regulation is needed. *Yet a similar array of horror stories could easily be assembled about highly credentialed psychiatrists and psychologists, all of them licensed.* (Hogan, Vol. 1, 1979:65)

Referring to empirical research on encounter groups, Hogan states that:

When reviewers conduct a comprehensive analysis of outcome studies in the encounter field, they generally find little evidence of a high level of risk. Parloff (1970:289) was one of the first to comment on this fact.... he concluded: "The circumspect clinician who wishes to advise prospective group participants regarding possible dangers can, with confidence, offer only the following kind of advice: participation in most encounter groups is likely to be more dangerous than attending an office Christmas party and somewhat less dangerous than skiing...."
 ... Cooper(1972) ... argued that from his review of the literature the danger had definitely not been proved, and that some evidence existed that encounter groups were less stressful than university examinations.... (Hogan, Vol. 1, 1979:68)

The finding of a low rate of casualties is fairly uniform among those who have conducted an overall analysis of outcome studies in the encounter field.... [for example Easton, Carr, and Whiteley (1972) found that] most of the concrete evidence available indicates that casualties are comparatively rare and usually involve people with some previous history of psychological difficulty. (Hogan, Vol. 1, 1979:75)

... In fact one cannot help but be struck by the number of studies that have found encounter groups to pose only minimal dangers. (ibid.:69)

Thus encounter groups would seem to pose even less risk than conventional verbal psychotherapy.

Having surveyed the evidence available regarding the risks involved in both conventional verbal psychotherapy and encounter groups (as representative of the human potential movement) Hogan concluded that:

> ... psychotherapy, whether traditionally defined or including the newer encounter groups and humanistic therapies, does not appear to be gravely dangerous. This does not deny the existence of isolated instances of serious harm, but to suggest that overall the dangers may be overstated.
>
> The percentage of people who deteriorate as a result of psychotherapy is somewhere around 5%, while the research on encounter groups generally reports figures of 1% or less. *These dangers are not of such epidemic proportions that the arm of the law should intervene to curb the problem....* (ibid.:370)

Thus, even though the bias of research is liable to favour a medical model (a model which I personally do not favour in this area), the evidence available does not appear to indicate that psychotherapy and personal growth work pose a particularly significant threat of harm to the public. Those who seek to justify the licensing of psychotherapy on this basis need to prove their case.

How much of the risk that psychotherapy does appear to pose is attributable to the practitioner - and attributable in a way that can be addressed by a licensing system?

As indicated in Chapter 5, the Sieghart Report cites with favour the opinions of the Royal College of Psychiatrists, the British Medical Association and Sir John Foster that psychotherapy can cause harm if carried out by 'unqualified' as opposed to 'qualified' practitioners, however the dissenting view of the behaviour therapists appended to the report refutes this view on the grounds of lack of evidence. Both points of view however beg the question as to what meaningfully counts as 'qualified' in this area.

Establishing causation is problematic. The case of supposed provocation of mental illness cited by Foster from the Anderson Report, which I quoted in Chapter 5, dramatically illustrates the perils of too readily jumping to conclusions as to causation. Lonie (1991a:122) has suggested that rather than a simple Newtonian 'billiard ball' model of cause and effect which implies that the client is a passive recipient of the 'effects' of the psychotherapist, a more appropriate paradigm for looking at psychotherapy is that of 'Chaos Theory', in the light of which psychotherapy may be conceptualized as a non-linear system of mutually cueing feedback loops.

Furthermore, the application of general findings to a particular individual case is fraught with difficulty, the more so when, from one perspective at any rate, the essence of the psychotherapeutic activity is a focus on the individuality of the client. It is over-optimistic to suppose that individual outcomes are predictable. Such a view presumes that this sort of activity is more 'scientific' than it actually is. In discussing the difficulties of predicting which 'patients' are liable to be provoked into 'breakdown' through going into psychotherapy, Rowan (1983:12) cites the example of David Malan of the Tavistock Clinic who has this to say on the matter:

> During many years at the Tavistock Clinic, I have accumulated a long list of patients in whom this question arises [relief versus increased disturbance]; and, even being wise after the event, I have found myself quite unable to distinguish between these two possibilities. I am constantly being surprised by patients whom I would not expect to break down who do break down, and those whom I would expect to break down, who don't. This remains an area where systematic research is badly needed. (Malan, 1979)

Maybe so, but unfortunately one cannot do a 'double-blind' trial on a particular individual's life for the purpose of a control study. Reincarnation aside, we each only have one shot.

Bergin's studies of the 'deterioration effect' mentioned earlier, focused on 'therapist-induced deterioration' and Strupp refers to 'negative effects' to describe his findings which implicated the therapist as a factor in harmful psychotherapy, particularly 'noxious personality traits' of the psychotherapist, though also 'deficiencies of technique' (Striano, 1988:81,119). Mays and Franks: "... use the term 'negative outcome', which does not implicate the therapist in blame for the failure. Franks focuses on 'patient characteristics and extratherapeutic events' that may be responsible ..." (ibid.:119).

As will be discussed in Chapters 14 and 16, it does seem that the so-

called 'non-specific factors' (Lonie, 1991a:118) such as the personal qualities of the practitioner, for example empathy, the personal qualities of the
client, for example motivation to change (rather than simply to satisfy
dependencies or narcissistic needs) and a congruent match or helping alliance between practitioner and client are the sort of factors most strongly
related to positive outcomes (Russell, 1981/1993). Presumably the absence
of such factors also relates to negative outcomes, however such criteria
are difficult ones on which to build a licensing system.

Hogan concludes that: "Assuming, however, that psychotherapy represents a significant public danger, the lack of consensus as to what causes
danger and how to measure it should prevent the enactment of laws restricting a person's right to practice.... factors quite apart from the practitioner such as the initial level of a patient's mental health, may account for
a large share of the harm that occurs in therapy" (Hogan, Vol. 1, 1979:370).

The question of harm for *whom* will be addressed in Chapter 17. The
chapters in Section II are also highly relevant.

In the context of the push for registration by the UK therapy bureaucracies it has been claimed that: "While many people have been helped by
therapy, there is increasing evidence that vulnerable, traumatized clients
are being abused by badly trained therapists working without supervision
or regulation..." (Pepinster, 1993). And, Dr. John Marzillier, chairman of
the British Psychological Society's Standing Committee on Psychotherapies is reported as claiming that statutory registration of psychotherapists
will provide safeguards against unscrupulous, untrained and unmonitored
individuals whose practices are "causing untold misery and damage to
many hundreds or thousands of people" (Illman, 1993). Bear in mind here
that the British Psychological Society is not an independent research body
but rather should be viewed, in this context at least, as more like an academic psychologist's trade association or guild, albeit one with a Royal
Charter. (I wrote to Dr. Marzillier in September 1993 requesting supporting references for his statement but I did not receive a reply.)

Certainly the risks of therapy have increasingly become a subject of
interest for the media (Bond, 1993:5) but has there been a recent flurry of
substantial new evidence indicating a degree of risk greater than that outlined above? Has substantial evidence come to light showing that unlicensed practice bears a significantly greater degree of risk than licensed

practice? If so, I failed to find it.

It seems fair to assume that the number of people engaged in psychotherapy and related activities has grown over the last twenty years or so, and one would expect there also to be an increase in reported cases of harm, however this does not signify that psychotherapy is more risky than previous studies have indicated. Obviously, the amount of harm occurring needs to be compared with the volume of activity to give a meaningful assessment of risk.

Bond (1993:8) indicates that of the 9000 members of BAC only 0.25 per cent (23) have been involved in formal complaints (complaints that is, not 'convictions'). One might argue that this low level of complaints is *because* of BAC - the type of practitioner and/or client that it attracts and the nature of counselling, rather than reflecting the generally low levels of risk for psychotherapy across the board, as indicated in previous studies. By the same token however, the case for the statutory regulation of counselling is weakened if a voluntary arrangement appears to work so well and is available to those clients who need such reassurance.

In the absence of reliable new evidence showing a significantly greater risk than that indicated by the research I have cited, such statements as Pepinster's and Marzillier's must be regarded as unsubstantiated. I am reminded of the situation regarding encounter and other such groups in the 1960s and 1970s mentioned above, where anecdotal scare stories evoked public curiosity, fear and media attention. As we have seen, the considerable body of empirical research that followed did not by and large bear out anecdotal reports of significant risk.

The current UK registration advocates do not appear to have built their edifice on the basis of sound empirical evidence of a high level of risk to the public. *Nor do they provide evidence to support their contention that any risk to the public can be best remedied by the schemes they propose.* Rather, they fall back on emotive statements of the "untold" variety as cited above. (I think we should be told!) Given the hidden agenda of professions and the wealth of evidence indicating that licensing systems (statutory regulation) often fail to protect the public in the way intended and have serious negative side-effects, such vague justifications should not be allowed to become the basis for licensing without adequate supporting evidence.

One may argue as does Rowan (1992b) that outcome research: "is perhaps about the weakest area in the whole field of psychological research" and that: "the best controlled studies tell us virtually nothing about psychotherapy as ordinarily practised" and that we therefore cannot take outcome research at face value. But then *nor can we take at face value the unsubstantiated arguments of licensing advocates, particularly when they speak for professional organizations who stand to gain from the restrictive practices thereby invoked.*

Much of the recent concern about the risks of harm in psychotherapy has focused on abuse of power in the therapy relationship. It is often argued that inherent inequalities of power between therapist and client, and transference wishes on the part of the latter, provide an open invitation for the abuse of power by the therapist and consequently a significant risk of harm for the client. (Note that if this is the case, it has not revealed itself in the empirical evidence cited above.) Aveline for example argues that:

> The arena in which individual therapy takes place is constructed essentially by the therapist. Though subject to negotiation, the therapist decides the duration, frequency and form of the therapy. Ultimately, beginning and ending is in her hands, the latter being a powerful threat to the patient who is dependent or not coping. With rare exception, the meetings take place on the therapist's territory. The therapist, whether trainee or trained, is held to be expert in what goes on in the arena, certainly by the patient, who is relatively a novice in this setting. What procedures the therapist propounds, the patient is predisposed to accept. Because the sessions take place in private, the therapy is not subject to the natural regulation of the scepticism and even incredulity of outsiders. All this gives therapists great power and, consequently, exposes them to great temptation. (Aveline, 1990:324-5)

Such an account presents a one sided view that only looks at the possible powers that may be abused by the practitioner rather than also addressing those that may be abused by the client. Furthermore it bristles with assumptions that may or may not apply in a particular type of work or a particular case. For example it seems predicated on assumptions of an extremely passive and non self-directing client/patient and/or a setting such as where the 'patient' is assigned to a practitioner rather than choosing freely with whom to work. The practitioner's 'expertise' may give a power advantage if the model of work has an explicit or underlying treatment ethos, however if the model of work is more one of an adult to adult contract or a dialogue between equals (Dryden, 1990:274) then this power advantage cannot be assumed to be the case. Moreover in terms of encountering any particular client the practitioner is a relative novice. The client knows him/herself better than the practitioner ever will. In private practice even if the therapist decides the duration, frequency and form of therapy, the client has a choice of therapists and can choose a 'recipe' of such variables to suit their needs. In my experience more often than not it is the client who decides when to end. It is true that sessions are likely to take place in a space provided by the therapist, in private and often in the therapist's own home. This however also gives the client power which can make the therapist vulnerable to malicious acts, verbal abuse, intimidation and assault by clients and intrusion into privacy. Remember that strong feelings are often what is being dealt with and that the client has often come for that very purpose. Moreover whereas the therapist will usually feel bound by principles of confidentiality, the client is not usually so bound and may talk freely, making the therapist vulnerable to any one-sided or distorted accounts that may be put about, without the therapist usually being in a position to refute them. In the humanistic field, where simultaneous participation in individual and group work is commonplace, individual work may have a semi-public nature in that the client can refer to it in the group if so desired. Thus it is by no means inevitable that an unequal balance of power and potential for abuse lies in the practitioner's favour. Such a view assumes that the situation is seen through the lens of a medical model or some near relative thereof, whereas so much depends on the type of work and the type of client.

As regards the role of transference wishes in this, I will explore this in more detail in Chapter 17, suffice it to say here that transference reactions are also a source of vulnerability for the practitioner, depending on their nature. 'Negative' transference reactions on the part of the client may lead to various forms of destructive 'acting-out' including 'blaming' and 'accusations' that more appropriately have a historical focus. Moreover those transference reactions that make the client more vulnerable to abuse are unlikely to be ameliorated by professionalization and statutory recognition - in fact they are more likely to be exacerbated thereby (see Chapter 17). Furthermore, as outlined in previous chapters, the potential for 'abuse' of the public as a whole by practitioners as a group would be enhanced by the actual social power so engendered.

With regard to the abuse of power, particular attention has centred on the question of sex between practitioners and clients/patients (both current and former). Such sexual activity has been regarded as inherently abusive in nature (by parallel with child sex abuse) and that a client/patient (especially a woman) is incapable of freely consenting to sexual activity with a practitioner (Austin, 1990:148; Rutter, 1989:25). Furthermore, under the laws of some states in the USA, such activity is a felony and in the case of the laws of Florida, for example, the psychologist-client relationship, and hence this incapacity to consent, is deemed to continue "in perpetuity" that is, for ever (Austin, 1990:145).

This issue of practitioner-client sex has also captured the attention of the media (as matters sexual have a way of doing) and has led to adverse comment about the 'unregulated' status of psychotherapy and 'alternative' practitioners.[3] Moreover, the high profile of the issue has led to renewed nervousness about any form of physical contact between practitioners and clients after a few decades in which there has been: "... an increasing acceptance of physical and emotional intimacy between psychotherapists and their patients under the guise [*sic*] of humanistic approaches to psychotherapy ..." (Garrett, 1994:431).

At the 1993 annual conference of the British Psychological Society, new empirical research was presented that revealed that of a group of 580 clinical psychologists studied, four per cent admitted to having had sex with their patients. These findings were used as a basis for the Society's bid for statutory regulation of 'psychologists', even though all of the practitioners cited were already members of BPS (Hall, C., 1993; Garret, 1994).[4]

For the purpose of this particular discussion the key thing to note is that practitioner-client sex occurs in professions that are *already* licensed and have specific sanctions against it. Furthermore, as far as I know, there is no clear evidence to that its incidence differs between licensed and unlicensed settings (Garrett, 1994:432). Rutter (1989:35) cites six to ten per cent of psychiatrists as having had sexual contact with a patient. Kardener et al. (1973) carried out an anonymous random survey of Californian psychiatrists in which five to ten per cent self-reported having had some kind of erotic contact with patients, while five per cent reported having intercourse. A more recent survey in the USA reached the similar conclusion that nine per cent of medical doctors have had some form of sexual contact with their patients at least once in their careers (Gwyther, 1992:70). So this issue, whatever its consequences, is not in itself a sound argument for traditional forms of licensing as is often maintained.

Moreover, the cases of abuse in therapy referred to by Masson (1988, 1992) mainly involved practitioners who were *already* licensed professionals (i.e. medical doctors, clinical psychologists) and their resulting status in community if anything made it *harder* to challenge their abuses.

As Nick Totton says: "... Looking at the highly regulated medical profession, we find much the same problem - a handful of abusers. It doesn't happen often, but it does happen whatever the controls. We would need to look much deeper into the structure of our society in order to defeat this sort of abuse. Curiously though, if psychotherapists ever do abuse their role, they are in some ways more open to retribution than members of high-status professions such as medicine and law. The latter are protected by the closing of ranks, by self-policing systems and by a general belief in their semi-godhood. Furthermore, an independent therapist who isn't very good is far more likely than a doctor or lawyer to stop getting clients" (Totton, 1992:26).

In sum, as Carl Rogers has said: "There are as many certified charlatans and exploiters of people as there are uncertified" (Rogers, 1973).

Even if psychotherapy did pose a more significant and widespread risk of harm to the public than appears to be the case, in view of the harmful side effects outlined in Chapter 10, licensing (statutory registration) as a remedy would still not be justified unless simpler, less deleterious methods to accomplish the same purpose were unavailable.

Striano (1988) describes ways in which she believes psychotherapists can hurt their clients - by mistakenly diagnosing symptoms of a physical illness as 'psychological', by sexual or financial exploitation, by encouraging dependency, by entrapment in cult-like systems, by pathological labelling, by extreme passivity, by encouraging introspection at the expense of practical action in the real world, and by compounding low self-esteem. No doubt the implantation of false memories would now be added to the list.

The likelihood of a conventional licensing system providing an effective means of protection or redress in these cases is pretty slim. As discussed in Chapter 9, we have little reason to be confident that statutory systems of regulation based on restrictive entry requirements, the disciplinary enforcement of professional codes of ethics and practice and the outlawing of unlicensed practice will effectively protect the public. If protection of the public from harm has not been a proven consequence of such systems *in general,* there is little prospect that such a system would protect the public in a field as indefinite as this one. To believe otherwise represents a triumph for wishful thinking.

However, pitfalls such as those cited by Striano can be addressed by other means that are less harmful to the public interest. For example, educational endeavours directed at both practitioners and the public, the application of general laws (such as those concerned with contract, deception, truth in advertising, assault and non-consensual sexual behaviour) and the other alternatives explored in Chapter 28.

The vast majority of what goes by the name of psychotherapy consists of little more than two people conversing in a room and not even a case of one of them giving professional advice to the other. As Combs points out so elegantly in the quotation that opens this chapter, the question of regulating such an activity by licensing is actually quite a sensitive issue in a free, democratic society - and not one to be undertaken lightly. Being 'licensed to talk' has civil liberties implications!

Chapter 14

Licensing and Psychotherapy - Qualifications, Standards and the Requirements of Entry to the Occupation

The fact is that consumers of mental health services choose therapists on the basis of their credentials and licenses granted by government, but neither credentials nor licenses bear any relation to patient improvement.

... The studies all indicate that long years of academic training are not a prerequisite for competence....

(Roberta Russell, 1981/1993)

... Accreditation procedures tend to be forced back onto the most easily measured parameters, which in this situation are the least significant. Books read, courses attended, training analysis, or numbers of hours spent under supervision, intellectual understanding of the issues involved - none of these are necessary, let alone sufficient criteria of competence in the therapeutic engagement. One thing that does emerge from outcome studies is that it is not so much the paradigm, the ideological framework, or the particular skill set involved that makes a difference, but the quality of the interpersonal relationship established between therapist and client. Seen in this light truly the therapist has no clothes and accreditation is an attempt to generate a veritable Emperor's wardrobe of nonsense.

(David Wasdell, 1992:5)

This chapter addresses precondition for licensing *(h) - the purpose of licensing must be the prevention of harm.*

Hogan argues that a licensing system *may* be justified if the conditions for licensing are fulfilled. However the purpose of such a system should be to establish *minimum* requirements for safe practice, not to maximize standards (however conceived) because of the aforementioned detrimental effects of licensing such as increased costs of services, reduction of supply of practitioners and the stifling of innovation.

As we have seen, UKCP is pursuing a path of accreditation and is concerned to promote a situation in which no one would be able to call themselves a psychotherapist without first having to meet the "high" standards it espouses. It claims that this will protect the public from the "unqualified" (UKCP, 1993a & f).

The agreed baseline criteria for acceptance of training organizations by the Council include the requirement that entry to training should be "at a postgraduate level of competence" and that the training be at a postgraduate level, have M.A. equivalent content and not normally be shorter than three years part time (UKCP, May 1993f; Pokorny, 1992). Exceptions are made for those without degrees in some cases and ways around this requirement offered (the UKCP literature, e.g. UKCP, 1993c, makes reference to Accreditation of Prior Experience and Learning (APEL) whereby previous experience and learning can be accepted as an alternative to satisfying normal entry requirements to courses) but the overall values espoused are those of promoting psychotherapy as a *postgraduate* occupation. APEL is the back door not the front. In 1991 UKCP (then UKSCP) reached agreement on: "forming a postgraduate level profession with specific entry and training criteria" (UKCP, 1993b). Whatever other purposes they may serve, these UKCP criteria are also clearly intended to be compatible with European Community legal requirements for the recognition of professional 'diplomas' at the university level (see Chapter 3).

The possession of academic credentials from an accredited institution is a traditional prerequisite in licensing systems but one which is difficult to defend in this area. UKCP is promoting an increased academic content and higher academic prerequisites for training when the evidence available is that this skewing towards intellectual skills is not particularly relevant to competence in this area. *There is little if any evidence that the possession of academic qualifications by psychotherapists relates to basic competence or protects the public in any way.*

... The existing empirical evidence suggests that licensing efforts to date have focused on the wrong variables. No evidence exists that possession of academic credentials protects the public. Surprisingly little if any evidence exists that the particular school of the therapist, the techniques used, the amount of knowledge, diagnostic ability, or extent of training makes any difference in achieving minimal therapeutic results. Instead, the findings indicate that personality factors may be the most influential in determining whether a therapist is competent to practice.... (Hogan, Vol. 1, 1979:370)

As indicated above, statutory licensing should be concerned with the prevention of harm, rather than fostering the highest quality of practice because of the negative side effects of licensing. This is relevant here where what can at best be regarded as enhancements are put forward as baseline criteria. (The over-intellectual focus of the typical academic degree, especially in the realm of psychology, may actually be counter-productive as a prerequisite for work in this area. All too often, degree courses in psychology are a disappointment to those in search of self-knowledge.)

In many countries where there are legal restrictions on the practice of psychotherapy, for example some of those in Europe and many states in the USA, an academic background in medicine or psychology is regarded in law as an appropriate training, or necessary prerequisite, for the practice of psychotherapy. Even where psychotherapy is registered as a distinct profession, medical practitioners will often be exempt from registration. There is no sound basis for this (see also Appendix E).

In most US states the academic criterion for licensing as a psychologist, and hence often for practice as a psychotherapist, has escalated from a master's degree to a doctorate - a research degree with even less relevance to basic competence.

Encouraging such irrelevant criteria for access to training and practice constitutes an effort to raise the barriers to entry for the occupation and has various deleterious effects as previously indicated, including discriminating against those social groups such as the poor, ethnic minorities etc. that are less likely to possess academic qualifications. Raising barriers to entry to a market is a common monopolistic strategy. In the case of the professions it is usually effected by gaining legal privilege, in other areas such as say, soap powder, it is effected by tactics such as multiple product lines to swamp the market and huge advertising budgets which raise the cost for new entrants to the market.

Likewise, extending the required duration of training to cover things that are not essential to basic competence but are at best enhancements, obviously also restricts access to the occupation through the resulting increased cost of training and the increased commitment of time involved.

The claim that statutory registration will protect the public from the "unqualified" is also challenged by the finding that *there is no clear evidence that professionally trained psychotherapists are in general more effective than paraprofessionals* (Berman & Norton, 1985; Russell, 1981/ 1993).

This is not altogether surprising when one realises that the "wrong variables" have been focused upon. Privileging those with a background in medicine or psychology, lengthening the courses, increasing the academic prerequisites and content do *not* favour the most important variables that relate to basic competence in this area. Pre-existing personality factors are of: "overwhelming importance in promoting personal change" (Aveline, 1990:321).

This does not imply that training is unimportant. I would not advise anyone to go to a practitioner who has not been trained in the work that they are offering (but I would not want to prevent them from doing so either). Rather, the point here is to highlight the issue of what factors it is most relevant for training programmes to promote.

The personal qualities that are prerequisites for competence in this sort of activity cannot be 'trained in', they can only be encouraged out. There are skills to be learned and knowledge to be acquired (and as discussed in Chapter 18, the guidance of experienced practitioners is crucial here) but without the personal qualities of the practitioner being regarded as fundamental, the 'heart and soul' of the matter may be left out of the process.

Personal integrity, inner ethical standards that reflect that integrity, an ability to be empathetic and the capacity to be autonomous are the sort of qualities that need to be encouraged. What training environments best facilitate the emergence of these qualities in the budding practitioner? Does the direction in which training is encouraged to go by UKCP foster this? Can, for instance, required conformity to irrelevant academic criteria set by an authority with little claim to democratic validity foster independence of mind and spirit? I think not. The structure of training environments should *at least* not suppress or inhibit those personal qualities known to be of particular significance to the activity for which training is being undertaken and should not discourage those who manifest these qualities but lack academic qualifications or abilities.

The skewing towards academia promoted by UKCP obviously in part reflects the significant presence therein of conventional and established bodies with a particular interest in preserving the importance of academic qualifications as the 'front door' to this 'profession'. The British Psychological Society,[1] the Royal College of Psychiatrists and the Association of University Teachers of Psychiatry are already Special or Institutional members and are apparently to be joined by the University Psychotherapy Association allowing graduates of University courses in psychotherapy a direct route onto the register (UKCP, 1993i). University courses in psychotherapy are apparently "mushrooming" (UKCP, 1994). Universities eager to get in on the act are also forging links with independent training programmes who are thereby able to offer the 'carrot' of a university M.A. on completion as an inducement to potential trainees.

The cost of all this, for those people who are still able to afford the inflated cost of training, will of course be passed on to the clients and, maybe, third party payers.[2]

For human potential organizations to have become a party to all this accreditation myth-making and inveigled into traditional 'hoop jumping' when it has so little relevance to the task at hand is, to my mind, a particularly poignant state of affairs.

Chapter 15

Licensing and Psychotherapy - Hogan's Conclusions

Psychotherapy and laws prohibiting unlicensed practice

Psychotherapy does not meet the criteria for licensing through laws that restrict a person's right to practice....

Apart from the definitional quagmire, psychotherapy does not meet many of the other criteria to warrant restrictive licensing. Although the degree of public impact is sufficient for licensure to be warranted, the evidence ... indicates that the negative impact of licensing is more likely to outweigh the positive benefits that are likely to flow therefrom. In addition ... other methods of regulation are available that promise adequate protection, but with less adverse impact. [See Section III.]

One of the basic reasons that licensing laws restricting practice to the credentialed few have little to recommend them is that sufficient information is not available about the extent and type of danger involved in the therapeutic process, whether the dangers are attributable to the actions on the part of the therapist, and what specific activities lead to dangerous results. Since so much disagreement exists on these fundamental issues, the value of licensing is seriously jeopardized. Until consensus exists on how to identify those therapists who are *not* dangerous, licensing standards will continue to be arbitrary and capricious. *Their actual effect will be to mislead the public into thinking it has protection from the incompetent practitioner.* (Hogan, Vol. 1, 1979:368-70)

Psychotherapy and title-protection acts

Psychotherapy should not be regulated through licensing laws, even if it is only the use of certain titles and representations

120

that is restricted. Even where licensing laws do not restrict a person's right to practice, requiring certain standards to be met before a person has the right to use specific titles is not advisable. Although title-protection acts have fewer disadvantages than laws restricting practice, their positive utility probably does not outweigh their negative potential.

It is true that title-protection acts do not present problems in defining what constitutes psychotherapy, since it is only the use of certain titles that is in question. It is also true that their impact in terms of raising the cost of services and restricting the supply of practitioners is less, since nonlicensed persons are not prohibited from practicing. On the other hand, if no impact occurs, the value of the law disappears.

The critical question is whether states are performing a valuable service by identifying practitioners possessing certain credentials as being competent. The problem is that little consensus exists as to what credentials are a sound measure of therapeutic competence, and the skills that seem important, such as empathic ability, are difficult to operationalize. Thus it is premature and misleading for the state to give approval to any one set of standards at this time. Instead, its policy should be to recognize this state of affairs and to teach the public that not enough is yet known about the ingredients of therapeutic success to warrant the use of restrictive licensing.

There is another political reason against title-protection laws. Professional associations are generally the sponsors of licensing. When initially seeking licensure it is common to recommend title-protection acts, since they generate less political opposition. Once these laws have been enacted, however, these same associations frequently seek amendments to transform the law into one that prohibits unlicensed practice as well. These Amendments often only involve minor word changes, and it is difficult to organize opposition to such changes. If for no other reason, this danger warrants extreme circumspection in advocating the adoption of any title-protection acts. (Hogan, Vol. 1, 1979:370-1)

Chapter 16

The Bases of Competence -
Significant Criteria for Practitioner Selection

> The selection of a therapist must be based on qualities as diverse
> and comprehensive as those applied to the selection of partners in
> other relationships - spouse, workmates, friends. The variables in-
> volved may be as basic as values or conceptual level, or as superfi-
> cial as shoe polish, but the patient must be able to pick a therapist
> who talks his language, with whom he shares a mutual regard.
>
> *(Roberta Russell, 1981/1993:56)*

Roberta Russell in her *Report on Effective Psychotherapy* (1981/1993)
has comprehensively surveyed research into what factors have been shown
to be positively related to the efficacy of psychotherapy and what factors
have not. Russell's original report published in 1981, was supplemented
in 1993, at which point the accuracy of its conclusions was confirmed by
an American Psychological Association panel of distinguished therapy
outcome researchers. This panel, which included Strupp and Grawe, also
felt that the conclusions of the report could be refined by some of the
results of the latest research on therapeutic alliance (ibid.:85) - findings
which are included in the summary that follows.

   The research surveyed by Russell indicates that the effectiveness of
psychotherapy *does not* appear to depend upon any of the following:

(1) The practitioner holding academic qualifications.
(2) The length of training of the practitioner.
(3) The school to which the therapist belongs.
(4) The practitioner having had a training analysis. That is, personal therapy
undertaken as part of a training process has not been found to relate to
increased competence of the practitioner. Moreover, personal therapy will
not render competent someone who lacks a basic talent for the role.

The effectiveness of psychotherapy *does* however appear to correlate positively with the following:

(1) The degree of experience of the practitioner.
(2) The personal qualities of the practitioner. Those qualities which can be roughly summed up as 'empathy' are particularly important. These include acceptance, genuineness, warmth, trust, and understanding. [Note however the point made by Smail: "... Empathy is of course important, but arises between people, and is not a quality (or 'skill') possessed by individuals in some finite amount" (Smail, 1983:14).]

The practitioner's ability to perceive what is happening accurately is also important to outcome: "... Some therapists are better at this than others and this ability has more to do with effective therapist selection than formal training. One's sensibilities may be formed out of the clay of our inherited temperaments and shaped by the interstices of life. The training of would-be professionals who do not have inherent therapeutic talent may be a poor use of resources" (ibid.:92). So, it seems that perceptiveness, (intuition?), talent and wisdom and are also important factors.

Personal skills, seem to be more important than particular techniques. Jerome Frank believes that the therapist's personal qualities are the most significant factors and that techniques merely provide the ritual by which the personal changes are mediated (ibid.:89). [I myself believe that, for the humanistic area at least, both personal skills and those skills that can be regarded as the 'craft' of practice are important.]

(3) The personal qualities of the client. Included here are motivation to change (rather than for example satisfy addictive propensities) and the ability to form a working partnership.

(4) The quality of the interpersonal or helping alliance - the congruent matching of client and practitioner. This is even more crucial than 'empathy': "... Alliance as judged by the client, is an even better predictor of outcome than empathy" (ibid.:94). Asked what makes for a good therapist Arnold Lazarus said: "Being good doesn't mean very much, and I'll tell you why. 'Good for whom' is the question ..." (ibid.:51).

Such a congruent and effective match between practitioner and client depends upon: (a) the strengths and weaknesses of the particular practitioner that make them more suited to some clients than others; (b) shared values and an agreement on the aims of the endeavour; (c) idiosyncratic factors are also very important. Luborsky has studied this latter issue and found that seemingly trivial factors such as whether or not the practitioner's shoes were well polished can be crucial in forming the necessary bond (ibid:52).

Given the importance of this congruent and personal matching between practitoner and client, Luborsky suggests that encouraging clients to try several therapists, and to make a selection on the basis of their feelings, will lead to better outcomes.

On the basis of this survey of psychotherapy outcome research, such as it is, the bottom line seems to be this: given access to appropriate information as discussed in Section III, clients are the best judges of who are the competent practitioners for them, and on the basis of their *personal responses* to practitioners (and the approaches that they offer) rather than on the basis of misleading criteria such as those that UKCP promotes. 'Upping the ante' to the practice of an occupation by establishing entry requirements that are not highly correlated with effectiveness restricts the size of the pool of people from whom the prospective client can choose an appropriate practitioner for themselves. The chances of them then finding someone with the appropriate personal characteristics - the major criterion of choice - are correspondingly reduced. This is all the more so when one realises the importance of idiosyncratic factors.

As mentioned in Chapter 13, Rowan has expressed grave doubts about the validity of even the best controlled outcome studies and he has responded in a similar vein to the conclusions in Russell's original report (Rowan, 1983:150). The studies surveyed by Russell indicate that factors which UKCP is promoting, such as extending the duration of training, raising both the academic content and academic prerequisites for training courses, and fostering links with universities, will *not* produce more competent practitioners. If this evidence is discounted, that still leaves us in the position that there is apparently little or no sound empirical evidence to support the notion that such moves *will* produce better practitioners. There is however, as previously discussed, a great deal of evidence to support the proposition that the establishment a regulatory system on the basis of non-proven criteria is detrimental to the public interest.

Chapter 17

Practitioner Selection
and the Perils of Transference

... A national register of accredited psychotherapists would hopefully solve all such problems [involved in choosing a therapist],
reducing the anomia and anxiety and ensuring that any client who
wished to engage a therapist could pick a name from a list in full
confidence that the service rendered would be competent, uniform
and effective. Tragically, any such confidence is misplaced. A register of accreditation would provide a token or symbolic anxyolite,
while in fact hiding the realities of confusion, uncertainty and
unpredictability that underlie the choice making procedure. In this
sense the drive toward accreditation that stems from client anxiety
is a defensive manoeuvre, colluding with the public desire for a
simplified and irresponsible decision making process.

(David Wasdell, 1992:5)

Competence in handling transference by its very nature is the one
thing that cannot, without serious distortion, be professionalized and
legalized in an emotionally repressive society. The professionalization of it takes it away from the public domain into mystification
and expert knowledge accessible only to a few and this exacerbates
and reinforces the very processes which it is supposed to be dealing
with....

(John Heron, 1990:19)

Practitioner selection for the 'decisionally challenged'

Protagonists of statutory control of psychotherapy frequently present the
image of the potential purchaser of psychotherapy as being in such a state
that they are incapable of making a sensible choice of practitioner. They
are presented as vulnerable, distressed, traumatized, disturbed, lacking in
autonomy or 'rationally impaired'. Holmes and Lindley for example hold

that: "The patient is usually not in the position of a free purchaser. She is in distress, and is prone to grasp uncritically at any offer of help. The market does not protect old ladies whose pipes burst in winter from exorbitant and incompetent plumbers, and *a fortiori*, the desperation of someone in need of therapy may frequently lead to bad therapy choices being made by patients" (Holmes & Lindley, 1989:118).

The Foster Report holds that: "... it will not have escaped attention that those who feel they need psychotherapy tend to be the very people who are most easily exploited: the weak, the insecure, the nervous, the lonely, the inadequate, and the depressed, whose desperation is often such that they are willing to do and pay anything for some improvement of their condition" (Foster, 1971:178).

There is a certain circularity about all this. If someone is seeking psychotherapy they are *ipso facto* insufficiently 'together' to be fully responsible for choosing their psychotherapist!

Granted that *some* seekers are in such a state of distress that their adult functioning falls below a minimum level needed to retain adult responsibility for their choices and for whom the social role of being 'sick' (Parsons, 1953) is appropriate - they are indeed 'patients' in relation to the potential psychotherapist. However it is disingenuous to presume that *all* or most seekers are so impaired in their decision-making that they are sitting ducks for exploiters and that therefore special legislative arrangements should be made. This is all the more so if, as is the current tendency, the term 'psychotherapy' is being stretched to cover self-actualizing approaches such as in the humanistic area as well as remedial treatments for psychological disorders or mental illnesses.

In addition, the potential customer for psychotherapy is presented as being faced with a dauntingly difficult task of selection in a disorganized and complex field, crowded with a plethora of different types of work to choose from. Hence the need for systems of accreditation to sort the wheat from the chaff and ease the burden on this less than adequately functioning individual:

> [A psychotherapy profession] would also help to overcome a real difficulty which exists for the consumer faced with the variety of psychotherapies.... The person in search of help is faced

with an array of different treatments, and is often not in a position or state to evaluate the distinctions between them, and so make an informed choice of therapy.... (Holmes & Lindley, 1989:217)

However, as David Wasdell points out above, the notion that the registration of psychotherapy would really help the potential client to choose is illusory and misleading. There are no easily applied external qualifications that you can trust. As discussed in the previous chapter, having selected a type of work that suits your intentions and values, the basis for deciding on a practitioner must essentially be personal. Moreover, since the available evidence does not strongly favour any particular approach as being generally more effective than any other, the choice of what type of work to undertake is less critical than it might at first appear and can be approached on the basis of what sort of work attracts you or by experimenting and trying out several types. In addition, rather than assuming that the consumer cannot become sufficiently well informed to become 'aware' enough to 'beware', and must instead leave fundamental parts of the selection process to a statutory board, the potential consumer can be 'informationally enriched' as discussed in Chapter 28.

The perils of transference

'Transference' is a term derived from psychoanalysis that refers to the unconscious assignment to the practitioner (or other person) of feelings about important and usually powerful figures in one's past (such as parents). Although this term is usually used in relation to a therapeutic setting, the phenomenon to which it refers is not confined to that context but is widespread, though seldom acknowledged as such. Transference is also a phenomenon which varies in its manifestation depending upon the expectations associated with the setting. The more it is 'the done thing', the more it will be done.

Much of the discussion about statutory control of psychotherapy has been heavily influenced by the psychoanalytic model in which transference is actively encouraged, since the analysis of the transference is the primary '*modus operandi*' of that approach: "... 'Deep' transference is an extension and exaggeration of everyday transference which occurs mainly, but not exclusively, in analytic therapies whose arrangements, for example the passivity and reticence of the analyst, are especially designed to evoke it" (Holmes & Lindley, 1989:117). Frequent, regular sessions also tend in this direction. As we have seen (Chapter 5) Sir John Foster was heavily influenced by the psychoanalytic lobby in his report and the Sieghart Report was the outcome of a working party dominated by analytic bodies. Holmes and Lindley (one of them a psychoanalytically trained consultant psychiatrist/psychotherapist, the other a philosopher) favour a statutory profession and likewise seem to view these matters through a lens coloured by that model. However, from perspectives other than that of psychoanalysis, such as 'holotropic therapy' for example, transference would not be regarded as something to be encouraged but rather as a complication of the therapeutic process, a form of resistance rather than as necessary to successful treatment (Grof, 1988a:225). In humanistic and transpersonal approaches such as gestalt, psychodrama or psychosynthesis the relationship between the client and practitioner would be regarded as important, for example as a 'container', but transference would not be regarded as the main instrument of the work as in analytic approaches. Though awareness of the phenomenon would be included, actual encouragement of a transference would not necessarily be involved or considered appropriate.

Early in his career, Freud himself regarded transference as a form of resistance that impeded progress. The fact that he later abandoned this viewpoint should not be automatically taken as a sign of its redundancy. After all, Freud also abandoned the 'seduction hypothesis' of hysteria (that emphasized the importance of memories of actual childhood sexual abuse) in favour of a 'phantasy' interpretation, and he felt that this marked the beginning of psychoanalysis as a therapy and a profession (Masson, 1984).

There is no conclusive evidence that psychoanalysis or analytic psychotherapies are more effective than other forms of therapy (not to mention *cost*-effective!).[1] Therefore, it hardly seems fair that they should be used as the touchstone for legislative decisions - the more so if the 'psychotherapy profession' is supposed to include a gamut of other approaches, such as the humanistic ones mentioned above, as intended by UKCP.

Encouraging transference involves encouraging regression and dependency. Holmes and Lindley refer to therapy creating a temporary dependency *en route* to a state of increased 'autonomy', the promotion of autonomy being the essential goal or outcome of psychotherapy. In a section describing: "some common elements in various types of psychotherapy", they say that: " Psychoanalytic therapy attempts, through the concept of *transference*, to make the issue of dependency-in-the-service-of-autonomy a central vehicle for therapeutic change..." and that: "... it remains true that some of the ethical dilemmas of psychotherapy do arise out of the *cultivation of dependency* in the service of increased autonomy" (Holmes & Lindley, 1989:5-7). Despite Sir John Foster's claim that: "... More than ever today, psychotherapists regard the ultimate dissolution of the transference at the end of treatment as the most difficult, and yet most crucial, part of their task." (Foster, 1971:177), the concept of 'countertransference' and the usual inhibition of post-therapeutic contact between therapist and client, carry an implication that the 'resolution of the transference' is actually a theoretical possibility rather than necessarily the norm.

Autonomy, here, is a variable state of being. With regard to the safe selection of a therapist, discouraging transference and concomitant regression and encouraging what adult functioning and autonomy the person *already* has is the more appropriate stance. This means not colluding with any urges in the prospective client to forsake what adult status and responsibility they do have and the responsibility for choices that only they can make - including the choice of a practitioner.

Institutionalizing the transference

The accreditation route fostered by UKCP promotes the myth that the public can be protected from the difficulties of choice in this area.

The promotion of this myth is indicative of a process that I will refer to as *institutionalizing the transference*. This represents a further effect of licensing in this area that if anything actually *increases* the potential risk of harm to the public over and above the negative side-effects of licensing that generally occur.

Many institutions, individuals and professions appeal to and exploit transference - for good or ill. As we have seen some types of psychotherapy and related fields address transference itself and work with it directly and indeed an awareness and understanding of transference can be regarded as a basic competence in this field - and should be a basic social competence. As Heron explains in the quotation above, promoting the handling of transference as the rightful province of a special professional enclave mystifies it and removes it from the public domain - where an awareness of it as a pervasive phenomenon rightly belongs. Demonstrating this awareness collectively as practitioners (and individually) would mean refusing to collude with a 'fear of freedom' that makes people yearn for someone else to relieve them of the burden of decision and take charge of their lives.[2] It would also involve practitioners refusing to act out their own urges towards aggrandizement.

Instead, we have the very occupation which should know better pursuing the myth of accreditation in this area and seeking 'official recognition', statutory privilege and monopoly. By so doing transference would become institutionalized in the sense that the practitioner's status as 'expert' would become endorsed by the state and his or her authority commensurately enhanced. Transference, and regression, are encouraged by anything that encourages you to 'look up' - from the couch onwards!

Potential clients can become lulled into a false sense of security and suspension of judgement by such a system. It encourages them to defer to the authority of the practitioner and the institutions backed by the state that give him credibility - to 'leave their brain at the door' - in a way that fosters dependency and a letting down of appropriate self-protective guards.

As with transference, so with hypnosis, suggestion, and subliminal influence. These are not techniques or phenomena confined to the 'therapy' room. Nor are they phenomena so discrete that they can be readily defined for the purposes of law without infringing on civil liberties. Can hypnosis and meditation, for example, be legally differentiated? Our culture is awash with appeals deliberately aimed to bypass conscious awareness. Our media are full of subliminal cues and emotive inducements and our politics full of 'feel-good factors'. Perhaps politicians should be licensed.

Once again the golden rule is to let personal judgement or recommendation be your guide. Remain circumspect and do not allow status to cloud your personal assessment of the practitioner and what they do and say. As sociologist Dr. Eileen Barker of INFORM - Information Network Focus on Religious Movements - has said of the so-called 'mind-control' techniques used in some cults: "the point is, the techniques they use are not irresistible" (*Focus*, 1995a:36).

The latest 'hazard' of psychotherapy to cause concern is the notion of the 'false memory syndrome'. Alongside the encouragement of transference, interpretation is a favoured psychoanalytic technique. In the past, Freudian dogma has led psychoanalysts to erroneously interpret the emerging memories of sexual abuse of some of their patients as 'phantasy'. The 'false memory syndrome' can be seen as a consequence of the further misapplication of that technique, whether by psychoanalysts or others, but in this case the error is in the reverse direction. A medical model notion of the practitioner as diagnostician of the underlying cause of symptoms is also implicit here and it is the attribution of a status of 'expert' to the practitioner that is likely to raise the client's suggestibility and make them more vulnerable to such errors.

Much is made by registration advocates of the need to protect 'the vulnerable', but vulnerability in this context is not an isolated condition of personal make-up. It is proportional to the power that the prospective client gives away to the practitioner. Official recognition based on unconfirmed criteria *begets* vulnerability.

Safety here lies in retaining an appropriate degree of circumspection - appropriate to the degree to which competence *can* be assured. Supporting the potential client's existing autonomy, whatever degree of 'adult' they already have, by empowering them with information and relevant questions to help them make the judgements that *only they* can make, is more appropriate than enhancing the official status of the practitioner with the accompanying assumption that competence has been assured. Greater safety lies in an encouragement to evaluate rather than to take on trust.

As Schutz says: "In the present situation [USA. 1979], I rely on the state to tell me who is competent. I passively submit myself to a professional, and if I do not like what he does, I sue him for malpractice. My role is very inert and childlike. If I, as a consumer, know that I am responsible for selecting a counselor, I am likely to assume a more responsible stance. In many cases, the very act of being responsible will have a therapeutic effect" (Schutz, 1979:157).

For those people whose autonomy really is already well below a necessary minimum for adequate adult functioning, the 'low status' system discussed in Chapter 28 may provide a form of practitioner regulation that is appropriate to state funded settings.

Chapter 18

The Training Business
and the Business of Training

Sadly, the correlation between training and effectiveness as a therapist is low....[1]

(Mark Aveline [UKCP board member 1993], 1990:321)

Wouldn't it be handy if newcomers went through a long and expensive training which offered lots of teaching and supervision work?
Within psychotherapy people have begun jockeying for position,
putting their training courses and accreditation procedures in place,
inventing hurdles for the next generation - hurdles they themselves
will never have to jump!

(Nick Totton, 1992:26

Notwithstanding the significance of personal factors in practitioner competence, training *is* important. This chapter addresses the detrimental impact of the current bureaucratic endeavours on training opportunities and
some of the less than altruistic factors that may come into play in relation
to training programmes and lead to inflated costs of training.[2]

Trainers are not necessarily amongst the 'best' or most experienced
practitioners (though they may be amongst the most ambitious) and yet
they have the overwhelming say in UKCP compared with non-training
practitioners (never mind clients, etc.).

Becoming a trainer in this field has significant appeal over and above
being simply a practitioner. It often seems to yield a higher status and the
power afforded to trainers by UKCP is likely to exacerbate this. People
will be likely to assume that a trainer has sufficient experience to train
others, whether or not this is the case (and certainly UKCP does not require it). This is an assumption that is likely to be compounded if any
'official' status is granted to UKCP.

In addition, being a trainer gives the possibility of a more 'captive' group of people to work with - trainees - who will be tied in for the duration of the course - three or more years and getting longer - a situation fostered by UKCP. This does not necessarily correlate with increased competence as we have seen. Trainees are also often more willing to pay over the odds for groups, etc. on the grounds that it is an investment which will pay off in terms of future earning capacity, rather than a non-recoverable (financially speaking) expenditure on their 'self' development. It is perhaps not coincidental that psychotherapy registration has become such a 'hot' issue during a period of economic recession. Traditionally, professions become more self-protective at such times.

Furthermore, where training requirements include personal experience in the modality in which one is training, as is the case in say the Humanistic and Integrative Psychotherapy Section of UKCP, trainees will be committed to be 'in therapy' for reasons beyond those of personal need or motivation, thereby 'steadying' the income for the therapists concerned and indeed providing a guaranteed flow of clients, especially if there are 'in-house' requirement regarding with whom the trainees may work.

Prospective trainees are commonly not required to have had significant experience of the work in which they are training *before* being accepted for training - as a positive experiential basis for their ambition. This would severely limit the catchment for the training course and reduce the economic basis of the enterprise. Instead (or as well as) there will often be a requirement for trainees to have their own personal therapy during training in the modality espoused by the particular organization and their choice of practitioner may well be restricted to someone 'in-house' or a graduate of the organization. This produces a virtuous economic circle for the organization concerned. Where such a restriction is not the case, if current trends continue, it is increasingly likely that choice may be restricted to UKCP registered practitioners.

I am doubtful about the quality of personal growth work that can be effected as a course requirement. If it is being done in order to 'qualify' it is no longer really 'personal'. The pace and rhythm of it is no longer determined by personal growth factors alone and instead is subject to career ambition and compliance with outer pressures. For example, as discussed above, under these circumstances the 'client' is not entirely free to choose who to work with but must instead work with an 'approved' practitioner and the frequency and duration of the work will often be specified by the trainers. Moreover, personal growth work that is too closely entwined with a career assessment process is in my experience very likely to be compromised by the actual (never mind transferential) power and authority relationships with one's trainers. Revealing oneself is less likely when there is a potential career penalty for personal revelations which may be adversely judged. In practice, it is unlikely that personal therapy and career assessment can be effectively separated when the former is a concurrent requirement of the latter. Szasz takes a similar view (Szasz, 1965, 1974:116). These factors may go some way to explaining the finding that, as mentioned in Chapter 16, having undergone a training analysis does not appear to correlate with therapist effectiveness. In a similar vein, I think that the ambition to be a psychotherapist, or whatever, of a particular school is one deserving particular scrutiny *unless* it has emerged as a result of an extensive prior positive personal experience of the modality in question - personal work during the course of training is just not the same thing. In practice, course administrators are under economic pressure to forgo such scrutiny - unless they have so many applicants as to be able to pick and choose. Significant personal experience of the modality in question, *prior* to training, is to my mind far more relevant as a prerequisite for training than, say, postgraduate level entry requirements.

As discussed in Chapter 6, the mere *prospect* of statutory recognition of UKCP may make it harder to start up a new training organization, effectively 'freezing' training in the hands of existing member organizations and stifling innovation. Michael Wibberley, an exponent of encounter groups since the 1970s, thinks that: "it is extremely unlikely that the kind of creative group work we do today could ever have evolved if the kind of restrictive measures proposed now had been in force before, and they may well restrict future developments" (Wibberley, 1994b:22).

Bureaucratic structures like UKCP are not the appropriate structures for regulating practice or training in this area. Just as the working alliance between practitioner and client is crucial to the positive outcome of that activity (and is not best served by such a bureaucracy) so a training relationship with an experienced practitioner is crucial to the business of training. Much of what needs to be learned will be done so more appropriately by a process akin to 'osmosis' or 'resonance' - being taught by example - rather than by didactic presentation. The apprenticeship model, a model which involves working alongside a more experienced 'craftsperson' who can watch over one, from whom one can learn and to whom one can refer for guidance, is in many ways more appropriate (particularly for humanistic work) than training programmes modelled after traditional professional disciplines where a conceptual framework of theory is taught, learned and then applied. However, the apprenticeship system is one whose existence is likely to be less viable the more support there is for the deformation of training which UKCP and its ilk will produce. Perhaps this process is already more advanced than many realise. Guy Gladstone has the impression that: "new therapists are once again entering experiential groups outside of their trainings, informally reviving the vanishing apprenticeship model, a model which rests on the premise that becoming a therapist is a personally transmitted craft for which no amount of academic course work can substitute" (Gladstone, 1995:15).

Aveline (1990:327) is typical of those who favour a theory-followed-by-practice model of training as in a traditional professional discipline. He argues that theory should be the starting point (though it should be critically examined later in training). He comments that studying theory means that therapists do not 're-invent the wheel'. To my mind that is exactly the sort of thing they should be encouraged to do - to approach each client first and foremost with 'open eyes' and an open mind rather than be entrained from early on to see them through conceptual and categorizing lenses that become harder to remove the earlier one habituates to wearing them. After all, the conceptual frameworks of psychotherapists are hardly 'wheels'. Whatever their variations, wheels are at least perfectly formed in their roundness. If wheels were fashioned in the likeness of the conceptual frameworks of psychotherapists we would all be having a very bumpy ride! As with children, so with trainees and apprentices, preserving and encouraging an exploratory freshness of approach to each person - a 'Zen-mind, beginner's mind' (rather than an approach that is 'play-impaired' and fearful of making mistakes), is paramount. With that securely in place, conceptual schema can be drawn on as and when they are helpful like maps in one's pocket. Do it the other way round and they become spectacles wired to the head. (See also Appendices F and G.)

Chapter 19

Carving up the Field and Doing the NVQs

Relationships [with UKCP and BPS] from my point of view are good. There is endless goodwill on all sides....

*(Judith Baron, General Manager of the British Association
for Counselling, 1994:14)*

The more I hear about NVQs, the more I learn about them, the more I think they have the power to affect counselling as a profession and counselling in Britain and Europe. The reason is that they have government backing and a lot of money has been put into them....

(ibid.)

There are now at least five large professional organizations with an interest in statutory registration in this area - the UK Council for Psychotherapy (UKCP), the British Association for Counselling (BAC), the British Psychological Society (BPS), the British Confederation of Psychotherapists (BCP) and the Royal College of Psychiatrists (RCP). The problem of defining psychotherapy in any precise way means that there is considerable potential for overlap between the interests of these organizations. Despite the fact that some of them are also involved with each other, the prospect of statutory registration, being a form of monopoly at least over a title, puts these organizations into potential competition with each other - unless some form of territorial accommodation (cartel) can be reached. This is a process driven more by the 'needs' of the organizations to carve out territory in relation to statutory privilege rather than by any clear differentiations arising out of what their practitioners actually do on the ground.

As we have seen (Chapter 7), the psychoanalytic psychotherapists of BCP are unwilling to be subject to the hegemony of UKCP and in the event of statutory initiatives would want to be separately acknowledged. BPS has argued that state funded therapists should all be psychologists or social workers and that registration of psychotherapists is really a question of the control of the private sector. Since the establishment of UKCP, some BAC members who regard themselves as practising psychotherapy and think that counselling includes psychotherapy, are worried about having to be members of two organizations (and pay two sets of fees for the privilege) and argue a case for BAC to redesignate itself 'The British Association of Counselling and Psychotherapy' (Rawson, 1993; Townsend, 1993; Tantam & Rickard, 1992). As previously discussed, BAC regards psychotherapy and some forms of counselling at any rate as being barely distinguishable. The Royal College of Psychiatrists has shown an interest in a statutory register of psychotherapists provided it has a central role in its administration and is in consequence a Special Member of UKCP. The psychiatric profession also has representation therein in the form of the Association of University Teachers of Psychiatry (AUTP), an Institutional Member.

Depending on your point of view, 'psychotherapy' could be conceived of as a type of counselling, a form of applied or clinical psychology, a form of psychiatric treatment, a discipline in its own right or a *mélange* of different things defying overall definition. What really counts in this context are definitions for legal purposes, and for such things as access to employment and the recovery of health insurance payments. Hogan has shown how professional organizations in the USA lost interest in meaningful definitions once a legislative scramble was under way (see Chapter 12) and as previously discussed, once registers become statutory, they can become self-defining. For example in the Australian State of New South Wales, a 'psychologist' *is* someone who is on the psychologists register (see Appendix B). Thus the 'carve-up' or legislative scramble reflects issues of organizational 'sovereignty' and power and, as indicated in the next chapter, even in the absence of statutory control, eligibility for National Health Service (NHS) employment and third party payment of fees constitute a measure of *de facto* regulation to be fought over.

Furthermore, the National Council for Vocational Qualifications (NCVQ), set up in 1986 as: "part of Margaret Thatcher's attempt to recreate a nation of professional shopkeepers" (Sarson, 1994), has set up a 'Lead Body' to promote the establishment of National Vocational Qualifications (NVQs) in this area. NVQs are sort of occupational 'driving tests' based on demonstrable competence. A recent investigation of NVQs was less than complimentary about the system. Occupational 'driving tests' they may be, but they are driving tests in which your instructor is also your examiner since for reasons of cost, there is little in the way of external verification (BBC Radio 4, 1994d). The 'Lead Body for Advice Guidance and Counselling' has conducted a mapping exercise of counselling which includes - at the request of the BAC - a mapping of 'therapeutic counselling', defined as that form of counselling which goes into depth according to psychodynamic or other principles and lasts for more than a few months. UKCP supporters have expressed concern about whether there will be any territory left for 'psychotherapy' (and UKCP) to cover (Rowan, 1993c). At a June 1994 conference in London sponsored by the European Association for Psychotherapy (EAP) along with UKCP and BAC, the speaker from UKCP seems to have emphasized the importance of establishing clear boundaries between psychotherapy and counselling whereas the speaker from BAC seems to have played down the differences (Collis, 1994b).

At the behest of the Department of Employment the 'Lead Body' has commissioned a report on the feasibility of developing national standards for psychotherapy and encompassing psychotherapy within the 'functional map' of Advice Guidance and Counselling (AGC) (Consultants at Work, 1993).

At its annual conference in January 1994, UKCP voted to join the Lead Body for Advice Guidance and Counselling as urged by Sue Slipman, the Chair of that body, and to thereby participate in writing standards for NVQs in psychotherapy. The motion was carried despite much unease within UKCP about the prospect of NVQs:

> ... The general feeling reported by the twelve groups was that we really had a gun at our heads. If we refused to join the Lead Body, therapeutic counselling (BAC accredited) would step in to fill the place of psychotherapy. NVQs would probably become an essential requirement for employment in the NHS and that this would have a detrimental effect on the intake to training centres in psychotherapy if they did not offer these for training therapists.... (*Self & Society*, 1994)

The Lead Body's 'draft functional map of the psychotherapy domain' was produced by applying 'functional analysis' to the area in order to test the feasibility of: "... trying to "get at" the heart of psychotherapeutic competence in terms of *the distinctive characteristics which mark it out from other forms of human endeavour*" (Consultants at Work, 1993:7).

'Functional analysis' is a system borrowed from studies of engineering and factory management. It involves defining a 'Key Purpose' and then deriving from this 'units of competence' which can then be analysed into 'elements of competence' which are (supposedly) minimal, self-sufficient competencies with both a range and a set of performance criteria and which can (supposedly) be taught and assessed, independently of other elements.

Some of the psychotherapists who participated in the mapping process were disinclined to accept that a methodology which might be adequate for engineers could also describe what psychotherapists do. They felt that such a process would fail to mirror the intuitive aspects of psychotherapy and inevitably lead to a narrow, mechanistic, reductionistic approach (ibid.:4-5). How true.

Regarding these misgivings, the view taken by the consultants responsible for the analysis was that: "... As psychotherapists operate with at least one model of the mind which informs their actions and acts as a guarantor of their professionalism, then it must be possible to reference their actions against this model. In this way activity is rendered intelligible to others and hence amenable to assessment. *If this is not the case then much of if not all the assessment and accreditation currently taking place within psychotherapy would be open to the same criticism as that being levelled at functional analysis*" (ibid.:4). How true!

The basis for this 'Lead Body' 'functional analysis' of the 'psychotherapy domain' is the following proposed 'Key Purpose' statement for psychotherapy:

[To] assist people to address their experiences by creating a structured therapeutic setting informed by an accepted ethical framework and drawing upon a developed body of psychological theory in order to produce psychological change.
(ibid.:annex:1)

Applying a bit of 'analysis' to this 'Key Purpose' statement for psychotherapy is instructive:

[To] assist people to address their experiences ...
Is that different from meditation? contemplation? the arts?

... by creating a structured therapeutic setting ...
It is tautological to use 'therapeutic' to define 'psychotherapy'. Is a "structured setting" different from a church, a confessional, an ashram, a retreat, a club, a theatre, a school or a pub? What would an unstructured setting be like? Some practitioners might find working outside of a 'structured setting' more conducive for some clients.

... informed by an accepted ethical framework ...
How is this different from any other meeting other than say a 'mugging'? 'Accepted' by whom? - the two or more people concerned? If so will not a contract suffice?

... and drawing upon a developed body of psychological theory ...
Some of the best practitioners may not be applying a 'developed body of psychological theory' (though there are so many to choose from and so many that contradict each other) but rather may be working intuitively. They may not be consciously applying a 'developed body of psychological theory' nor subconsciously applying one they may previously have been conscious of. Do good mothers mother on the basis of 'a developed body of mothering theory'? Also, what is the boundary between a 'developed body of psychological theory' and a spiritual discipline?

... in order to produce psychological change.
Does 'psychological' include the body? the soma? the spirit? If so, where is the boundary with massage? with bodywork? with spiritual practices?

In addition as Rowan rightly points out in criticism of the 'Key Purpose' statement: "... It seems to me that the therapist does not ***produce*** change in the client. It is the client who produces or does not produce the change" (Rowan, 1993b).

The 'Key Purpose' statement does not distinguish the activity of psychotherapy clearly from others and is so broad a catch-all that human potential work for example could clearly be trawled in by it if such a broad definition became the basis for a practice act.

Subsequent levels of the Lead Body's 'functional analysis' of psychotherapy read like a design for the toy box of an 'obsessional neurotic' with 'schizoid' aspirations. It is an exercise in 'relationships by numbers'. (Perhaps friendships and the choice of an intimate partner might also benefit from this rigour?) It is not really relational at all and assumes that the locus of change lies primarily in the psychotherapist's skills.

The whole exercise of attempting to measure the 'elements of competence' reminds me of the application of 'cost-benefit analysis' in relation to social policy such as the siting of a new airport or road development. The *appearance* of accuracy that the analysis presents simply misleads. What are at root issues of competing values and special interests (i.e. political issues) become disguised by a spurious coating of rigorous analysis. Thus the choice of whether or not to go ahead with a road development may hinge on the numerical values attributed in the analysis to the journey times of pedestrians versus car users or the numerical values allotted in the analysis to the loss of a view or a woodland.

One may doubt, as I do, the feasibility of *measuring* performance in this area in the way proposed by the 'Lead Body' but at least it has the virtue of shifting the focus of attention onto competence as such - however acquired - and away from the promotion of irrelevant prerequisites for practice or title usage.

So far the occupations to which the NVQ system has been applied have not been amongst the most prestigious, whereas UKCP has until now been aiming resolutely 'upmarket'. Instead of real 'standards', what we are liable to end up with from either system are bureaucratic standards - whether it be practitioners brandishing their NVQ 'empathy scores', or flaunting their UKCP approved postgraduate, professional status. (See also Brown & Mowbray, 1994b.)[1]

Chapter 20

Third Party Payments
and 'de facto' Regulation

... I feel the licensing procedure here in the US is humiliating, irrelevant, non-seeing and certainly unrelated to competency and commitment. It is a procedure entirely controlled by the Insurance Agencies and seems motivated by greed....

(Miriam Dror, 1990:35)

Unfortunately, the mental health establishment continually attempts to tighten state licensing requirements. These laws supposedly are aimed at protecting the public from unqualified practitioners, but their main aim is to encourage health insurance companies to pay for costly services. Overall, licensure laws enable groups of professionals to monopolize the psychotherapy market by locking out unlicensed competitors while guaranteeing a steady flow of clients and high fees for themselves....

(Peter Breggin, 1991/1993:496)

... In the past, especially, health insurers were prone to pay for bills generated by psychiatrists but not by other mental health professionals. In order to qualify for reimbursements from health insurers, these other professions have tried increasingly to make themselves over in the image of psychiatry. In a field where innovation and variety should have top priority, limiting health insurance reimbursement to traditional look-alikes stultifies the field.

(ibid.:456)

In the realm of alternative and complimentary medicine, the debate in the UK about official recognition and statutory registration of such disciplines as osteopathy, chiropractic and acupuncture has focused not only on the protection of the public, but also on the eligibility of these methods for recognition as treatments available under the National Health Service (NHS) or under private medical insurance schemes.

This 'eligibility of the treatment' issue is also a factor to be considered in the case of psychotherapy. For patients there is a question of having access to psychotherapy funded by the state or by private medical insurance as an alternative to the typical resort to symptom suppressing drug-based approaches with attendant risks of addiction and side-effects (see Appendix E). For practitioners there is a question of what status qualifies them for reimbursement of fees or employment in the NHS. That is, who would be recognized to offer psychotherapy?

Eligibility for medical cover, whether state or private, categorizes the activity in question as a remedial treatment. Holmes and Lindley argue a case for state-funded psychotherapy on the grounds that emotional autonomy is an essential part of human well-being and that therefore the state should be responsible for funding activities directed towards the restoration, maintenance or development of a reasonable level of emotional autonomy in the same way that state provision of education is accepted (Holmes & Lindley, 1989). This may be a desirable vision, but setting aside the question of to what extent the education system is really concerned with promoting individual development rather than conformity and preparation for economic activity (Illich, 1971), I think one would be extremely fortunate to get treatment paid for by others unless one is seen by them as 'sick'. Psychotherapy when provided under the NHS or private medical insurance is almost by definition a remedial, medical model activity - 'psychotherapeutic treatment' - rather than a personal development activity. In pursuing access to NHS employment UKCP is by implication moving (closer?) towards an implicit medical model definition of psychotherapy. If not, self-actualization is to be funded by the taxpayer and the Department of Health has changed its spots.

As indicated by Peter Breggin above and as Juliana Brown and I have outlined elsewhere [see Appendix A], eligibility for medical insurance payments has been a factor in the development of licensing systems in this field in the USA. This has favoured a medical model rather than a growth model and has encouraged both practitioners and clients to classify aspects of the latter's experience or behaviour as pathological, as psychological disorders, in order to render attending to them a claimable item.

The 'bible' for this is the *Diagnostic and Statistical Manual of Mental Disorders* (DSM) which is modelled on the *International Classification of Diseases* (ICD). According to *Psychology Today*, the latest edition, DSM-IV: "... continues the classification mania set in motion in 1952 with the debut of the original DSM" (*Psychology Today*, 1993:17). And, according to psychologist Mark Hubble who regards DSM-IV as a fashion catalogue for mental health workers: "It's been a road to hell paved with expert consensus" (ibid.). From this perspective, DSM-IV is a catalogue of deviations from cultural norms. A classic example is that homosexuality was classed as a disease until dropped from the DSM in 1973 on the basis of a vote by the American Psychiatric Association (Grof, 1985:329).

According to Mitchell Wilson, DSM-IV furthers the medicalized "narrowing of the psychiatric gaze" by teaching doctors et al. to focus only on "the superficial and publicly visible" (*Psychology Today*, 1993:17).

> How to make sense of psychiatry's diagnostic swelling? It may not accurately reflect the nature of human problems, say Hubble and Wilson, but it follows the widening scope of medications and the need for strict classification codes by insurers. (ibid.)

Having a diagnosis of 'mental disorder' may be financially beneficial in that you may be able to claim the cost of psychotherapeutic (or other) treatment against medical insurance or have it 'free' under the NHS. In the latter case this makes such an activity available to people who might not otherwise be able to afford it. However there is also a downside that needs to be taken into account. Psychotherapy categorized as treatment becomes part of your medical record and if you've received psychotherapeutic treatment *ipso facto* you've had a psychological disorder. Given the stigma that attaches to 'mental disorders' (often regarded as weaknesses or defects of character) having this on your medical record may have effects on your employment prospects, visa worthiness, etc. Of course, going to a practitioner privately need not in most cases become part of your medical record - nor your 'social' record.

There may be less stigma attached to going to see a 'counsellor' rather than a 'psychotherapist' as the associations with medical treatment are looser. However, it is worth noting that the UK government investigation into the case of Beverly Allit (a nurse who killed and injured children in hospital whilst suffering from 'Munchausen syndrome by proxy') recommended that access to the nursing profession should be denied to people with a history of heavy use of counselling services (amongst other things) (BBC Radio 4, 1994a).

For practitioners, reimbursement of session fees by health care schemes and access to employment in the NHS are amongst the main economic cherries to be picked from the regulation tree. As indicated in Chapter 19, the prospect of access to NHS employment and competition from BAC has tempted a reluctant UKCP to join the Lead Body for Advice Guidance and Counselling (*Self & Society*, 1994:42). Counsellors are already making a home for themselves in the NHS. Under the new GP contract of April 1990, GP's may employ counsellors in their practices and it is estimated that 49 per cent of all fund-holding practices already have one, and 70 per cent or more of their wages may be reimbursed by the local funding authorities (Harris, 1994:24). Members of the recognized 'core professions', psychiatry and clinical psychology, are already regarded as directly eligible for NHS employment. There are posts for over a hundred consultant psychotherapists (medically qualified) in the NHS, the first having been appointed in 1964 (Holmes & Lindley, 1989:84) and there are approximately 2,500 clinical psychologists in the UK: "most of whom consider their primary responsibility to include the provision of psychological therapies" (Kosviner, 1994:289).[1]

When work such as psychotherapy is undertaken under the NHS or the fees are recoverable under private health insurance schemes, a question of whether or not practitioners would be subject to medical supervision also comes into play. This issue of professional autonomy *vis-à-vis* the medical establishment has been a particular cause for concern for practitioners of alternative medicine contemplating the incorporation of their services into the NHS but reluctant to be subject to 'allopathic' control. In the context of NHS employment, except in those cases where the practitioners are themselves also medically qualified or perhaps members of that other NHS 'core profession' - clinical psychology, psychotherapists or counsellors are by and large regarded as 'professionals supplementary to medicine' and this seems something unlikely to be easily changed. As discussed in Chapter 7, the types of non-biological approach currently favoured in the NHS (psychoanalytic and behavioural/cognitive-behavioural) have historically been subject to the influence of, respectively, medically qualified psychoanalysts and the championing of behaviourism by clinical psychologists in the course of their bid to carve out the status of a profession separate from medicine. Other approaches are now apparently making inroads.

The choice of criteria for employment or reimbursement involves the same sorts of issue as discussed for licensing systems generally, in particular the issue of whether competence as such will be targeted. On the one hand, where public money is being spent there is a strong incentive to do so accountably, on the other hand, state bureaucracies have tended to favour input criteria - the traditional reverence for professional status rather than output regulation and the monitoring of performance. There are also issues of immediate versus long term costs and of symptom relief versus 'cure' to be considered. Roberta Russell has referred to the: "age of accountability" in which insurance reimbursers and state funders of psychotherapy are increasingly counting the cost of psychotherapy provision and demanding clinical evaluation (Russell, Summer 1993:6). NVQs in this area may be seen as indicative of this trend and the creation of competing NHS Trusts leads in the same direction. It has been argued that, in this climate of increasing accountability, the need for practitioners to monitor and evaluate the outcome of their clinical work will become more urgent if renewable licenses to practice are introduced (Wilson & Barkham, 1994:50).

In Section III, I will discuss an alternative model for the provision of psychotherapy-as-treatment in those health care settings where third party payments apply, a model which avoids many of the pitfalls of existing approaches.

In those countries where there is no specific statutory regulation of psychotherapy, restrictions on eligibility for employment and reimbursement can provide a measure of regulation of an indirect nature. In much of the European Community/Union, for example, eligibility for reimbursement of fees for psychotherapy under health insurance schemes is limited to psychiatrists or in some cases psychologists as well (European Parliament, 1993; Young, 1990).[2] Given sufficient acknowledgement by state and private health care funding systems, even without statutory registration, professional organizations may come to exercise a degree of power over access to employment and fee reimbursement that amounts to a form of indirect, *de facto* regulation - at least of psychotherapy or counselling offered as *treatment*.

What may be referred to as 'self-regulation' may in fact become a case of market control - *de facto* licensing not too far removed from that achievable through statutory means. Moreover, acting alone or in concert with others (as a cartel), professional organizations may dominate the market sufficiently to control access to such things as advertising in journals, using/renting premises and employment by agencies in the private or voluntary sectors as well as the public sector. A tie-in with insurance companies may occur whereby employers may require prospective employees to carry professional indemnity insurance (see the next chapter) and yet insurers only recognize members of the professional organizations as being eligible or the employing agency's insurance may require membership of, say, UKCP or BAC by employees as a prerequisite for cover. Domination of training and accreditation is of course a main avenue to such control of the market-place.

Even in those countries where statutory licensing does exist, such factors may in fact operate as a main form of control. For example in the North American context even where a practice act applies, 'in practice' the main mode of enforcement of unlicensed practitioners may be via the restriction of access to a 'billing number' (and thereby to third party payments for treatment i.e. state or private medical insurance payments) to licensed practitioners. The unlicensed are in effect 'starved out'.

It is really quite remarkable how professions in numerous fields and many countries have managed to accrue to themselves such monopoly powers, whether of a *de facto* or *de jure* nature, in a way that would be quite unacceptable in other parts of a market economy. 'Protection' has been sold to a trusting public and all too often skillfully massaged into protectionism.

Chapter 21

The Codes of Practice
of 'Defensive Psychotherapy'

... this form of market-failure analysis [which centres on the issue of quality assurance by seeking to relate the quality of outcome to the nature of services] is predicated on an assumption that *someone* (if not the consumer) can reliably determine "satisfactory" outcomes and "appropriate" services. In other words, if ignorance about what is a good or bad outcome, or what is a good or bad procedure, is not asymmetrical but pervasive [i.e. it is not only the consumers who are ignorant of these things], then psychotherapy begins to resemble astrology in that no settled bench marks can be identified upon which to base any regulatory strategy directed to promoting service quality....

(Michael J. Trebilcock and Jeffrey Shaul, 1982:276)

For the past few weeks, the attention of the legal and medical communities in the United States has been focused on an extraordinary civil case being played out in the Napa County courthouse in the heart of California's wine country. There, Mr. Ramona is seeking to persuade a jury that he should be paid more than eight million dollars damages by his daughter's therapist and a psychiatrist because, he says, they planted false memories in her mind. The trial is considered a landmark case. Legal experts believe it is the first example of a non-patient suing a therapist for damages over allegations resulting from "recovered" childhood memories....

(Phil Reeves, 1994)

It is a requirement of UKCP registration that practitioners take out professional indemnity insurance (UKCP, 1993g). BAC counsellors are "encouraged" to do so (BAC, 1993), as are BPS members (Dobson, 1995:3).

Professional indemnity insurance may be considered a badge of a 'proper' profession. It betokens the hazards that might arise through professional negligence and from which the public needs to be protected - over and above the legal obligation to exercise reasonable care and skill that behoves anyone offering a service. The case for the restrictive practice which is brought into being when a profession is legally backed is demonstrably weakened without the implication of such hazards awaiting the potential consumer.

Professional indemnity insurance insures the practitioner against claims of professional negligence or malpractice. Malpractice presumes a standard of good practice. In a field such as surgery, for example, where there is more of a consensus about the relationship between practice and outcome, malpractice may be quite easy to specify - leaving a pair of forceps in the patient, for example, is obviously bad practice. However the field in question is even less of an exact science than medicine or surgery, if it is a science at all. Despite the prevalent assumption of a medical model (which has given rise to the issues addressed in this chapter), there is in fact no consensus as to aims or means in this area. Rather than an evolved homogeneity there is a host of divergent opinions.

For example, what should be the role of touch? Is touching clients/ patients a reprehensible practice as it might be regarded in psychoanalytic circles or is its absence a cause for concern as might be the case in the humanistic world? Are active techniques advisable? Does thrashing a cushion discharge rage or encourage violent behaviour? Does accepting a gift from your client represent an exploitation of them or not doing so a snub, a rejection of an urge to give, which would be counterproductive to the work in hand? Should 'dual relationships' be allowed? Is socializing with a current or former client acceptable?

The answer to such questions is usually "it depends". It depends so much on the context and the nature of the relationship between the two or more people concerned. It depends on their goals and their values, and cannot in many cases be reduced to clearly differentiated 'good' and 'bad' practices. There will be things that warrant a great deal of caution in a good many cases but may be appropriate in some. Furthermore the critical factors in this field seem to be personal factors rather than practice factors.

Guidelines, ethical and otherwise, and discussions of ethical dilemmas such as that by Tim Bond (1993) are valuable as cautionary pointers to what may be potential problem areas - hazardous turning points on the road which the sincere practitioner will consequently negotiate with particular care. However, such guidelines will have little hope of having impact on the unscrupulous practitioner unless as part of the process of professionalization they become rigidified as *codes* of practice that have the status of rules and hence are capable of enforcement. Unfortunately this means of addressing the problem of the morally deficient practitioner has the effect of requiring a standardization of practice. In an area that should be concerned with the individuality of the client above all (from a personal growth point of view at any rate), this standardization of practice is akin to throwing the baby out with the bath-water. Moreover the presence of a code of practice is unlikely to really deter the seriously unprincipled practitioner, who may in fact be protected by the status that being a member of a recognized profession affords. Codes of ethics and practice are no substitute for inner integrity on the part of the practitioner. Clients should not be encouraged to believe otherwise and be lulled into a false sense of security thereby. Furthermore, if the history of other professions is anything to go by, the potential for self-serving behaviour and iniquity is more than likely to be constellated at the collective level by the process of professionalization.

In the absence of an evolved consensus, that is a reasonably homogeneous 'profession', malpractice (and hence malpractice insurance) cannot be grounded in clear unambiguous functional criteria. The basis for defining malpractice becomes the norms set by the professional organizations which have statutory recognition or dominance in the field, so that in effect good practice becomes what the profession says it is. Under this regime 'good practice' so easily veers towards what is 'good' for the profession - judged as what is safest for the reputation of the profession (remember that as discussed in Chapter 9, the 'Index of Visibility' bears the strongest correlation with disciplinary enforcement action).[1] These standardized criteria of practice then tend to become used by the courts to assess suits for negligence and by insurance companies as the basis for assessing professional indemnity claims - leading to further ossification.

What is fostered by such circumstances is not a fertile and innovative field but conformity of practice based not so much on true standards that are inherently related to the nature of the activity as on practitioner self-protection - the practice of 'defensive psychotherapy'. Practitioners will do or not do things in order to avoid disciplinary action, malpractice suits and/or the invalidating of their insurance cover, rather than solely on the basis of whether or not the client would benefit.

In litigation-happy USA, where it is possible for plaintiffs to initiate an action without any financial risk to themselves, the increased prevalence of malpractice suits in the field of medicine has resulted in rocketing professional indemnity costs and widespread practice of 'defensive medicine'. The effect on the quality and availability of care has been: "disastrous" (Holmes & Lindley, 1989:184). For example, doctors are reluctant to practise as obstetricians at all in some states because of the risk of being held responsible for, and sued for, negative outcomes. Those who do practise tend to 'play safe', and if in the slightest doubt about the delivery, prefer to deliver by Caesarean section rather than risk the natural route since the Caesarean route gives them more control over the process. Consequently, for this and other reasons the USA has a much higher rate of Caesarean section than elsewhere.

Defensive medicine is expensive. Billions of dollars are spent each year in the USA on unnecessary investigative procedures which are primarily undertaken to protect the doctors from negligence suits - although they also add to physicians' incomes. For example, even a minor bump on the head will call forth a brain scan (BBC Radio 4, 1994e). The USA pays a higher percentage of GDP (Gross Domestic Product) on health care than any other country and paying for medical care is the leading cause of bankruptcy there. The practice of defensive medicine is a significant contributory factor to this level of expenditure (ibid.).

In the field of psychotherapy, malpractice insurance and malpractice suits have also become increasingly commonplace in the USA - and expensive/lucrative. Striano (1988) cites California's then costliest psycho-- therapy malpractice case as resulting in a six million dollar settlement to former clients. There is reason to believe that the proliferation of psychotherapy malpractice suits in the USA in part reflects the fact that the prevalence of professional indemnity insurance makes a suit worth pursuing (Hogan, Vol. 1, 1979:315,323). Moreover the level of damages that may be awarded is linked to the income of the defendant rather than just to the nature of the injury. Provided the practitioner has not invalidated the policy by 'non-standard' practice, his or her own assets are not on the line, so the practitioner will refer it to the insurance company who may pay up to avoid litigation costs, whatever the justice of the claim:

> ... You may be upset with the insurance company's willingness to settle out of court. Resist the impulse to clear your name.... Although settlement is not in the best interest of the professional [or justice], most malpractice cases are settled out of court at the pretrial stage due to the prohibitive cost of trial proceedings.... (Austin et al., 1990:20)

As discussed in Chapter 13, the question of harm in psychotherapy, especially with regard to causation, is problematic. Expedient bypassing of issues of causality and responsibility in the short term sows spores that will eventually manifest as decay in the system as a whole. With regard to the medical profession in the USA, such a system has been a costly and spurious exercise. Applied to psychotherapy where the risks of harm are low and the likelihood of establishing causation slim, it has done little to provide regulation and done much to smother innovation:

> You should be aware that, if your practice deviates from what is considered standard treatment procedures by most other respected and qualified professionals in your particular discipline (i.e. experimental or nontraditional therapy) you risk being sued ... using experimental or nontraditional therapy leaves one vulnerable to both a malpractice charge and a charge of unethical conduct. "Generally, suits against innovative therapies have been based on negligence in techniques, assault and batteries (apprehension of and/or harmful or offensive touching without consent), or infliction of emotional duress" (Schutz, 1982:33).... (Austin et al., 1990:155)

When this sort of working environment prevails, practitioner self-protective caution gains the ascendancy. Whereas the practice of defensive medicine leads to a proliferation of unnecessary and expensive interventions so that the doctor can be shown to have taken all possible steps to counteract a disease process, the practice of defensive psychotherapy tends towards passivity and a retreat into an interaction that is, at most, verbal - as foreshadowed by Freud's retreat from direct work with primary process and a cathartic approach. Unless there are standard 'treatment' procedures that you can fall back on, doing nothing very much is the best defensive option - just mirror what the client has said. Any physical contact with your client becomes circumspect. Don't touch or do bodywork - you may get sued for sexual malpractice or accused of having caused injury. Austin et al. specifically warn that initiating hugs with your client is risky behaviour (ibid:161). Don't suggest tasks or offer opinions on outer life issues - you may be held liable if they backfire. Don't suggest a causation - you may be sued for 'implanting' a false memory.

Apparently, not only have malpractice suits against practitioners proliferated in the USA but through the doctrine of 'vicarious liability' their supervisors have become implicated as well. According to Austin et al. (ibid.:230), a new trend in the USA is for supervisors to be named as defendants in malpractice suits brought against counsellors they are supervising. Some of the instances cited involve yet-to-be-licensed trainees, but it is not clear that this is so in all cases:

> ... Slovenko (1980) predicted that litigation involving supervisors is certain to be the "suit of the future." When one undertakes to supervise the work of another therapist, one also assumes the legal liability not only for one's own behaviour but for the acts of the supervisee.... (Austin et al. 1993:230)

So far, in the UK the likelihood of being sued, never mind successfully sued, for professional negligence as a psychotherapist has been almost zero. According to Kenneth Cohen, a solicitor who has studied the legal framework for the practice of counselling and psychotherapy in Britain, there has been only one case of negligent psychotherapy published in the English Law Reports and that concerned a psychiatrist. Furthermore it is his belief that: "... we are unlikely to see a dramatic increase in such cases because of the uncertain state of our knowledge about counselling and psychotherapy, and because of the general obstacles placed by the law in the path of any plaintiff in a negligence action ..." (Cohen, 1992:11).[2]

So, members of UKCP are required to insure themselves against a risk that is virtually non-existent at the present time. A similar situation applies in the world of Alexander teachers and Feldenkrais practitioners where professional indemnity insurance is compulsory for membership of professional organizations and yet there is a minimal recorded level of risk. According to Dobson (1995:3), more than 5000 psychologists and counsellors in the UK have been persuaded to take out insurance against negligence claims, including allegations of planting false memories of child abuse. Most of them have opted for cover of around £1 million. Perhaps it is time to buy some shares in the insurance companies concerned!

Unlike the US legal system, the British one has so far exhibited what is to my mind an eminently sensible reluctance to make hurt feelings in themselves a ground for compensation through the courts, unless they are such as to amount to mental illness or accompany a physical injury (Cohen, 1992:14; Bond, 1993:49). This is a position that reflects the difficulties of allotting responsibility in the area of hurt feelings.

I do not think it is wise to encourage a litigious adversarial approach to the sort of difficulties that may arise in relationships of this nature. Seeking redress of a financial or punitive nature via the legal and insurance systems is rarely appropriate for an activity whose stock in trade is 'unfinished business' of an emotional nature. Encouraging a settlement on the level at which the problem exists - the emotional, the relational, perhaps with the aid of a facilitator or mediator, is usually more relevant than fostering an escalation to the level of litigation and insurance claims.

In the USA the incentives to pathologize experience built into the US medical insurance system have combined with the stultifying effects of licensing, the promotion of 'defensive psychotherapy' through professional indemnity insurance and an escalating risk of litigation. The 'standards' promoted by such a system are not necessarily ones that correspond well to the nature of an activity where so much depends on personal qualities and environmental support for a very individualized response. This is a system that promotes standardized and conservative practice - practitioners and clients afraid to deviate from the average. It is a system that encourages a legitimized mediocrity rather than the variety of responses that the kaleidoscope of human nature requires. In my opinion such a system should not be allowed to take root here.

Section II

Human Potential Work and Psychotherapy

A Suitable Case for Differentiation

Chapter 22

Human Potential Work
and the Rise of the Therapy Bureaucracies

We are concerned that if these moves [towards statutory registra-
tion] gain ground there will be a deterioration in the prevailing ambience of openness and choice. One of the fundamental principles
of growth is choice, and introducing a system of regulation or licensing into the growth movement is liable to restrict choice. We
feel that measures towards empowering the public to make more
informed, responsible choices would be more in keeping with the
spirit of the human potential movement....

Despite areas in common with existing institutions this field
should not be subsumed under any of them. It is important that it
retains its autonomy and continues to establish itself in its own right.
It is important that the structures we develop reflect the underlying
model and that we do not 'regress' and adopt structures appropriate
to other models.

(Juliana Brown and Richard Mowbray, 1990)

Are human potential work (personal growth work), psychotherapy and
counselling basically all the same thing? It has been argued that they are
(e.g. Rowan, 1988:77). Certainly the activities that these terms have been
used to refer to may employ techniques in common and from a superficial
perspective they might appear to be the same sort of thing. However from
a deeper perspective, the focus of human potential work differs markedly
from, say, behaviour therapy, hypnotherapy, or psychoanalysis - as does
the target clientele.

The issue of statutory regulation prompts a need for a clarity of definition and terminology that so far we have managed without in this area -
witness the reams that has been written about psychotherapy, counselling
and personal growth without specifying the differences.

At the political and legal level, the relevant definitions of psychotherapy et al. are intertwined with social role definitions such as adult/ minor (child); healthy/sick; able/disabled; normal/abnormal and with questions of autonomy versus diminished autonomy and responsibility versus diminished responsibility. These are roles that are socially defined and self or socially allotted.

There are also the associated questions of which social categories the activity is bracketed with for purposes of law (whether existing law or new laws specifically targeted at the activity in question) and what categories it falls in for the purpose of funding and other matters. The question of whether the activity is regarded as a medical/mental health concern, an educational process, a religious endeavour, a cultural/artistic pursuit, a recreational activity, or simply a business activity has very practical consequences. For example, does the activity fit with town planning permission for the premises in which it is conducted? Is the activity regarded as a 'health profession' for the purposes of law or is it perhaps too spiritual or educational in orientation for that category? In the UK, categorization as a 'health profession' relates, for example, to the status of client/patient records. Under the UK's *Access to Health Records Act, 1990* , the records of 'health professionals' have the same status as medical records in terms of the patient's right of access to them. Medical records have social consequences in terms of employment and insurance assessment and may be called for as evidence in a court case or insurance claim. Clinical psychologists are defined as 'health professionals' under the Act, as are child psychotherapists, but practitioners of other types are not so far explicitly defined as 'health professionals' (Cohen, 1992:23-4). Lister-Ford and Pokorny take the view that psychotherapists generally will be regarded as 'health professionals' under the Act "once they have a register" (1994:155-6). 'Health professionals' may also be called to testify as 'expert' witnesses in court. Take the question of advertising. Under which section of the 'yellow pages' or other directories should the activity be classified?

In this light the *aims* of the activity and the *status* of the recipient are crucial to defining its nature rather than its methods or current labels. In the chapters that follow, I will be guided by this sort of perspective in spelling out the case for a clear differentiation between remedial 'psychotherapy' and human potential work (personal growth work) on the basis of goals, values and intended clientele. In my opinion, the activities of human potential movement do not readily fit into the pre-existing social categories mentioned above and really deserve a category of their own.

Currently, because of the ambiguous use of such terms as 'psychotherapy' and 'counselling', some of what occurs under those labels would constitute human potential work and some would not. I propose a terminological clarification to prevent human potential work becoming inappropriately subsumed, to reduce a source of client confusion, and also to attempt to distance clients involved in human potential work from the stigmatization of the 'patient' that so frequently accompanies remedial mental health treatments.

The chapters in this section go on from the general case against psychotherapy registration outlined in Section I to address the question of how such professionalization would affect the human potential movement.

If the case against psychotherapy registration is strong, the case against human potential work (personal growth work) becoming involved in that process is all the more so. Some people seeking psychotherapeutic treatment do so as an alternative to suppressive approaches such as drug treatments and may be functioning with less than 'average' autonomy and therefore may be willing to define themselves as 'unwell'. However human potential work is directed at people who are 'as healthy as the next person'. They may be seeking change or personal transformation but would not fall outside of a category of 'average maturing adult'.

Without an appropriate differentiation between human potential work and approaches that focus on remedial treatment (and unambiguous terminology to match), policies and structures aimed at people who do not have sufficient autonomy to function adequately in our society may also become applied willy-nilly to those who do.

In addition, the introduction of a system of regulation into the field of psychotherapy when, as has been argued in Section I, such a system is neither warranted nor effective is liable to have a detrimental 'knock-on' effect upon human potential practice even if a clear differentiation from psychotherapy is maintained.

In my view, those who would like to retain a healthy human potential movement would be well advised to oppose the ambitions of UKCP and the other therapy bureaucracies - rather than participate in or acquiesce to them.

Chapter 23

Humanistic Psychology Joins in - the Humanistic and Integrative Psychotherapy Section of UKCP

Humanistic psychology looks up to people rather than looking down on them. One of the founders of the movement, Abraham Maslow says that he sees people as living organisms with an inherent need to grow or change. This is born inside them, part of their basic nature and it leads to a never-ending process of going into the self and going beyond the self. People involved in humanistic psychology study and try to experience ecstasy, creativity and transpersonal states as well as everyday functioning. These approaches emphasise a moving away from safety, and towards a set of values which Maslow calls the Being-values: the values found amongst people who have grown into something approaching their full potential as living human beings. In recent years a number of methods and techniques have been developed for fostering this kind of unfolding of human potential. *You* are invited to find out how humanistic psychology helps to generate a way of life, not only for you in your own private self, but also for you as a social being, a member of society.

(Introduction to "Self and Society" from 1975 to 1979)

It is well understood in sociology that nonconformist movements often mimic what they seek to change. The new professions of counselling and psychotherapy run this risk. Bureaucratic training bodies, accreditation bodies, brokers who sign up therapists and market them to companies, universities and hospitals teaming up with hitherto independent training centres all mimic the status system in British society.... The language of personal growth has been replaced with the lexicon of clinicians, clinical training, and psychiatric diagnostic systems. We risk going back to the oppressive, authoritarian culture of the head, emphasising theory and labelling at the expense of integration. We will lose the power of 'being with' in the

transformation of suffering. Personal growth and empowerment risk going out of the window.
(David Jones, editorial, "Self and Society", 1994)

As with so many things, wide acceptance is even more dangerous than rejection....
(John O. Stevens & Barry Stevens, 1975:ix)

The journal *Self and Society* quoted above has been a mouthpiece for humanistic psychology in Britain since 1973 and has been closely associated with the Association for Humanistic Psychology in Britain, AHP(B), for most of that time. For its first 20 years in addition to various other subtitles such as "European Journal of Humanistic Psychology" it has carried the message: "A channel of communication for the Human Potential movement." This description was dropped in 1993 and *Self and Society* became simply "A Journal of Humanistic Psychology".

As will be discussed in greater depth in Chapter 25, humanistic psychology, pioneered by Maslow and Sutich, was a major contributor to the formation of the 'human potential' or 'growth' movement. As humanistic organizations in Britain have sought the bosom of UKCP, there has been a tendency to write off the human potential movement or reduce it to a humanistic psychology described as: "consolidating itself" and: "now part of the mainstream" (Rowan, 1992a:74).[1] Along with this, no doubt to avoid being: "condemned to practise psychotherapy as a 'therapist' " (Young, 1990:5), humanistic organizations and practitioners that would once have loosely referred to their activities as 'therapy' or 'growth', have increasingly gravitated towards the use of the term 'psychotherapy'. Thus for example the 'gestalt therapy' of Fritz Perls has for some now become formalized as 'gestalt psychotherapy' (see e.g. the brochure for The Gestalt Centre, 1994). Also, 'humanistic psychotherapy' has become increasingly adopted as a generic term and human potential modalities are in danger of being 'gathered' under such a term in a way that favours their regulation by the statutory body that UKCP hopes to become.[2, 3]

The Humanistic and Integrative Psychotherapy Section of UKCP (HIPS) comprises 19 organizations most of which both train and accredit.[4] In terms of number of organizations in a Section this is the second largest

Section in UKCP, however as most of its constituent organizations are fairly small, its membership of approximately 500 practitioners amount to only about 20 percent of the practitioners on the register.

The "flag statement" of the Humanistic and Integrative Psychotherapy Section of UKCP holds that:

> Humanistic psychotherapy is an approach which tries to do justice to the whole person including mind, body and spirit, and thus humanistic psychotherapists believe psychotherapy is not a medical practice and thus most often speak of clients and not patients.
>
> Humanistic psychotherapists recognise the self-healing capacities of the client, and believe that the greatest expert on the client is the client. The humanistic psychotherapist works towards an authentic meeting of equals in the therapy relationship. (UKCP, 1993g:156)

However, although "patients" are not referred to in the *Criteria and Guidelines for Membership of the Humanistic and Integrative Section of the United Kingdom Council for Psychotherapy* (UKCP, 1993j), the document is littered with other examples of medicalized language and thinking. There are, for example, references to "psychotherapeutic treatment", "psychopathology", "clinical competence", "clinical practice", etc.[5] Apart from the "Ethos" statement discussed below and a limp assertion that: "We also *favour* courses that take a holistic approach, paying attention to mind, body, and soul/spirit ..." (ibid.:1) inserted in amongst all the 'shoulds' and 'musts' there is to my mind very little in these criteria that is 'humanistic'.

The document ends with a statement of "Ethos" which refers to the value system that the Section "holds as fundamentally important" (ibid.:9) and contains the principles by which they are to be guided in the shaping of a psychotherapy profession. However, try as I might, I could find little congruence between the criteria in the rest of the document and these fundamental principles from which they are supposed to have emerged.

Take their first stated principle: "that life itself brings as much if not more learning than any organized training. Therefore, *as much emphasis* needs to be placed on relevant life experience as on recognized qualifications or expertise" (ibid.).

How does this principle manifest in the criteria? It is not apparent to me. The criteria consider psychotherapy training as a: "postgraduate level activity" (ibid.:1) and include requirements of intensive study of theory as well as practice and some form of substantial written work or presentation. I see nothing there to indicate that a particularly rich personal background might lead someone to be accepted straight on to the register without passing through one of their approved training courses.

Take the principle that: "authority and responsibility shifts over time from the outer teacher or expert to the inner authority of an individual. In recognizing this, organizations and individuals need to protect the rights of self-determination within certain agreed guidelines" (ibid.:9). And similarly, that: "principles of empowerment of both individuals and organizations within which individuals are either working or training are highly valued and are embodied in the structures and systems of the organizations" (ibid.).

How do these principles manifest in the criteria? I've no idea. Practitioners are usually put on, and maintained on, the register by the organization that trained and accredited them. This is not a once and for all placement. Accreditation is seen as: "a renewable licence to practise" (ibid.:1). The organization reviews practitioners' accreditation regularly and also their: "ongoing personal and professional development" (ibid.:4). So, unless there is an alternative route for them onto the register (which to some extent is provided by AHPP in this Section) practitioners are tied into, and subject to, their 'parent' organization. The UKCP complaints procedure also operates initially via the training organization.

In order to get onto the register, having completed the required number of years of training etc., the practitioner is subject to an evaluation which requires a minimum of four persons including at least one: "who has not been one of the candidate's primary trainers, supervisors or therapists" (ibid.:2). That is three-quarters of your assessors could be your trainers, supervisors or therapists and not, for example, your peers. The choice of external moderator who, amongst other things, participates in and assesses the graduation process is: "*entirely* up to an individual organization", though the Humanistic and Integrative Section: "*could* question a choice of moderator" (ibid.:9).

Although one of the other principles in the "Ethos" statement is a strong valuation of unanimity or consensus in decision-making there is not even a mention of graduate participation in decision-making even though they are still dependent on the 'parent' organization for continued validation. Likewise, student/trainee participation in decision-making is not referred to, whether regarding accreditation or otherwise. What is more, unlike their 'progeny', the trainers themselves are rather free from prerequisites and scrutiny: "... *We are not necessarily concerned with the credentials and intentions of the organization's founders or present directors.* We are more concerned with its actual existence and performance as a professional organization." (ibid.:1) So the trainers are not for example required to participate in any form of self and peer assessment (see Appendix D). So much for the empowerment of trainees and a shift towards their inner authority! What hope is there of the clients - the supposed beneficiaries of all this - being inspired to empower themselves in the presence of the graduate output of such a system? If they do so it will be despite the system rather than because of the system.

As John Rowan has reminded me (Rowan, 1994), representatives of humanistic psychology were amongst the first to get involved in the development of UKCP, particularly those representatives who were associated with the Association of Humanistic and Psychology Practitioners (AHPP). AHPP was formed in 1980 as a sub-section of AHP(B) with a view to grasping: "the nettle of accreditation" (Rowan, 1991:32) and: "to act as a professional organization existing to promote the highest standards of excellence amongst practitioners of humanistic psychology" (AHP(B), 1992). AHPP was founded two years after the Sieghart Report (and two years before the first Rugby conference), with the therapy world awash with fears of UK government intervention. Later, fears of European Community/Union requirements were to take the ascendency. AHPP is a member of the Humanistic and Integrative Psychotherapy Section as an accrediting body and does not do any training itself. It is one of the few accrediting bodies that accredits individuals rather than courses (Jelfs, 1992:17) and it has 73 of its practitioners on the UKCP register, a majority of its 100 full members (Collis, 1995:45).[6]

This practitioners' 'arm' of AHP(B) seems in some respects to be more like a 'tail' wagging the dog. AHP(B) has a membership of about 870 (AHP(B), 1994) and is a registered charity whose constitution states that its objective is: "to advance the education of the public about humanistic psychology." (AHP(B), 1992) and yet the interests of the professional group - all of whose members are also required to be members of AHP(B) - have in some cases come to override this charitable objective. For example AHP(B) operated a referral service or resource directory of humanistic services for many years. By 1989 this had 240 people on the list. This original resource directory was unvetted and explicitly disclaimed any recommendation. This has been all but killed off because of opposition from AHPP who wished to convert it into : "a proper register of qualified practitioners" (AHP(B), 1989) and to foster AHPP recruitment by restricting the list to its members, thereby foreclosing on an alternative to membership of AHPP. An emasculated version of the AHP(B) resource directory remains but this is only distributed to members of AHP(B) on request and not to members of the public at large - AHP(B)'s constitutional target. Only the AHPP directory is distributed to the general public. In 1989 when the issue of AHPP taking over the list arose, Juliana Brown and I wrote to AHP(B) favouring its retention as an *information* service to the public but with the information therein to be verified on full disclosure lines (see Chapter 28). Unlike AHPP's activities, this proposal is in line with AHP(B)'s constitution as an educational charity and, we felt, also in tune with humanistic principles of encouraging informed choice.

AHPP is said to operate "semi-autonomously" of AHP(B) (AHPP, 1991b). Proposals were made in 1994 to change the structure of AHP(B) including trying to incorporate AHPP to the fullest extent, however this may cause difficulties with the Charity Commissioners (Burgess, 1994).

John Rowan has warned of the danger of humanistic psychotherapy becoming "absorbed into the medical system and treated as some kind of auxiliary medical aid" (Rowan, 1988:103), and the risk of the work being "twisted out of recognition" if legitimation is sought through NHS channels. He cites AHPP as an alternative route to recognition (ibid.).

With a view to preserving psychotherapy as an activity independent of medicine or psychology, AHPP supports the establishment of psychotherapy as an activity with the status of a profession (AHPP, 1991b), and is party to UKCP's drive for a statutory monopoly, a goal which is arguably antithetical to the essence of humanistic work.[7] The presence of AHPP and those other humanistic organizations which have joined UKCP[8] has helped to modify the latter's institutions in a more humanistic direction than might otherwise have been the case. However, in pursuit of professional status, these humanistic organizations have gone along with all the non-humanistic features of UKCP, such as the academic bias, the aim of a postgraduate profession, the medicalized thinking and terminology, the lack of representation and the absence of any humanistic form of accreditation such as true self and peer assessment (see Appendix D). This has resulted in a situation where much humanistic training has become encumbered with excessive and inappropriate baggage[9] and the whole endeavour fosters reduced choice and stultification. Yet these 'humanistic sacrifices' have been made when risks of absorption into the medical system or of statutory restrictions on the right to practise in the UK (other than as a consequence of UKCP, that is) have actually been rather slight. Instead, the medical model and the model of a profession akin to medicine have been allowed to creep into humanistic psychology. As John Heron, a founder member of AHPP, has said of the 1989 guidelines for full membership of AHPP:

> ... [They] represent a sorry mess ... [falling] between the stool of self-assessment and self-selection of practitioner categories, and the stool of imposed criteria for the category of psychotherapist imported from the UK Standing Conference for Psychotherapy. These criteria are not only imposed, they also appear to be restrictive and outmoded, implying a total separation within a closed, hierarchical professional enclave - of psychodynamics from sociopolitical dynamics. It is all very unhealthy, and looks as though humanistic practitioners are incongruently choosing a form of professionalization quite at odds with the interrelated values of self-realization and social transformation which have so far distinguished Humanistic Psychology. (Heron, 1990:23)

Perhaps it is time for a humanistic 'true self' to emerge from behind all this status seeking? An HPA (Human Potential Association) or an HPPCA (Human Potential Practitioners and Clients Association), perhaps?[10]

Chapter 24

Human Potential Work and Psychotherapy - Ambiguous Terminology and the Right to Practise

> Why should all this bother me? I don't do 'psychotherapy' anyway.
> I don't like the term and its medical model associations and I don't
> use it. I'm a human potential practitioner, I call myself a 'personal
> growth facilitator'.
>
> *(Group-leader-with-his-head-in-the-sand, 1994)*

> I have used the words "therapy," "psychotherapy" and "patient".
> Actually, I hate all these words and I hate the medical model that
> they imply....
>
> *(Abraham Maslow, 1971:53)*

An essential ingredient at the start of the human potential movement was
the promotion of a growth model that focused on the development of *potential*, on self-actualization, on becoming more fully human, rather than
the medical model's remedial focus on 'disorders', repair and cure. That is
a focus more on "growth motivation" than "deficiency motivation" as
Maslow would say (Maslow, 1968).

In our article "Whither the Human Potential Movement?" Juliana
Brown and I argued that: "The current moves towards regulation and licensing derive from an implicit association with the medical model and
with the medical professions as a model for professionalization." And that:
"... in common with John Heron [and others] *we feel that terminology
associated with the medical model (in particular the terms 'psychotherapy' and 'therapy') should be avoided by human potential practitioners*, at least officially ..." (Brown & Mowbray, 1990:33).

The term 'psychotherapy' is derived by combining two words with
roots in classical Latin and Greek. The prefix 'psycho' derives from 'psy-

che' meaning: "breath, soul, life" (*Shorter Oxford English Dictionary*, 1973). The word 'therapy' derives from the verb 'therapeuo' meaning 'wait on, cure' ('therapeia' = 'healing'). Similarly, 'therapist' comes from 'therapeutikos' meaning 'a servant or attendant' (Taft, 1933; *Concise Oxford Dictionary*, 1990; *Shorter Oxford English Dictionary*, 1973). These ancient Greek meanings offer a possible interpretation of psychotherapy as involving healing through attending to the soul of another, and may therefore appeal to those of a holistic bent, but it must be remembered that these meanings derive from a time when there was no clear-cut distinction between medicine and religion and the 'therapeutes' were attendants of a *god*.[1] We, however, live in a time when medicine and religion are for the most part sharply divided and these ancient terms have already been borrowed by secular scientific medicine and psychology and applied in ways far removed from their classical meanings. Do you think of academic psychology as the study of 'breath, soul, life'?[2]

The combination of these root words into the term 'psychotherapy' was not undertaken by the ancient Greeks but is of quite recent origin. The initial use was by Johann Reil in 1803 in an article entitled "Rhapsodies in the Application of Psychic Methods in the Treatment of Mental Disturbances" (Hogan, Vol. 1, 1979:12). This first use was in the light of a medical model and the term is very similar to many other medical model terms. It is not so much that the term 'psychotherapy' has become medicalized and corrupted as Peter Breggin (1991/1993:463) has argued, but rather that, as with many other medical model words, the term was devised during the early years of scientific medicine using classical vocabularies as building blocks. Thus, like 'psychiatry' which combines 'psyche' with 'iatreia' (Greek for healing), 'psychotherapy' is a nineteenth century medical model word and the *Concise Oxford Dictionary* (1990) still defines it as: "the treatment of mental disorder by psychological means". The same source defines 'therapy' as: "the treatment of physical or mental disorders, other than by surgery" and as a suffix or second term, '-therapy' is standard usage in the world of medicine and psychiatry for 'remedial treatment' by the means referred to by the prefix or first term. For example, physiotherapy, radiotherapy, pharmacotherapy - or electroconvulsive therapy (ECT).[3]

The human potential movement has failed to give birth to a generally accepted term that succinctly makes clear the nature of its focus and, for want of a catchy alternative label, has slid into the widespread use of the terms 'therapy' and 'psychotherapy' despite their simultaneous medical model use to describe a remedial activity. After all, 'therapy' slips so easily off the tongue and it's then but a short step to 'psychotherapy'. Can anybody think of a really catchy alternative? [4]

In a world where legality may depend upon the words that you use to describe your work (title protection), the choice of labels with which you ally yourself and with which you build up an association in the public 'mind' becomes a matter of *crucial* importance. After all, the drive for statutory registration in the UK is (initially at least) all about the control of the use of a label. Human potential practitioners have not fostered sufficient public awareness of an unambiguous distinguishing label for their work and have instead laid themselves open to a risk of losing autonomy by resorting to the use of pre-existing, ambiguous labels which for many people are strongly associated with medical models of curative treatment.

Practitioners may be clear about the differences between these models sharing the same terminology but I doubt that the 'man in the street' (never mind the government) is so well informed. In the 1994 Times/Dillons debate: "The Curse of Therapy" attended by about two thousand people, Fay Weldon, the protagonist, declared (unchallenged) that "therapy is cure" (and only a handful of those present voted against the proposition that therapists should be registered). Furthermore, many people have trouble distinguishing between a psychiatrist, a psychotherapist and a psychologist. Consequently, going to see anyone with 'psych-' on the front of their label carries a measure of stigma. They are all 'shrinks' to some (see Appendix E). This public ignorance compounds the use of ambiguous 'psychotherapy' or 'therapy' terminology for human potential work, and provides a ready avenue for the existing medical/health and/or psychology establishments to gradually move into a position of dominance or control of human potential work, a position unwarranted by any allegiance to the model of growth espoused or their actual involvement in the movement.

Despite the insidious ambiguity of the terminology in this area, I did not initially regard the existence of UKCP as other than an indirect threat to human potential work. Not regarding my own work as a form of psychotherapy anyway and having no desire to use that term, I adopted a line of argument akin to that of the group-leader-with-his-head-in-the-sand quoted above. I did not believe that this sort of work could be regulated by some crude statutory approach and thought that nobody would be absurd enough to try. How could two people talking, or a group assembling, be legally regulated in a 'free' society? I now recognize that this was politically naïve and that a more active opposition is required involving a removal of as many heads as possible from the sand before eager register builders add the cement.[5]

As Hogan has pointed out, title protection is often all that is sought initially by professional associations because less political opposition is generated thereby. Once such a law is enacted it is relatively easy to extend it to include practice as well as title. Thus, if say the UKCP register is legitimated by government and allowed to become statutory, there is a significant risk of a shift from title protection to the restriction of activity also.

Eventually what may ensue is the restriction of the practice of whatever actual activity is deemed by UKCP to be 'psychotherapy' - and note that they have not so far defined what the limits of this activity are. Lack of definition has not been a bar to this sort of thing happening elsewhere.

Even without this risk of an escalation to a practice act, title protection of the term 'psychotherapist' would not necessarily be a benign event in relation to the right of human potential practitioners to pursue their craft. The restriction on use of that label is not all that is involved. (Note that, as mentioned in Chapter 6, UKCP also has ambitions regarding the labels by which various types of psychotherapy are to be known). Once a board is established, alternative labels can be 'mopped up' as and when they become popular. Remember also that the regulation of the medical profession in this country is essentially on the basis of title protection. In the Australian state of New South Wales, the Act that gives title protection to the term 'psychologist' also restricts the use of any title that:"is capable of being understood to indicate that the person practises psychology" - without defining what psychology is! Few alternative practitioners there seem to realise that their right to publicize themselves in any meaningful way is already in the hands of the psychology board! The alternative therapists of the state of Victoria only woke up to a similar legal reality twenty years after the Act had been passed. (See Appendix B.)[6]

For all these reasons, not least the risk that UKCP may attempt to go beyond the title protection of the term 'psychotherapy', I feel that its attempt to legally restrict the use of this term should, from a human potential movement point of view, be resisted *even if one does not wish to use it.*

By the same token, the British Psychological Society's ambition to secure title protection for the term 'psychologist' would presumably mean that the title 'humanistic psychologist' would also be ruled out of use unless you were on the register of that society. (For example, in the Canadian province of British Columbia the term 'humanistic psychology' hardly features at all in the local growth movement since the term 'psychology' is legally restricted to those on the psychology register. See Appendix C.) Such a move could also be the prelude to a practice act governing the practice of psychology, including humanistic psychology, that could restrict human potential work to those on its register, *unless* such work were explicitly specified as religious and thereby benefit from the cultural support for religious freedom - such as enjoyed by the Scientologists!

Similarly, moves to have a statutory register of 'counsellors' would impinge on human potential practice. In North America the term 'counselor/counsellor' is often used in the growth movement (rather than 'psychotherapy' which has even stronger medical associations over there than here, and is in any case frequently unavailable unless you are a licensed psychologist or medical practitioner).

If each of the therapy bureaucracies is granted statutory privileges, scenarios that could transpire include a situation where title acts for 'psychotherapist', 'psychologist' and 'counsellor' coexist without any definition of practice. This might not be a such a problem for human potential practitioners who are content not to have access to these terms (other than by signing up) were it not for the risk of extension to cover practice and other labels as well, as discussed above. In that case, what might ensue would be a situation where there is a psychotherapy act, a psychology act and a counselling act each with title protection and a broad definition of practice (that could be overlapping or more or less the same in each case). Each act would be likely to have exemptions for people registered under the other acts (and as usual, medical practitioners) so that no one other than a registered psychotherapist, psychologist, counsellor or medical practitioner could practise, albeit under their different titles.

Chapter 25

Human Potential Work and Psychotherapy - a Subtle but Important Boundary

The key thing for us is that the Human Potential Movement is a manifestation of a *different model*, a holistic growth model. It is a "new" field that is not medicine, not religion, not art, not even education, but something in between, which has similarities with aspects of each of these but has an essence of its own. It lies closest in principle to education, however, in practice education is often focused on the development of the intellect or the acquisition of utilitarian skills. This new field is educational in the sense of a holistic learning about oneself ... human potential work is not a medical matter. There is a danger of this holistic work becoming split: saddled with a quasi-medical framework on the one hand or going the religious route on the other.

(Juliana Brown and Richard Mowbray, 1990)

In the USA in the 1960s, a 'heady' mix of ingredients combined to form a new movement. The openness to experimentation that existed in California in the sixties and to a lesser extent elsewhere in the USA provided a conducive environment for the integration of influences from Asia, England and continental Europe along with those that were 'home grown'. These included: imported eastern religions and mysticism, an interest in consciousness expansion (resulting in part from experimentation with psychedelic drugs), a throng of ideas and practices brought to the USA by people such as Moreno, Reich and Perls who had sought refuge from the attentions of the Nazis in the thirties, the teachings of British 'mystical expatriates', notably Aldous Huxley and Alan Watts and the work of American humanistic psychologists Maslow and Sutich and encounter group pioneers Rogers and Schutz. Huxley's 1960 lecture "Human Potentialities" gave a name to the movement and inspired Richard Price and Michael Murphy to turn the latter's inherited spa property into the first 'growth centre' - "Esalen" (Lawson, 1988).

Bill Swartley was one of the less well known figures involved in the early days of the human potential movement although he started one of the earliest growth centres, the Centre for the Whole Person in Philadelphia in 1962 and later was a founder of the International Primal Association. He developed the form of human potential work (personal growth work) called Primal Integration. He described this as a process for average maturing adults to undertake within an educational rather than a therapeutic framework and was emphatic that Primal Integration was not a form of psychotherapy (Swartley, 1975). This is the form of work that I myself have practised since training with him in the 1970s (see Mowbray, 1990; Brown & Mowbray, 1994a).

Writing in 1971, Swartley explained the : "subtle border between the science of psychotherapy and the new science of humanology" in the following way:

In general, psychotherapy has ignored normal people and has exhibited even less interest in people who have super-normal mental health, or who I call super-sane. This has left a scientific gap which during the last eight years has begun to be filled by members of a new profession. The practitioners of the new profession do not even have a generally accepted name yet. Usually we are called encounter group leaders. Our infant science is usually called the Human Potential Movement. The place we practice our new profession is called a growth centre. The normal people with whom we work are called group members. I like to call myself a humanologist or one who practices the science of humanology. Humanology, I define as *the science of becoming fully human*. In statistical terms, humanology is the science of helping average people continue to mature into a state of super-normal mental health....

... [The client] who is attempting to grow (or mature) psychologically retains the responsibility for her own growth.... To make the contrast with psychotherapy as clear as possible,

humanologists do not even try to make a diagnosis and have no
therapy to offer. (Swartley, 1971)

I fully agree with the viewpoint expressed above, though the label 'humanology' has not (so far) caught on. The clarity of this position has not
been maintained over the years. Human potential work has often been
lumped in with psychotherapy generally (or 'humanistic psychotherapy'
in particular) thereby obscuring the boundary between human potential
work and psychotherapy. UKCP represents a significant 'hazard warning'
on a road to the 'potential' submerging of the essence of the human potential movement by too close an association with the remedial world of conventional psychotherapy and psychiatry.

One pioneering figure who writes clearly about the distinction between personal growth work and psychotherapy and who has lived to see
the muddying of the boundary between the two is Charles Kelley, the de-
veloper of the form of neo-Reichian personal growth work known as 'Radix'. Writing in 1991 he reflects:

> ... I have never had difficulty keeping Radix work as I do it sepa-
> rate from psychotherapy, though both clients and the psycho-
> therapists do not all find it that easy. And it is easy to understand
> how Radix Teachers trained as psychotherapists and saturated
> with the parent-child medical/therapeutic model of the therapist-
> client relationship will often lose the personal growth perspec-
> tive Radix work should have.... (Kelley, 1991a:8)

> The confusion between psychotherapy and personal growth edu-
> cation in Radix work has become much worse through the years,
> as more psychotherapists have become Radix Teachers, and as
> some of them have become able to collect medical insurance or
> other third party payment if they can diagnose and call their Ra-
> dix sessions 'therapy'. (Kelley, 1991b:4)

As argued in the previous chapter, I believe that this blurring of the distinction between human potential work and psychotherapy stems in no
small measure from a failure on the part of human potential practitioners

to develop an association to a distinctive label (such as 'humanology'). Instead, human potential practitioners have tapped into existing (but unsuitable and confusing) public associations to the term 'therapy'. This in part reflects a tendency to give priority to 'feelings' over clear thinking in the human potential movement. It also represents a succumbing to societal pressure to adopt more mainstream cultural models and a succumbing to the temptations that associating to the 'therapy' model may represent in terms of the rewards of client referral and financial gain. The human potential practitioner is often under sustained pressure from clients and the wider society to revert from the human potential model to the dominant cultural model of 'therapeutic treatment'. As Kelley puts it:

> As soon as Radix Teachers start thinking of their work as therapy, their focus will inevitably change from potentialities to problems, from understanding the student's structure to diagnosing their illness, from teaching and training to treating and therapizing, from walking beside them and being their friend to leading them, like a conscientious parent. This trap is easy to fall into, because our culture so encourages it. It has to be resisted consciously by the Radix Teachers who understand the basic educational, personal growth nature of Radix services, or that nature will continue to be distorted and in time destroyed. (Kelley, 1991a:9)

However, I have the impression that other factors are also involved in obscuring this distinction. The human potential movement fostered opening and release rather than suppression. It favoured 'experiencing it' and catharsis - 'letting it out', both bodily and vocal expression rather than just verbal 'talking about'. In the human potential movement, screaming tended to be encouraged. In the world of psychiatry, screaming would more than likely incur the "chemical cosh" (Prince Charles, 1994). In the world of psychoanalysis it would be likely to incur disapproval and be labelled as 'hysteria' or 'acting out' (besides, the sound-proofing in Hampstead was generally inadequate).

Once the human potential movement became better known, it presented an attractive possibility to those seeking sources of help for emotional problems but who were disillusioned with the medicalized approaches to psychological disorders offered by psychiatry, or the verbal offerings of psychoanalysis and conventional psychotherapy. For such people, the human potential movement presented a less suppressive alternative and they gravitated towards it. This changed the mix of the client base for the human potential movement and tended to dilute the principles of self-responsibility, 'owning' your feelings and so forth, that gave it strength. The human potential movement became increasingly expected to fulfil remedial functions and these tended to swamp the 'potential' orientation. Moreover this trend towards the remedial threatened the turf of established purveyors to the distressed.

In more recent years, the 'holism' of the human potential movement has also been fissured by other trends. Some practitioners have allied themselves with alternative medicine and work in 'natural health centres' rather than 'growth centres'. More important has been the aforementioned gravitation of many human potential practitioners towards the world of conventional psychotherapy - through fear and temptation, a process accelerated in Britain by the presence of UKCP. In a contrary direction, the human potential movement has drifted more towards the 'new age' end of the spectrum. I would not equate the human potential movement with the new age movement, but the boundary is by no means distinct. Nevill Drury has referred to the 'new age' as the: "more visible but less discerning counterpart" of the human potential movement (Drury, 1989:103). Moreover, some in the human potential movement, leading practitioners amongst them, became members of 'therapy cults' or worshippers of 'gurus' of various persuasions, some of whom proved unworthy of the honour. Such trends, the drift towards professionalization, the drift towards the 'new age', and the deification of 'dodgy' gurus have been at the expense of a more holistic movement encompassing work with emotions and intrapsychic issues as well as transpersonal levels and which, at its diverse and unfettered best has the potential to foster true self-determination rather than ill-considered submission to temporal or religious patterns of central authority - whether 'official' or otherwise.[1]

I have the impression that in those countries where the human potential movement was confronted by the more vigorous application of existing 'psychology' legislation, or by new legislation, these trends were exacerbated. In particular, the 'new age' end of the spectrum was favoured since this represents less of an infringement upon established groups with political power such as psychologists and doctors and it also benefits to some extent from traditional respect for religious freedom, which can act as a bulwark against such sectional interests.

The human potential movement pioneered numerous techniques that have subsequently gained more mainstream acceptance. Various techniques have been adopted in areas such as business management, the school system and in psychotherapy training institutes - although the more expressive ones do not fit too snugly with conventional institutions unless tamed or watered down - perhaps to a homeopathic degree (but without the consequent 'potentization'). Some of the methods used in the human potential movement recycle active and body-oriented approaches which had been discarded in the early days of psychoanalysis as the latter movement sought recognition and respectability (just as some parts of the humanistic world are doing now). Catharsis, touch, bodily approaches and direct work with primary processes were not methods that could readily be fitted into the respectable version of psychoanalysis. By the 1960s and 1970s however their time was ripe - for a while at least (Swartley, 1975, 1978).

These techniques may have been taken to be hallmarks of the human potential movement, but do not however represent the essence of human potential work. That is more a question of the particular model espoused, the model of 'self-actualization' or 'personal growth'. This is a model which stands in marked contrast to what is commonly referred to as the 'medical model' (or metaphor), and its analytic and behaviourist associates, all of which reflect an underlying Newtonian-Cartesian world-view.[2]

The 'medical model' presupposes a state of 'sickness', 'illness' or 'disorder' on the part of the 'patient', a state of 'dis-ease' as it is fashionable to emphasize. The 'patient' is 'unwell'. The practitioner will make a 'diagnosis' of the patient's condition on the basis of his 'symptoms' and apply an appropriate 'diagnostic label' to the 'disorder' or 'syndrome'. He will then 'treat' the patient by administering an appropriate 'therapy' as a 'remedy', thereby hopefully 'curing' the condition or counteracting the disease process and restoring the patient to normal health - seen as the absence of the 'disease' or 'disorder'. This is a model which is about 'normalizing' and carries an implicit or explicit notion of 'normality'.

The patient is not expected to have full adult responsibility in relation to his treatment. Some of this is passed over to the practitioner - the patient does not treat himself. Either his illness renders him incapacitated, or the treatment of his illness involves procedures that he may not fully understand or be able to carry out for himself. There is likely to be some form of legal or 'official' recognition of this special status of being 'unwell' in the form of eligibility for treatment under the state or private health insurance and also the possibility of being relieved of the need to work via a 'sick note' from a doctor. The patient's role here is quite passive. He is 'in the care of' the practitioner with whose treatment he is expected to cooperate. By contrast the practitioner's role is rather more active in the sense of it being he who diagnoses, prescribes, advises and does things to and for the patient to make the patient better. He has the status of an expert, who takes responsibility for the patient; takes care of the patient (Parsons, 1953). "... The doctor-patient relationship as defined by the medical model ... reinforces the passive and dependent role of the client. It implies that the solution of the problem depends critically on the resources of the person in the role of scientific authority, rather than on the inner resources of the client" (Grof, 1985:319).

In response to criticisms of medical profession 'hauteur', a notion of the need for the patient's 'informed consent to treatment' has been making inroads (British Medical Association, 1993). However, this concerns the patient being more consciously involved in the choice of treatment to be supervised by the doctor rather than more responsible for, or actively involved in, the treatment itself.

Thomas Szasz has argued that the 'mental illness' that psychiatry addresses is essentially a myth (Szasz, 1961). Applied to matters of the psyche, the use of the term 'illness' was originally metaphorical and intended to provide a form of protection for the behaviourally deviant: "... To save people from being labelled witches, (Sarbin, 1969:15) they were looked at *as if* they were ill. With the passage of time, and the development of a psychiatric nosology that equated behavioural with somatic symptoms, the 'as if' component became lost, and people were simply considered mentally ill" (Hogan, Vol. 1, 1979:205).

This had the positive effect of providing access to the 'special' status usually afforded to the sick in a society ('he can't help it, he's not well in the head'). However in the area of the psyche the designation of being 'sick' is double edged - it confers special 'treatment' and a protected status but at the same time marks you out as being 'abnormal' and may lead to labelling that is likely to involve stigmatization - which I suppose is better than being burned at the stake.

Furthermore, the application of a medical model in this area established a prescription in favour of the medical profession as the main social group involved with these issues and helped to bias research in the direction of a search for the relevant 'brain lesion' or 'biochemical imbalance' and treatment in the direction of drug or physical approaches. Without an underlying 'disease' process, the medical profession's status with respect to this area and claim to a dominant role is more open to question (see Breggin, 1991/1993; Pilgrim, 1990 and Appendix E).[3]

However, the fact that a particular biochemical configuration may correlate with a particular mental state does not necessarily mean that state was *caused* by the 'biochemical imbalance'. As Steven Rose has said, the fact that aspirin may take away the pain of your toothache does not mean that your toothache was due to a shortage of aspirin in the brain, nor does the presence of snot in your nose prove that it caused your cold (Rose, 1994). The absence of any proven disease process underlying many 'mental illnesses' (see Breggin, 1991/1993; Grof, 1985) means that the treatment of them under a medical model will often be a question of treating the 'symptoms' rather than the disease. That is, suppressing or counteracting them in some way.

The Pandora's box of genetic tinkering has yet to be fully opened (though genetic 'tendencies' or 'predispositions' have become concretized as diseases in the hands of insurance companies) but in the meantime, an important associated process alongside the biodeterminism of much of psychiatry is the medicalized labelling of human experience, whether or not serious claims to organic aetiology are made. References to 'avoidant personality disorder', 'post-traumatic stress disorder', 'attention deficit disorder', 'intermittent explosive disorder', 'impulsivity', etc. characterize aspects of human experience as if they were legitimately within the medical realm when they may not really be 'medical' problems at all.[4]

In the area of psychotherapy as such rather than psychiatry, the notion of an organic aetiology would seem to be more or less ruled out by the nature of the approach. However, elements of a medical model attitude, both in relation to symptoms and the practitioner-client/patient relationship, are to be found in numerous approaches, including psychoanalysis, behaviour therapy, and hypnotherapy (see e.g. Rowan, 1983:3 & 57). *Medical model attitudes are also to be found in the minds of many practitioners and clients/patients, whatever the approach, even when a different premise appears to be involved in the approach in question.*

Historically, psychoanalysis developed in close association with the medical field[5] and the analytic model retains many features of the medical model such as diagnostic labelling and arcane terminology, an emphasis on the alleviation of symptoms and restoring normal functioning through sublimation and adjustment to society - the 'taming' of the 'id' (but not, as so often in psychiatry, the 'encaging' or 'breaking' of the 'id'): "Where id was, there ego shall be" (Freud, 1933:112). Save for periodic 'expert' verbal interpretations which, whatever else they may do, also serve to set the acceptable conceptual framework, the analyst tends to be rather passive (by humanistic standards at any rate), though not as passive as the patient: "The patient contributes free associations, but it is the therapist and his or her interpretations that are considered to be instrumental in therapeutic change. The therapist is seen as a mature and healthy individual possessing the necessary knowledge and therapeutic technique. The influence of the medical model in the psychoanalytic situation is thus very strong and clearly discernible in spite of the fact that psychoanalysis represents a psychological, not a medical approach to emotional disorders" (Grof, 1985:154).

In addition to underlying medical metaphors, our western culture is saturated with conceptions of mental ill health which have an underlying *malfunctioning machine metaphor*. A person is as likely to be referred to as having 'maladaptive' responses or 'dysfunctional' behaviour these days as they are to be labelled as suffering from a 'neurosis' or 'nerves'. Along with this is an associated ethos of problem-solving and 'repair' - the 'technical fix' - for a machine needing repair or 'adjustment' to deal with patterns of faulty learning. In our secular, machine and computer dependent age, the medical model of 'cure' (with earlier echoes of salvation and Jesus performing miracles) coexists with this model of us as machines or computers in need of fault correction and restoring to smoothly efficient functioning. Behaviourist approaches that, in the extreme, bypass the issue of consciousness altogether, are particularly prone to such a mechanistic conception as apparently also are cognitive approaches (Rowan, 1988:243).

These medical and mechanistic metaphors merge and overlap (all the more so when the medical model is applied in the absence of clearly discernible disease processes in the psyche) and indeed they have common roots in a Newtonian world-view. The notion of the psyche being generated by organic processes which may fail, leading to mental disorder (bio-determinism), mates with the machine metaphor to produce an incestuous offspring - the 'human bio-computer' - "is it a hardware problem (genetic) or a software problem (your early 'programming')?"

Whether of the 'cure', 'repair' or 'reprogramming' variants, the remedial world-view informed by these sorts of model is so culturally ingrained that it is often very hard for people to think outside of it in relation to what may emerge from the psyches of themselves and others. The enlightenment of a self-actualizing orientation is all too easily obscured again by the low clouds of the prevailing cultural climate.

Like verbal clues to unconscious processes, the terminology that people adopt or drift into using, and the associations that those terms have in the culture can be taken as signs of the underlying metaphors. Terms such as 'clinical', 'treatment', 'symptoms', 'diagnosis', 'disorder', 'psychopathology' and 'therapy' associate to underlying 'medical' metaphors.

Compared with medical model activity, the focus of human potential work (humanology) is upon a different goal and a different target clientele. Rather than being primarily focused on curing 'neuroses', solving problems, and getting 'well', human potential work is informed by a different model and is focused on self-actualization. What may have seemed to be problems may well resolve *as well* but that is a by-product of growth and not the main aim. In human potential work the approach is non-clinical and the orientation is towards growth (Maslow's 'Being-values') rather than deficiency (Maslow's 'Deficiency-values'). There is no 'diagnosis', no treatment - and no medical insurance eligibility!

When a medical model is applied to matters of the psyche, the model itself defines the status of the 'patient' - if one is psychologically 'unwell' one's autonomy is *ipso facto* diminished. In human potential work by contrast, the criteria that distinguish it - that of the underlying model of growth and of the autonomous status of the client - are not mutually inclusive but rather remain separable and both are necessary to define the activity.

Firstly, the focus of the 'personal growth model' that human potential work espouses is on what can be variously described as 'self-actualization', 'individuation', 'self-realization', or 'self-knowledge'. It is concerned with processes of 'emergence' or 'unfoldment', with experiencing as fully as possible, with expression and integration, and with a goal of fulfilling more of the potential to be who you really are, rather than narrowly focusing on the cure of a 'disorder', the relief of symptoms or the resolving of a problem. Its concerns are educational, but not, as is so often the case in conventional education, narrowly focused on the academic or the technical - 'extrinsic learning' (Maslow, 1971:53 & 175). It is concerned, rather, with the emergence of authentic being - an education for the whole self - 'intrinsic learning' (ibid.). Bill Swartley remarked that it was significant that he, like many of those who were involved in the start of the human potential movement, came to this work through a study of religion rather than medicine (Swartley, 1971:2). Unlike much conventional religion however, this model encompasses the whole self, and is inclusive of emotions and sexuality as well as spirituality. The 'goal' in a growth model is a path rather than an end-point. The 'goal' is about becoming rather than arriving. It is about 'knowing yourself' - more.

A growth model usually involves the acceptance of an existing state of being. Acceptance of that state is what is usually required for growth to occur anyway. The sort of psychological or emotional phenomena which under a medical model would be labelled as symptoms would under a growth model be regarded as manifestations of consciousness and part of the 'self' - and their meaning for the person explored rather than efforts being made to cure, suppress or eliminate them. Thus at any level such phenomena can be seen in the light of a growth model and 'owned', opened to and experienced, or through the lens of a medical model, regarded as defects to be got rid of and 'disowned', 'cured' or suppressed.

It is of course unwise to assume that all psychological and emotional 'symptoms' are simply expressions of consciousness rather than signs of a genuine disease process. The consequences of such an assumption are regarded by Striano as: "the foremost hazard of faulty therapy: the neglect of physical illness [for example diseases of the endocrine glands, notably the thyroid] as the source of 'mental' symptoms" (Striano, 1988:4). When in doubt, consult your doctor. However, in the absence of sound indications that such experiences are indeed manifestations of a true organic disease process, their designation as symptoms should be regarded as presumptive and an application of the medical metaphor rather than as 'fact'. From a growth model point of view, many of such 'symptoms' would be seen as forms of communication, means of defence, signs of regression, 'altered states', as: "stages of a transformative process in which the client has become arrested" (Grof, 1985:329) - rather than illness.

Secondly, human potential work is intended as a form of growth work for *'average maturing adults'* to use Bill Swartley's phrase (Swartley, 1975), or *'autonomous functioning adults'* to use Chuck Kelley's phrase (Kelley, 1989). That is, it is a form of work for people who are regarded and regard themselves as 'normal' (and 'super-normal'!), or "ordinary" (and 'extraordinary'!) rather than in some way less autonomous than the average level prevailing in the society. This of course begs the question of whether 'normal' is 'healthy', but does correspond to society's recognition of the status of 'adulthood' with respect to responsibility and choice, except in certain specified cases such as when one is 'sick' and a degree of 'diminished' responsibility is usually allowed. Thus it is a necessary precondition for human potential work that clients have *Sufficient Available Functioning Adult Autonomy (SAFAA).*[6] At and beyond this level of functioning, *healing* could be said to become *'wholing'* and it is to this that human potential work addresses itself.[7] In my view, being an 'average maturing adult' engaged in a 'wholing' process does not preclude having deep life issues which may be addressed thereby.

In consequence of the combination of these two criteria, the roles of client and practitioner in human potential work differ markedly from those in a medical model activity.[8] Firstly, the decision as to whether the SAFAA requirement is met is one for mutual agreement between potential client and practitioner.[9] Furthermore, unlike in the case of activity operating from a medical model where the practitioner takes responsibility for the treatment of the patient, in human potential work the practitioner does not apply treatments to the client, instead the client is seen as the 'expert' - on himself. Hence the client directs the exploration - the process is one of self-exploration and the client does the 'work'. In human potential work the client retains responsibility for his growth process, his actions and his feelings - which he is encouraged to 'own'. The practitioner's role is to facilitate, to 'be with', to sit alongside. As Bill Swartley put it, in human potential work the practitioner is to be the 'patient', the one who waits with calmness (Swartley, 1971).

The relationship between practitioner and client is a non-hierarchical partnership between adults with differential roles rather than the practitioner having the status of a 'healer' and the client being regarded as in need of the practitioner's healing actions.[10] Clients are not regarded as being sick or unwell, rather they are 'average maturing adults' concerned to 'know themselves', capable of taking responsibility for themselves and of being self-directing. They have sufficient 'adult' functioning - a *good-enough adult*', as Winnicott might have said.[11] In human potential work the client is not 'in the care of' the practitioner. That does not mean that the practitioner does not care about the client or has a licence to be 'careless' but rather that the practitioner is not in any sense 'in charge' of the client. The basis for relationship is one of 'informed agreement to explore' rather than 'informed consent to treatment' as in the 'new' medical model. The 'client' role is equal, contractual and more active than that of the 'patient', however well informed the latter may be.[12]

The above may lead to a mistaken assumption that human potential work is necessarily superficial. This is not the case. It can be deep. In the case of some modalities like Primal Integration it can be very deep. It is not the *presence* of intensely experienced feelings or distress that is the limiting criterion but rather the *absence* of access to a functioning 'adult' self.[13] The requirement of a sufficiently available 'adult' in the sense of 'here-and-now-self' and ability to be in contact with 'here-and-now' and 'consensus' reality does not, for example, preclude the exploration of states of regression and of projections and transference feelings. The trick is that such feelings are explored on a 'twin-track' basis, that is on the basis of an adult-directed journey - exploring things from the past while maintaining contact with the present. Allowing one's 'inner child' (or whatever) out, in the presence of one's 'adult'.

In the following chapter I will return to the question of appropriate labelling and apply the above discussion to that issue.

Chapter 26

What's in a Name?

... how things look to us is determined (or at least strongly influenced) by how we sort and name them. Experiments on human subjects show things we learn to put in the same categories and give the same name to, come to resemble one another more, and things we put in different categories and give different names to look increasingly different....

(Stevan Harnad, 1995)

... So here [Austria, 1926, where a law forbade non-doctors from undertaking the treatment of patients] the question whether laymen (= non-doctors) may treat patients by psychoanalysis has a practical sense. As soon as it is raised, however, it appears to be settled by the wording of the law. Neurotics are patients, laymen are non-doctors, psychoanalysis is a procedure for curing or improving nervous disorders, and all such treatments are reserved to doctors. It follows that laymen are not permitted to practise analysis on neurotics, and are punishable if they nevertheless do so....

(Sigmund Freud, 1926:2)

... According to Scull (1979) and Bynum (1974), a strategic error of Tuke, the patriarch of moral therapy [an early attempt to operate psychological rather than physical methods to correct mental disorder] at York, was his terminology ('treatment', 'illness', and so on, which were medical terms although Tuke was not a physician) along with a deliberate emphasis on the ordinary non-expert features of his approach (such as paternalism and kindness, which were not peculiar to experts). This error made Tuke's approach vulnerable to attack from biological psychiatrists, who could thereby protect their status and salaries. The use of medical terminology poses problems to this day when non-physicians use it in relation to a client group over which they hope to have some jurisdiction (Pilgrim, 1987).

Thus today the term 'psychotherapy' remains problematic for non-medical practitioners, in terms of their claiming autonomous status within health care contexts.

(David Pilgrim, 1990:3)

What's in a name? Well, actually rather a lot. The whole legislative scramble of registration is after all (initially at least) about *labels* - the control of title usage. The terms concerned are those that have widespread currency in the public domain - which gives them an appeal as potential generic terms. This does not necessarily mean that the public's associations to the terms are based on significant direct experience and understanding of the activities they are used to refer to, nor that the public's image and the practitioner's offering have much in common.

Many who call themselves 'therapists', 'counsellors', or whatever, are highly attuned to the question of 'boundary issues' in relation to their work with their clients and aware of the difficulties that can result from confusion in that area. Ironically however, when it comes to the terminology they use to set the boundaries of their own work-roles such a state of affairs is far from being the case. In fact, potential confusion for the recipients and public at large has been generated by ambiguous redefinition of existing terms with commonly understood meanings.

The previous discussion of the models or metaphors underlying activities in this area provides a basis for clarifying *functional differences* in the worlds of psychotherapy and personal growth work which can perhaps eventually *be matched by correspondingly appropriate distinguishing generic labels - labels that take into account the intentions of the work, the models which apply, and the status of the client regarding the level of adult responsibility required of them in order to undertake the work.*

As discussed in the previous chapter, if an activity is undertaken on the basis of a medical model the status of reduced responsibility on the part of the 'patient' comes 'with the territory'. In the case of a growth model however the degree of responsibility of the client does not 'automatically' follow. Whereas human potential work involves the client retaining full adult responsibility this is not the case with all growth model activities for example in the case of work with children or with people experiencing a 'nonordinary state of consciousness' such as the re-integrative episodes of 'madness' described by John Weir Perry (1974) or what Stanislav and Christina Grof have referred to as 'spiritual emergencies' or 'transformational crises' (Grof & Grof, 1991; Brown & Mowbray, 1991:36). In such cases, while the person concerned would retain responsibility for their inner growth process, the ability to be responsible for outer adult concerns is diminished and perforce in the hands of others.

In the following survey of terms, my particular concern is to make proposals for terminology that will support a clear differentiation between human potential work and psychotherapy as discussed in this section. *The nub of this position is that self-realization processes and processes concerned with 'adjustment' and remedial restoration to 'normality' should not be addressed by the same terminology.*

In the case of most of the terms discussed below, unlike some current usages, the usages proposed are ones that are neither inconsistent with everyday usage and associations nor with linguistic roots (and hence, I hope, not inconsistent with international usage and translations).

Labels are particularly important in this area because they shape people's expectations. They can be likened to verbal 'buttons' or 'triggers' that activate underlying models or metaphors and expectations appropriate to the model that is 'engaged'. A model of personal growth for average adults, especially one which *includes* addressing deep life issues, is not one that is securely lodged in mainstream culture. Sharing 'buttons' with activities based on models that are well embedded in the culture will activate expectations associated with them rather than develop a new and appropriate set. Hence human potential work needs a separate 'button'.

Activity title: *Psychotherapy*

Practitioner title: *Psychotherapist*

As discussed in Chapter 12, confusion reigns as to how 'psychotherapy' should be defined and this reduces its utility as an identifying and distinguishing label. Those who don't know anything about it (and that usually includes government and officialdom generally) will assume, sensibly enough on the basis of associations to similar terms, that it refers to a medical model activity of treatment for psychological or emotional problems - the 'talking cure', and that its recipients are patients and are 'unwell' and mentally or emotionally 'disturbed'. Some of what actually goes on under the label will consist of that sort of activity with that sort of intention, but there is also a whole load of other things that are not really operating on the basis of a medical model at all - including forms of human potential work that have also been referred to by the term 'psychotherapy'. Thus 'psychotherapy' is medical model terminology with 'remedial', mental, and medical associations that has also been used indiscriminately to describe approaches that do not assume a medical model. This partial 'colonization' by exponents of a growth model brings to them the benefits of the public's medical model associations to the term, such as access to potential clients and possible third party payments but also the detrimental effects that I have been at pains to point out.

I suggest that the most appropriate use for the term 'psychotherapy' is to refer to remedial medical model activities that are concerned with states of mental or emotional 'ill-health' and focus on them as problems to be solved or symptoms to be relieved but that do not consist of drug treatment or physical interventions and where full self-responsibility is not required i.e. 'psychotherapeutic treatment'. The appropriate term for the recipients is 'patients'.

Even where a growth model is employed, the work may involve people who have insufficient adult functioning available for them to be fully self-responsible, for example, work with children or people in a breakdown situation and people experiencing nonordinary states of consciousness including 'madness'. In such cases, the terms 'psychotherapy' or 'therapy' are liable to persist in use as descriptions for the work in question. Given such usage along with medical model usage, the terms 'psychotherapy' or 'therapy' would correspond to activities where reduced adult responsibility is the case - as is often assumed by common associations to those words. By contrast, 'human potential work' or 'humanology' could be used to refer to growth activities where full adult responsibility is retained, that is, where the SAFAA requirement is met.

I regard it as problematic and insidious to label *any* growth work as 'therapy' or 'psychotherapy' for the reasons discussed and hope that in time such use will give way to a new label, reflecting the different model and, hopefully, reflecting a decline of medical model pre-eminence in this area. Currently however, the medical profession retains a dominance over

the handling of 'nonordinary states of consciousness' and (most importantly) the funding for such situations. In accord with the medical model
such states will invariably be counteracted and suppressed. Other cultures
have been more accepting of such states and have recognized their potential value for healing and transformation (see Eliade, 1964; Harner, 1980;
Grof & Grof, 1991). In the course of time, the value of such states of
consciousness may become more generally recognized and alternatives to
routinely suppressing them chemically may come to be considered more
acceptable (with perhaps third party funding for spiritual emergency centres such as the Grofs suggest or perhaps a national asylum service with
medical support staff but not subject to medical control). In such circumstances the term psychotherapy could be limited to medical model uses
only - 'psychotherapeutic treatment' - concerned with curing, symptom
relief, and the 'normalizing' of 'maladjustment' and a new, more appropriate label instituted for growth work below the SAFAA level.[1]

Activity title: *Therapy*

Practitioner title: *Therapist*

The use of the term 'therapy' carries similar ambiguous meanings to the
term 'psychotherapy' and similar arguments apply, albeit to a somewhat
lesser extent since it is used more generally and is one of the looser generics in this area. With its medical model roots and associations, 'therapy' is
a synonym for 'treatment', and different therapies indicate varying types
of treatment. Where a type of 'therapy' is not specified, 'therapist' is often
taken as a shorthand for 'psychotherapist'. References to being 'in therapy'
would not usually be taken to mean, say, being 'in aromatherapy'.

However 'therapist' is also often regarded as indicating a lower status than 'psychotherapist', especially where the latter is being promoted
as a high status profession, in which case 'therapist' and 'psychotherapist'
would not be regarded as equivalent (e.g. Young, 1990:5; AHPP, 1993).

The term 'psychotherapy' illustrates the 'linear', cause-and-effect,
Newtonian-Cartesian basis for the medical model that held sway at the
time of its coining and becomes something of a terminological nonsense
when applied to a growth model activity. It may make sense for a physi-
otherapist to be regarded as the active agent who administers remedial

treatment of a physical nature to the patient. However, from a growth model point of view, it does not make much sense to think of a 'psychotherapist' as the active agent who administers remedial treatment of a psychical nature to the patient. The newly popular term 'body psychotherapy' is even more of a nonsense from this point of view, incorporating a dualism in which the body and psyche - 'breathe, soul, life' (*Shorter Oxford English Dictionary*, 3rd edn.) are separated.

The term 'therapist' (like the less familiar term 'therapeutist') has more going for it etymologically, from a growth model perspective, in so far as 'growth forces' (Kent, 1969) can be construed as equivalent to a manifestation of the God Asklepios of whom the 'therapeutes' were attendants (Meir, 1967).[2] Nevertheless, to use the term 'therapist' for growth model purposes in a cultural context in which medicine and religion are separate spheres of activity, in which the medical model dominates (and that includes the courts), and in which there are numerous overlapping medical model usages is to ask for confusion and best avoided in my opinion. As discussed above, as with 'psychotherapy', I think it would make more sense for the term 'therapy' to be used only for those approaches that assume a medical model or, at the very least, only for these approaches where reduced adult responsibility on the part of the client is assumed.

Activity title: *Facilitation*

Practitioner title: *Facilitator*

This is non-medical model terminology that is suitable for use where a growth model is applied. Facilitate means 'to render easier, to assist' (from the Latin root: 'facilis' - 'easy' (*Shorter Oxford English Dictionary*, 3rd edn.). It does however need a specification of what process is to be assisted with, as in for example 'human potential facilitator', 'personal growth facilitator' and 'transformational crisis facilitator'.

Activity title: *Counselling*

Practitioner title: *Counsellor*

Like 'psychotherapy' the term 'counselling' has been subjected to attempted revision of the commonly understood meanings of the word, in this case largely through the efforts of Carl Rogers and the counselling movement that has followed his lead. They have endeavoured to dissolve the linguistic,[3] common sense and wider cultural associations that the term has with activities concerning advice and guidance thereby making it available for what Myles Harris has disdainfully referred to as "confessional counselling" (Harris, 1994).

This apparently came about through an effort on Rogers part to avoid the term 'psychotherapy'. It seems that Rogers adopted the term 'counseling' (US spelling) as a description for his work because when he started to practise in the USA in the 1920s, psychotherapy was restricted to medical practitioners and his qualifications were in psychology (Thorne, 1990:106). Apart from this terminological lead by Rogers (who also pioneered the use of the term 'client' as opposed to 'patient'), his British followers have apparently tended to use the word 'counsellor' rather than 'psychotherapist' because:

> ... They have seen the word 'psychotherapist' as somehow conducive to an aura of mystification and expertise which runs counter to the egalitarian relationship which the person-centred approach seeks to establish between therapist and client....
> (Thorne, 1990:106)

For historical and legal reasons the term 'psychotherapy' has a tighter association with the medical model in North America than in the UK.[4] Moreover, Rogers did much to popularize the growth model in the USA and was a seminal thinker of the human potential movement. Hence, compared with their UK counterparts, practitioners of personal growth in parts of North America may be rather more tempted to use the term 'counselling/counseling' than 'psychotherapy' even if the latter is available to them. 'Facilitation' would perhaps be more appropriate still.[5]

I suggest that the most appropriate uses for the term 'counselling' are for work that adopts a helping orientation and involves a focus on *specific issues* such as bereavement counselling, crisis counselling, fertility counselling, marital counselling, sexual counselling, and pastoral counselling. 'Counselling' is also appropriate in relation to specific illnesses such as in HIV counselling. That is, work with a focused problem-resolving orientation, where the problems are in large measure associated with outer pressures rather than deeply embedded inner difficulties:

> ... In this sense, counselling is about helping people who have the capacity to cope in most circumstances but who are experiencing temporary difficulties, or making transitions or adjustments in their lives.... (Bond, 1993:25)

This view of counselling is closer to what Tim Bond refers to as the "narrow" usage of the term (ibid.:31) than the "wider" sense deriving from the Rogerian influence. It also makes sense to me to restore to the term 'counselling' the guidance and advice connotations that most people will assume it has. That is, to 'undo' some of the Rogerian influence on the term which has altered its meaning for practitioners but not necessarily for the public at large. Furthermore, if counselling focuses on a specific issue then an element of guidance is likely be assumed to be there anyway in terms of an expertise regarding that topic at least. This 'narrow' delineation of 'counselling' is closer to that of the originator of 'counseling' in the USA, Frank Parsons, who was a social activist and saw counselling as being very much linked to outer concerns. He pioneered the first 'counseling centre' - which was called the "Vocation Bureau" (Bond, 1993:18). The narrow view is however unlikely to appeal to large counselling organizations like BAC and the American Counseling Association (ACA) as it runs counter to organizational expansion. ACA has adopted a very broad definition of 'counseling' (ibid.:16).

Compare the above proposal for the use of the term 'counselling' with the use of the terms 'human potential work' ('humanology') or 'personal growth work' to describe general 'opening' work with self-responsible adults (see below). Compare also this proposal for the term 'counselling' with that for the use of the term 'psychotherapy' to describe remedial work that concerns 'curing' 'normalizing' or 'adjustment' of what are seen as primarily 'inner' problems, whether construed as 'neurosis', 'maladaptive learning' or otherwise, and which does not involve full adult responsibility and self-direction on the part of the recipient - the patient.

There is an apparent anomaly in this discussion of 'counselling' and that concerns 'co-counselling' ('re-evaluation co-counselling' or 'reciprocal counselling') which is more like 'human potential work' than 'counselling' as delineated above and has its origins in the USA (Jackins, 1965), where the use of the term 'counseling' has been the outcome of the social and political forces mentioned previously. However, unlike counselling, co-counselling is by and large a peer activity where financial reward is not involved and therefore statutory registration is not really an issue. Moreover the term is '*co*-counselling' rather than 'counselling'. (See also Appendix D.)

Activity: *Supervision*

Practitioner title: *Supervisor*

Like 'counselling' and 'psychotherapy', the term 'supervision' has been subjected to attempted 'therapeutic' revisions of meaning; for a discussion of this see Appendix G.

Activity title: *Human Potential Work* or *Humanology*

Practitioner Title: *Human Potential Facilitator/Educator/Practitioner* or *Humanologist/Humanology Practitioner*

As discussed in the last chapter, this work is distinguished by the twin criteria of (1) the work is on the basis of a personal growth model and (2) the appropriate clientele consists of 'average maturing adults' that is those who have a 'good-enough adult' and meet the 'SAFAA' criterion (Sufficiently Available Functioning Adult Autonomy). The work is more of a 'wholing' than a 'healing' nature.[6]

This work tends to be about a general opening and unfolding rather than focusing on specific issues or 'problems'. The only 'specific issue' focused upon is the 'true self' or 'real self', and 'know thyself' is the goal (compare with 'counselling' above).

'Human potential work' may not be a succinct or a catchy title, but it does have certain other virtues. It is accurately descriptive and does not involve the use of ambiguous terminology nor an attempt to redefine existing words. Nor does it stray over terminological territory that is jealously guarded, or avariciously desired, by ideologically incompatible occupations. Whereas a 'psychotherapist' practises 'psychotherapy', perhaps giving an impression that the 'psychotherapist' 'does' the 'psychotherapy' i.e. is the active agent - as in the medical model - in 'human potential work', it is in fact more appropriate to think of the client as doing the 'work' referred to in the activity title and the practitioner as facilitating it. Hence 'human potential facilitator' is a recommended practitioner title - a human potential facilitator (practitioner) facilitates the human potential work of the client. The work of the client is 'human potential work'. The work of the practitioner is 'human potential facilitation'. 'Human potential work' also carries an implication in the wording of 'normal or ordinary and beyond', that is, growth model work for average maturing adults and that the criterion of SAFAA, or 'good-enough adult' would apply. Being more accurately descriptive, the terminology 'human potential work' is arguably preferable to the more general terminology 'personal growth work' as a distinguishing label for this type of activity. The usual location for this type of work, especially if various modalities are offered and it is conducted on a group basis, has typically been referred to as a 'growth centre' but could also be referred to as a 'human potential centre'.[7] Collectively, this work has been referred to as 'the human potential movement' or 'the growth movement'.

'Humanology' is an alternative term that has the advantages of brevity (the bigger the mouthful, the more the temptation to fall back on 'therapy'), relative unambiguity and a linguistic association with 'human-[istic psych]-ology' (see below). It avoids the association that 'psych-' tends to have with 'mainly mental' (see e.g. Foster's view in Chapter 5), and linguistic overlap with other occupations with consequent potential for confusion 'twixt 'psych-ology', 'psych-otherapy', and 'psych-iatry'. Defined by Swartley as: "the science of becoming fully human" (Swartley, 1971), 'humanology' also carries within it the notion of beyond the average state of 'adjustment'. It is close in form to the conventional delineation of a discipline for example, theology, psychology, anthropology, geology and perhaps therefore more practitioner focused - as a label - than 'human potential work'.

Unlike 'counselling', neither 'human potential work' nor 'humanology' have common associations with advice or guidance regarding problems, that is conventional helping models.

Activity title: *Personal Growth Work/Personal Growth/Growth Work*

Practitioner title: *Personal Growth Facilitator/Educator/Practitioner*

This is general terminology that could be appropriate for any experiential work that is based on a growth model. Currently however, 'personal growth' and 'human potential work' are loosely equated (the 'personal growth movement' and the 'human potential movement' are more or less synonymous) and 'personal growth' will often correspond to the description of human potential work described earlier.

If human potential work is clearly specified on the basis of the twin criteria referred to, and labelled as suggested, the term 'personal growth' could be used for growth work generally - with people who do not meet the SAFAA/'good-enough adult' criterion as well as with those who do. 'Human potential work' would then be a *form* of personal growth work with a more limiting criterion as to clientele.

In that eventuality, the term 'personal growth' could be applied to growth model work with anyone for example with children or with people undergoing spiritual emergencies. 'Personal growth facilitator' could therefore become an appropriate title for, say, workers in genuine asylums or 'blow-out' centres, though 'transformational crisis facilitator', or such like, might be a better label for such roles. In practice, as explained above, because of the common factor of reduced adult autonomy I expect 'therapy' terminology will prevail in such areas ('transformational crisis therapist' perhaps?). At least in so far as the medical profession and the medical model retain dominance in state mental health care settings. So, 'personal growth work' and 'human potential work' are likely to stay more or less equivalent, at least for the foreseeable future (likewise 'personal development' or 'self development').

Activity title: *Humanistic Psychology*

Practitioner title: *Humanistic Psychologist/Humanistic Psychology Practitioner*

'Humanistic psychology' was the terminology adopted for what came to be regarded as the 'third force' in psychology (the first and second being psychoanalysis and behaviourism, and the fourth, transpersonal psychology). The phrase 'humanistic psychology' was originally coined in 1959 by Maslow's son-in-law for the title of a journal: *The Journal of Humanistic Psychology* (Drury, 1989:36). Since then it has been variously used to refer to a component of the human potential movement or as synonymous with the movement as a whole, though such use is more to be found in literature and academic circles than 'on the ground'. There is an Association of Humanistic Psychology Practitioners in Britain (AHPP) but few are heard to refer to themselves as a 'humanistic psychology practitioner' or 'humanistic psychologist' as titles. People are more likely to refer to themselves as a 'therapist' or 'psychotherapist'. My feeling is that 'human potential facilitator or practitioner' ('humanologist' or 'humanology practitioner') or 'personal growth facilitator' are more relevant titles for work posited on a model of growth. They are less compromised by medical model associations than are 'therapist' and 'psychotherapist' and are less threatened than are the terms 'humanistic psychology' and 'humanistic psychologist' by academic psychology's dominance of the term 'psychologist'. 'Humanistic psychology' and 'humanistic psychologist' are vulnerable to any further moves towards title protection by the British Psychological Society.

The existence of a humanistic psychology practitioners' organization in Britain in close association with the human potential movement seems to be something of a local anomaly that reflects the current terminological openness of the UK scene. As of 1988 such an organization had not been created anywhere else (Rowan, 1988:199). In many other countries where psychology acts are in force (California, for example, has had psychology licensing legislation since 1957), the term 'psychologist' and hence 'humanistic psychology practitioner' would be reserved titles and restricted to those with an academic background in psychology. A Ph.D. would now usually be required in North America. Consequently in countries like Australia, Canada and the USA such terms have little currency in the growth movement and therefore there is little prospect of them becoming international generics for the practice of growth work 'in the field', though they may have some currency in academia.

Moreover, AHPP's involvement with UKCP and the promotion of 'humanistic psychotherapist' as a title is likely to further compromise 'humanistic' terminology - if 'psychotherapy' is taken to indicate a medical

196

model, as many people appear to do, some of them in high places. AHPP has numerous categories of 'humanistic psychology practice' (AHPP, 1993) but the 'psychotherapist' category has had the most energy put into it, has the highest status, the most rigorous requirements, and contains the largest number of practitioners. Nearly three-quarters of AHPP full members are UKCP registered psychotherapists.[8]

Either 'human potential practitioner' or 'humanologist/humanology practitioner' provide a possibility for the rather neat redefinition of 'AHP' and 'AHPP', if their members should find the arguments presented here convincing - or for labelling their 'doppelgängers' - 'HPA' (Human Potential Association) and 'HPPCA' (Human Potential Practitioners and Clients Association).[9]

Activity title: *Bodywork*

Practitioner title: *Bodyworker*

From a human potential point of view, 'bodywork' is, I think, a more appropriate term for work via the body than 'body psychotherapy' or 'body-oriented therapy'. The term 'body counselling' does not seem to have many adherents. It does sound a bit of a nonsense and this illustrates the verbal and advisory associations of the term 'counselling'. In the USA, 'somatics' is an increasingly popular term.

The above suggestions, particularly those for more appropriate and less ambiguous use of the labels 'psychotherapy' and 'counselling' do not take into account the inertial factors of practitioner attachment and habit and of organizational sovereignty and aspirations - factors that are quite likely to stymie any such realignment. However continued ambiguous usage of 'psychotherapy' and 'counselling' need not prevent the further development of 'human potential facilitator/practitioner' ('humanologist') or 'personal growth facilitator/practitioner' as distinguishing generic terms, provided the titles 'psychotherapist' and 'counsellor' are eschewed by such practitioners. However, in the light of their current ambiguous use and the likelihood that inertia may well prevail, for the reasons already discussed it is important in my opinion that the expropriation of the latter terms by UKCP, BAC et al. should be prevented.

Chapter 27

Preserving the Fringe

Fringe - first used in the 1960s, the term was coined from the Edin-
burgh Fringe - a place for diversity and the yet to be discovered....
(Ruth West, 1993:4)

Despite the eventual eclectic integration of psychotherapy into the
mainstream workings of the British mental health industry, I fear
that it can no longer claim the role of the radical humanistic conscience of that industry. This is a result of the energy dissipated in
intra- and inter-professional disputes about ownership and regulation and in the obsessive desire to acquire the trappings of professional accreditation. The role of therapists as the 'conscience' of
the mental health professions was tenable only when psychotherapy
was on the margins, where it could snipe at scientism in psychology
and biological reductionism in psychiatry. Once professional self-
interest took over, client-interest inevitably suffered....
(David Pilgrim, 1990:15)

The human potential or growth movement offers a valuable resource - the
possibility of holistic growth for the 'ordinary' person. It attempts to address the holistic growth of members of society who are at least 'aver-
agely functioning' rather than those who choose to, or are elected to, occupy
the role of the 'sick' or the 'abnormal'. It focuses on 'Being-values' rather
than 'Deficiency-values'.

A 'wholing' process for the 'average' person addresses the society as
a whole rather than just those marginalized and categorized as 'sick' by
that society.[1] *Because* it addresses the 'normal', the movement that carries
that process must stay on the margin and not be 'absorbed', not be tempted
by the carrots of recognition, respectability and financial security into re-

verting to the mainstream but rather remain - on the 'fringe' - as a source that stimulates, challenges convention and 'draws out' the unrealized potential for 'being' in the members of that society.

A society needs a healthy fringe - a fringe that is on the edge but not split-off in cult-like isolation. It is the seedbed from which much of what is novel will spring. It is where ideas that are ahead of their time will germinate and grow, later to be adopted by the mainstream. In order to remain a fertile seedbed the fringe needs to be legitimate rather than driven underground or 'criminalized' - which would stifle it, but also it must not be absorbed into the mainstream - which would stultify it with 'establishment' thinking and respectability. The necessary ethos of positive experimentation would be smothered by a climate of negative anticipation. In many countries the 'fringe' in this area is already outside the law and its activities subject to the whim of some regulatory board, usually dominated by professional interests. The 'mavericks' have been made 'outlaws'.

Britain, the traditional home of the 'eccentric', has in the past tended to foster healthy fringes in the sense described. For example a Japanese assessment of worldwide sources of important inventions highlighted the UK as having been the source of a disproportionately large number of such inventions and consequently set up a unit to monitor British inventiveness. According to Richard Milton, author of *Forbidden Science,* a large proportion of the scientific inventions and ideas that we now take for granted were at their inception the products of people who were at the time regarded as the equivalent of 'scientific heretics' (BBC Radio 4, 1994c). Clearly conventional wisdom is often merely conventional and not necessarily wise.

However it seems that processes of bureaucratization in the world of science may be changing the situation in the UK: "Since the second World War, science in this country has become a single, monolithic bureaucracy, a hierarchical bureaucracy and like all large bureaucratic organizations it tends to attract and selectively promote a certain kind of person, the kind of person who thrives and does well in a hierarchy and that doesn't bode well for anybody who is of an unusual turn of mind ..." (ibid.). Such an environment does not foster the 'mavericks' upon whom future innovation depends.

In an age when developments in transport and communication technologies are 'shrinking' the world to a 'global village' - but a 'village' with the population of a whole *planet*, cultural supports for a sense of personal identity are threatened by global homogenization. Instead we are challenged to found our sense of identity more firmly within. The human potential movement is an important source of support for that endeavour.

However, for those not ready to face such a challenge the presence of a human potential movement may be felt as a threat. The assumption of human potential work that average adults can benefit from inner work carries an implication that average people bear a degree of splitting within them[2] and challenges conventional notions of 'normality' and identity, posing a threat to 'consensus reality'. This can provoke a counter-reaction from those who feel threatened by any suggestion that they too, and not just the 'disturbed', may have unacknowledged aspects of themselves (which may be, for example, unfinished business from their personal unconscious or denial of their superconscious). Thus the very existence of such work can lead to urges to suppress or neutralize it.

Wilhelm Reich used the term 'character armour' to refer to the defences of the 'normal' person against their inner life and, writing in a context of the historical rise of Fascism, he used the phrase 'emotional plague reaction' to refer to a defensive counter-reaction that can be applied against those who seek to go beneath the layers of defence in search of greater contact with life or against those who facilitate that process for others (Reich, 1950, 1972).[3] Such a counter-reaction to the growth of others can take the form of a destructive acting out by groups of people acting in concert on the basis of a mutually reinforcing social alibi as in the case of Fascism or it may take the less 'feverish' form - bureaucratization - a process which quietly smothers.

In the absence of clearly delineated functional distinctions and corresponding labelling such as I have outlined, the rise of the 'therapy bureaucracies' and the possibility of their statutory endorsement poses a threat to the vitality of the 'fringe' - a threat which, in my view, those who value human potential work would be well advised to resist.[4]

Section III

No Treatment Required

Chapter 28

Disclosing the Alternatives

... Let us allow patients themselves to discover that it is damaging to them to look for mental assistance to people who have not learnt how to give it. If we explain this to them and warn them against it, we shall have spared ourselves the need to forbid it....

(Sigmund Freud, 1926:80)

You will have noticed that I have paid no attention to the question of psycho-quackery and charlatanry. This is because I ... regard this problem as of minimal importance and as one which will decline proportionately with the dissemination of correct education among the public....

(Robert Lindner, 1950:440)

... In short, licensure, which has been the conventional policy response to information failures in many professional markets, seems an inappropriate response in the market for mental health services precisely because information about quality measures is so bad....

(Michael J. Trebilcock and Jeffrey Shaul, 1982:290)

... This suggests that self-disclosure statements would be more useful in selecting a therapist than the present system [in the USA etc.] of state licensing, which misleads the public because it is not based on functional criteria....

(Roberta Russell, 1981/1993:55)

Is psychotherapy a suitable case for statutory treatment? This book responds with a resounding No! The situation prevailing in this field does not warrant any such intervention. *The alternatives presented in this chapter are possible improvements rather than necessary 'therapy'. The situation does not require a remedial legislative intervention.* So, what improvements would be possible?

Education

According to Hogan: "Perhaps the most effective method of regulating psychotherapists and protecting the public is through education. This is especially true of any profession that is young and undeveloped, where standards of practice are still quite diverse.... On a broader scale, the public should become more informed about the professions, their importance in society, their power, and the ways in which that power may be abused ..." (Hogan, Vol. 1, 1979:382).

So, in the interests of an informed consumer choice, the public could be better educated as to the criteria which are most pertinent to consider when undertaking psychotherapy, including what to look for in selecting a practitioner. In that regard, this book and some of the sources that I have cited may be aids to the process of selection. As with other diversified areas, the personal recommendation of someone who shares your outlook and whose opinion you have learned to trust is also a valuable guide.

Information could also be made available about the potential pitfalls of the work, and what is best avoided or approached with caution on the basis of the evidence available. For example, the interpretation of physical symptoms as being of purely psychological origin rather than perhaps indicative of an undiagnosed physical illness is worthy of prudence (Striano, 1988:5). Indeed, practitioner interpretations of any sort should not be regarded as 'gospel'. Likewise on the basis of studies such as Garret (1994), Pope and Bouhoutsos (1986), and Rutter (1989), having sex with your psychotherapist is an area for caution if not avoidance. Promoting a better understanding of the nature of transference in general and its pervasiveness both inside and outside the therapy situation should be an important educational goal (Heron, 1990).

The current diversity in this field, which has been referred to as a sort of 'information overload', can be regarded as an asset if people are aware of the appropriate criteria of selection. In my opinion the greatest source of difficulty for the 'customer' derives from not knowing on what basis to make their judgement. As argued previously, the criteria for selection of a practitioner promoted by a licensing system in this area would be misleading and would lull people into a false sense of security that competence had been assured thereby. Such a system represents an appeal to the authority of status that so many of us have a tendency to defer to.

Client choice with regard to which type of work to undertake would be assisted by the sort of differentiations I have attempted to make in Section II. That is, clear functional distinctions between broad categories of work on the basis of the intentions of the practitioners and the types of clientele for whom the work is offered - along with appropriate unambiguous labelling. Similarly, linguistically distinguishing *particular* approaches which are reasonably consistent as to values, aims and methods, could assist clients in their choice.

Rather than waste public funds in the inefficiencies of a licensing system, it would be more appropriate and effective to finance endeavours to educate the public as to the relevant factors to look for in a practitioner and what to expect from different types of work (perhaps aided by full disclosure provisions - see below).

The application of existing laws

Problems associated with the practice of psychotherapy can also be addressed by the application of existing or general laws (see also the following chapter) rather than the promulgation of specific statutory measures. Laws that are applicable in this area as elsewhere include those concerning contracts, deception, truth in advertising (trade description), assault and breach of confidence [the creation of a legal obligation regarding confidentiality is not dependent upon professionalization (Cohen, 1992:19)].

However, given the nature of the risks, their low levels and the difficulties of establishing causation, as discussed in Chapter 21, an encouragement of excessive litigiousness is unlikely to benefit this field as a whole and mediation rather than litigation may be more appropriate for most of the issues that are likely to arise.

Full disclosure provisions

Full disclosure provisions are concerned with empowering the public to make informed decisions in their choice of practitioner by allowing them access to full relevant information. These could be effected as part of general legislative improvements in the area of consumer law and freedom of information since the same principle applies to many purchase decisions, such as 'full disclosure' product labelling, for example, whereby informa-

205

tion about pharmaceutical and pesticide testing, the presence of genetically engineered material or the ecological status of timber and other products could be provided. Access to pertinent information about goods, services and providers, and relevant criteria for selection, would be beneficial in most if not all markets, not just this one.

Will Schutz, one of the pioneers of the human potential movement who was mentioned in Chapter 25, has outlined a proposal whereby:

> All persons offering services aimed at enhancing the human condition [in whatever way] would be required to provide potential customers with a full disclosure of all information relevant to the competence of the professional. Such information would include the practitioner's education, training, philosophy, fees, membership in professional organizations, awards, and anything else the professional feels is relevant. (Schutz, 1979:156)

In addition to Schutz, Carlson (1975:233), Hogan (Vol. 1, 1979:381), Russell (1981/1993:55) and Gross (1977, 1978) are amongst those who have also advocated full disclosure provisions in this area.

The role of the law in a full disclosure system would be to determine the veracity and completeness of the information, and to police lying and deceit, rather than to decide who is or is not competent and thereby usurping the consumer's choice. So, rather than the client having someone else decide who is competent as with a licensing system, this decision would remain theirs but on the basis of full and accurate information.

Full disclosure provisions can become part of an agreement or contract with the client and subject to the laws of contract. Compare this with the 'status' basis for many client-professional relationships - 'trust me, I'm a doctor'.

By way of illustration, there follows a discussion of some of the information that could be made available to potential clients by full disclosure provisions.

The practitioner's terms and conditions 'for hire' can be part of the full disclosure statement as can the aims of the activity and any promises as to outcome that the practitioner may be bold enough to make. Any codes of ethics or practice that the practitioner adheres to can also be cited.

'Full disclosure' statements could also give details of what training the practitioner has had for the work being offered, specifying duration (years, hours); type (e.g. apprenticeship or more academic-style course); content (e.g. how experiential/theoretical, whether group or one-to-one based and whether significant personal work in the modality was required as part of the course, not at all, or as a prerequisite for commencing the course); and with whom (named persons, rather than just named organizations).

The actual track record of the practitioner could be specified, for example, amount of experience (years, hours). Many years of experience might outweigh the details of training undergone (if any) in the decision-making of some would-be clients.

Full disclosure provisions can be used to specify whether, and to what extent and under what circumstances, physical contact between practitioner and client may occur. This may range from the avoidance of even a handshake as in the extremes of psychoanalysis to the body-oriented approaches of the Reichians and many humanistic approaches.

Likewise, 'full disclosure' can specify whether or not sexual activity is precluded and, if not, to what degree and under what circumstances it may occur (for example, during a session, outside of a session, only after the end of the contract, how long after, never). The track-record of the practitioner with regard to this could also be included and thus be available for potential clients, and for other practitioners considering referral, to make their own judgement of suitability.

Such information as outlined above would be far more meaningful and relevant than an impressive diploma, or letters after the name (whether they be 'F.R.C.Psych.' or 'Mb.H.R.') whose significance may not really be known to the potential client, yet which hook the 'status reflex' and the often all too blind trust in the 'properly qualified'.[1]

The public would still be free to choose to work with 'just anyone', such as someone with no training or experience whatsoever, if they wished, but they would do so knowingly.

Full disclosure provisions can also encompass a distinction between psychotherapy (seen as psychotherapeutic *treatment*) and human potential work, on the basis of clear terminological distinction if this can be agreed and/or by specifying the degree of autonomy/self-responsibility necessary as a prerequisite for undertaking the work (such as 'SAFAA'), whatever that work may be called (see Section II).

By the same token 'full disclosure' can encompass membership of a voluntary register such as that of UKCP since this would be part of the relevant information of the member practitioner. Consumers could choose, if they wish, to select a practitioner whose background corresponds to the criteria of such an organization. However, education of the public as to the relevance of the required criteria of such organizations and of the hidden agenda of professions and the power they can exercise - even without statutory recognition - would also be required and could be part of a general information background pertinent to the area of activity to which the disclosure declaration applies.

'Full disclosure' principles can provide an alternative model for practitioner organizations generally. All too often such organizations present themselves as quasi-licensing bodies offering assurance of competence in the traditional professional mode. Instead of providing a list of 'approved' practitioners such organizations could provide a list of practitioners which disclaims any explicit or implicit recommendations as to competence but which provides full disclosure information for each practitioner as discussed above. The role of the organization would be to specify which information was pertinent to competence in their view (and their basis for claiming so), to verify the information provided by each member and to exclude practitioners in the event of falsehood.

The need for truth is an essential element in 'full disclosure'. The status of any statements or claims and evidence or arguments for any such claims can be specified as a necessary part of such provisions. For example, if scientific proof is claimed, what sort of 'proof' is there for the claim? Is empirical evidence available? Experimental evidence perhaps? Has a statistical survey been undertaken or a double blind trial? References could be cited, along with any contrary opinions. Perhaps the statements made are a question of belief? Or perhaps they are based on clinical experience? If so this could be specified. Such a provision would be a way of addressing claims such as were made for Scientology as a science and the first thoroughly validated psychotherapy (Holmes & Lindley, 1989:209).

Such a system would be infinitely preferable to systems where conventional scientific standards of proof are imposed on areas where they are not fully appropriate. For example the *Therapeutic Goods Act 1989* in

Australia and the *Food Drug and Cosmetics Act 1964* in the USA. Such legislation has been used to impose a conventional orthodoxy on holistic and fringe activities and has been a vehicle whereby powerful established groups such as the medical profession and the drug industry can suppress competition from alternative practice. In the UK, the use of traditional herbal remedies is under a similar threat from pressure to subject them to conventional drug testing without providing funding to do so. As they are not proprietary products, there are no monopoly profits to fund such testing, and the cost of obtaining a licence, as is the case with pharmaceuticals.[2]

Full disclosure is a system that can support a pluralism that reflects the variety in this area rather than the standardization and conservatism that tends to emerge from licensing systems.

Non-credentialled registration

Where a significant risk to the public from unregulated activity has been demonstrated, Hogan (Vol. 1, 1979:361-2; 371-2) recommends a system of regulation in which the would-be practitioner registers with a state board of control for a nominal fee and *without having to meet any educational, experiential or other prerequisites before being granted the right to practise.* This system is very different from the 'registration' currently under discussion in the UK where what has been proposed is a form of conventional licensing with high barriers to entry for the occupation. Therefore, for the sake of clarity, I refer to it as 'non-credentialled registration' to emphasize the absence of entry requirements.

Under a non-credentialled scheme, full disclosure of all relevant information would be required as part of the registration. In addition, practitioners would be required to inform clients as to how, if dissatisfied, they can file complaints with the state registration board (or an 'ombudsman' perhaps). Practitioners would be required to distribute evaluation forms to clients at the end of the working relationship. A sufficient number of negative responses would trigger the attention of a disciplinary board - a board whose composition would reflect a balanced representation of interests, including members of the public, clients and government officials along with practitioners, but it would *not* be dominated by members of the profession.

Non-credentialled registration is a system whereby a right to practise or use a title is easy to acquire but can be withdrawn in the event of evidence of harm. It is comparable to a fishing licence which can be purchased for a nominal sum, but withdrawn if you are caught 'grilling a tiddler'.

Such a system avoids the drawbacks of restricting entry to the occupation on the basis of qualifications that may not be related to competence or performance whilst allowing a means of halting those who do prove for whatever reason to be harmful.

One advantage of such a system as this is that it would provide a simple mechanism whereby a levy could be made on practitioners, the money to be used to finance research and fund the education of the public - perhaps to set up a public information agency or publish a small booklet that practitioners would be required to give to any potential client to explain what was known about the activity in question, what was the status of the evidence for it and what was controversial. This information would tend to be less dominated by the 'needs' of the profession than would be the case with information emanating from guild-like professional bodies such as UKCP or BPS.

Unlike statutory professional self-regulation which appears, erroneously, to be cost-free for government apart from the parliamentary time involved in enacting a bill (see the next chapter), a proposal such as non-credentialled registration does clearly require the government to commit money and resources to its administration. However, such a scheme is only really applicable where public money is involved and/or the risk to the public from the activity in question is significant and widespread. On the basis of the analysis in this book, such a system is not warranted in the fields of psychotherapy or counselling as a whole, that is, for all those activities jostling to be included under these supposed 'generic' terms. The risks involved in these activities are not such that any special legislation is required. Nevertheless, this proposal is important as a model for regulation if at some stage in the future the evidence presented in this book is superseded. It may also be appropriate as a model for the regulation of some parts of the this field, such as those where a medical model (whether allopathic or holistic) is appropriate, say in relation to psychotherapeutic treatment under national health schemes such as the UK's NHS.

One of the strongest arguments against an informationally empowered consumer choice as the basis for regulation in this area is that when people are 'sick' they are least able to make informed and wise choices about their 'treatment'. The functional distinction between recipients provided by the 'SAFAA' criterion of 'good-enough adult' (see Section II), forms a basis for distinguishing activities where diminished responsibility on the part of the clients ('patients') is accepted and to which a non-credentialled registration system might usefully be applied and for which eligibility for NHS funding could be sought. As discussed previously, whilst the medical model holds sway in this area the terms 'psychotherapist' (a practitioner of psychotherapy as 'psychotherapeutic *treatment*') or 'therapist' could be used as the title for those who work with people who do not have 'sufficient available functioning adult autonomy' and therefore have diminished responsibility. A non-credentialled system would avoid restricting eligibility for working with such 'patients' to practitioners with high 'overheads' that have not been shown to be relevant to basic competence in this area - such as clinical psychologists and doctors or members of such organizations as UKCP or BAC. This could provide an economic basis for meeting the increasing demands by patients for 'psychotherapy' rather than drug based approaches in the NHS (Pedder, 1994).

Such a system of non-credentialled registration for psychotherapeutic 'treatment' might link quite well with the NVQ system if the provision of psychotherapeutic treatment on the NHS is to made available on the basis of an assessment of outcome and performance rather than relying on the status and prior qualifications of the practitioner. Whereas it may not be realistic to measure performance in the way proposed by the 'Lead Body', an *ex post* assessment of the performance of a practitioner in the way provided for by this system may be more feasible.

There is also the question of the provision of genuine asylum opportunities for people who are in a crisis or breakdown situation and so distressed or out of touch with present time or consensus reality that they are unable to function 'on the rational plane' to any significant extent, as consumers or otherwise. For people in such a situation the provision of genuine asylums or retreat centres - non-hospital 'transformational crisis centres' with 24 hour non-invasive care such as pioneered at 'Kingsley Hall', 'Soteria House', 'Diabasis' and elsewhere (Perry, 1974; Berke, 1979;

Podvoll, 1990; Breggin, 1991/1993) and the more recently proposed 'spiritual-emergency centres' (Grof & Grof, 1991:242) - would in many cases be preferable to the chemical or physical intervention so beloved of psychiatry and upon which so much public expenditure is lavished.

Such non-drug alternatives to the handling of acute 'psychotic' episodes have failed to spread and flourish largely due to problems of funding (Grof, 1988b; Breggin, 1991/1993). State or private medical insurance schemes are reluctant to countenance non-drug approaches to madness and to fund or reimburse for that sort of treatment without the acceptance of such approaches by the medical establishment who, in conjunction with the drug companies (the 'psycho-pharmaceutical complex' (Breggin, 1991/1993) are understandably reluctant to undermine their dominance of this area by encouraging non-biodeterministic theories of aetiology and non-medical and non-pharmaceutical approaches to treatment (see also Chapter 25 and Appendix E). This difficulty apart, a system of non-credentialled registration for psychotherapeutic 'treatment' (whatever it may be called) might provide a framework for manning such facilities and accessing state or private finance.

Self and peer assessment and accreditation

For a discussion of self and peer assessment and accreditation and the idea of a peer accredited network as an alternative to conventional accreditation and licensing, see Appendix D.

Chapter 29

Politics, Politics

... Licensing does not protect the public. Licensing does not exclude incompetents. Licensing does not encourage innovation. It stultifies....

(Will Schutz, 1979:157)

The public is ill-served by exclusionary and anti-competitive licensing regulations whose correlation with proficiency and ethical behaviour has not been established....

(The Consortium for the Advancement of Diversified Programs in Psychology [CADPP], 1989)

No regulation is better than regulation based on standards that have nothing to do with patient improvement. Such regulations, which are currently in existence [in the USA etc.], are misleading to the public.

(Roberta Russell, 1981/1993:74)

... Dare we insist upon meaningful regulation, rather than government support of arbitrary standards?

(ibid.:58)

Opposition has begun to develop, but slowly. The informal and individualistic nature of the activity [psychotherapy] is such that many of its best practitioners are only starting to realise what is going on, and they are often not organization-minded people....

... Standardized, rule following therapy is not what the clients deserve. There will be opposition, but will it be in time?

(Nick Totton, 1992:27)

I hope I have been able to demonstrate that the case against statutory psychotherapy registration is, firstly, that the case *for* it is so poor. 'The case for' fails to stand up to close scrutiny and is even weaker than I had first supposed it to be at the outset of writing this book. Even where I had expected to find some solid evidence to back-up the arguments for statutory control, whether of the need for it or the efficacy of it as a response, the 'evidence' crumbled on closer investigation.

This experience of finding that the 'givens' had to be constantly questioned and could not be assumed to be sound on the basis of the status of their source is highly pertinent to a theme of this book - that personal growth approaches whether currently referred to as psychotherapy or not, are not the sort of activities where deferring to someone's opinion on the basis that they are the 'expert' is at all appropriate. In this area in particular, it is not appropriate to take things on trust on the basis of a 'professional' status.

Secondly, the case against psychotherapy registration is that the effects of it would, on balance, actually be negative and represent a deterioration of the existing situation. This 'treatment' would be worse than the 'disease'.

What appears to be on offer in such registration schemes is a sort of bogus insurance policy representing a collusion with regressive urges for a risk-free existence where responsibility for key life decisions is lifted from the individual by benevolent 'experts'. Moreover this is a curious 'policy' where the risks are low, the premiums are high, the settling of any claim unlikely, and where taking out the policy actually increases the risk!

Juliana Brown has remarked that as in an organic garden, it is perhaps better to put up with a few 'pests' for the sake of the well-being of the whole system rather than resort to 'chemicals and pesticides' with the prospect of developing long term negative side-effects, not least that of reducing the 'fertility' of the 'soil'. It is better to put energy into encouraging the health of the garden as a whole. A flourishing garden can cope with its 'pests' (Brown, 1994a). Furthermore as with the global ecosystem, 'species diversity' (pejoratively referred to as 'fragmentation' in this area) provides a greater prospect of long term health for the system than a 'monocrop'.

The conclusions of this book apply to the UKCP scheme and by the same token to the BPS attempt to gain statutory restriction of the term 'psychologist' and likewise the BAC's ambitions (along with other organizations) to obtain statutory recognition for a register of counsellors.

Granting these bodies a legal monopoly on the respective terms would not be in the public interest, rather, it would constitute the institution of restrictive practices that would, overall, be more detrimental than beneficial. From the practitioner's point of view the issue is one of the right to practise (or to use a particular title). From the point of view of the consumer it is a question of the freedom to choose with whom to work and how. Statutory registration, especially a practice act (remember that a title act is often the 'thin end of the wedge' for a practice act), represents a coercion of the would-be clients as well as the would-be practitioners since the former are forced to select from a smaller and less diverse pool. From the point of view of society as a whole, there are issues concerning the efficient use of resources, the variety, availability and cost of services, and the climate for innovation. There are also fundamental questions about the role of the state in relation to the rights of citizens to pursue paths of personal transformation and about the establishment of an official 'priest class' as an intermediary in that process.

UKCP is unlikely to disappear - it has too much support from conventional institutions and too many people have climbed aboard through fear or fatalism. Its presence has already had a deadening effect thereby. However, its register is only a voluntary one. The arguments I have presented lead to the conclusion that every effort should be made to discourage governmental compliance with UKCP's ambition to convert its register into a statutory one. Even if this were only to be a form of title protection, this should be resisted for the reasons outlined in this book (see in particular Chapters 15 and 24), and confirmed by Trebilcock as follows:

> The conferment on professional associations of legal ability to certify the competence of their members may set in motion a set of political dynamics that will tend to convert certification schemes [i.e. title protection] however desirable, into licensing schemes [here meaning practice acts], however undesirable.... (Trebilcock, 1982:95)

The existing situation regarding psychotherapy does not in general warrant any legislative changes other than what can usefully be effected as part of a general improvement in consumer legislation by legislative encouragement of the truthful, full disclosure of information relevant to any service, product or undertaking being offered for reward. Such a general improvement in consumer legislation requiring full relevant information about *any* product or service to be made available to the potential consumer would provide a cost effective way of improving the existing situation regarding psychotherapy without the negative side-effects of creating a statutory monopoly.

As has emerged in the course of this study, the likelihood of legislation being introduced in this area in the UK is nowhere near as great as has been trumpeted by those who would like to see it come about. This does not however mean that opponents of such a measure can be complacent. The supporters of 'the case for' are organized, known to government and have links with established power bases such as the psychiatric profession. Supporters of 'the case against', whether practitioners or consumers, are more dispersed, less organized and their voice is, so far, perhaps almost unknown to government. However unsound 'the case for' may be, because of these differentials of political power it may yet have its day if opponents fail to be vigilant and fail to speak out. Don't rest in the false security that because it doesn't make sense it won't happen. As Trebilcock says: "... Unfortunately the political forces that tend to promote concentrated producer [practitioner/trainer] interests over thinly dispersed consumer interests are formidable and are not likely to be easily denied these biases" (Trebilcock, 1982:104). All that may be required for a law to eventually be enacted is for there to be some sort of associated scandal, probably sexual, and for the government of the day to be tempted to toss the 'bone' of statutory control to placate the tabloid press hounds and the lobbying professionals. Moreover: "A licensing scheme once in place, is difficult to undo ... exclusive licensing laws, once enacted tend to be politically irreversible [since they create a vested interest], irrespective of their continued aptness" (ibid.:99).

Thus statutory registration is harder to reverse than to grant. If an aspiring profession can cite the precedent of other professions (at home and abroad) in favour of its case, it may be politically easier for the government to comply with the request than to endeavour to remove the existing privileges of what have probably become entrenched and powerful special interest groups. Similarly, faced with criticism of a particular regulated profession, the government may find the option of 'more regulation' or 'better regulation' more politically feasible than deregulation.

The profession of architecture provides a ready example of these sorts of issues. Uniquely in the UK construction industry, this profession has a statutory register and title protection. In the throes of deregulatory fervour in the early 1990s, the government instigated a review of that profession's statutory position. Representatives of the profession argued for an extension of title protection to cover similar terms and a protection of function as well. They cited the example of other countries in Europe and elsewhere as precedent. To their chagrin however, the resulting report (Warne, 1993) recommended the abolition of title protection and statutory registration. Consequently the government proposed to repeal the relevant laws. However, a vigorous campaign by the profession and other interested parties succeeded in securing a 'U-turn' by the government, who settled instead for a revision of the regulatory council, title protection being retained (ARCUK, 1995). Apparently, one of the clinching arguments put forward for non-abolition was that a question of existing consumer expectations was involved (NCC, 1994). In effect, after 60-odd years of title protection of the term 'architect', the public had become so used to expecting an 'architect' to be a qualified person that, it was argued, deregulation would create confusion and mislead the public (ARCUK, 1995). So, the existence of title protection had generated the justification for its own continuance.[1]

Statutory professional regulation also has certain other political appeals that may make it tempting to governments whatever its demerits. Such systems: "do not typically involve any commitment of government resources and therefore do not show up in government accounts or payrolls" and yet they create: "an appearance (an illusion) of protection for second and third party interests". Moreover: "[The vigour of a self-regulating professional group] in prescribing exacting entry standards and restricting post-entry conduct can be held out as symbolizing a strong commitment to regulatory redress of consumer concerns in the market in question, whereas the real impact on second and third party interests ... may be negative" (Trebilcock, 1982:103). That is, although seen from a wider frame statutory professional self-regulation actually exerts a heavy price on society as a whole in terms of deleterious effects on the efficient provision of the services in question, it may still appeal to government because at little immediate cost to itself (apart from the parliamentary time involved in the enacting of a bill) the government can give an appearance of 'doing something'.

Hence: "... the potential for conferring perceived (but illusory) benefits on relatively dispersed [consumer] interests while imposing relatively small real costs (and in many cases real benefits) on highly concentrated [professional] interests will often make [professional statutory] self-regulation a politically rational choice of instrument, despite its technical inefficiencies" (ibid.).

However, the more aware people are of what is really afoot and the more vocal the opposition, the less easy it is to generate such an illusion of benefits and protection and, therefore, the less likely will it be that government will acquiesce to the statutory ambitions of the 'therapy bureaucracies'. The intention of this book to raise such awareness.

Opposition could be made more demonstrable by, for example, forming a group in favour of retaining the current openness of the UK milieu, challenging proponents of statutory control to produce empirical evidence in favour of the need for it and of its efficacy, joining or supporting organizations promoting alternative forms of accreditation such as the Independent Therapists Network (see Appendix D), lobbying for full disclosure consumer legislation for goods and services *in general* and writing to the Department of Health, your MP and your MEP.[2] Amongst other things, these and other actions are ways of challenging any assumption that the 'therapy bureaucracies' UKCP, BCP, BAC, BPS and RCP represent all interested parties in this area. They do not. They do not represent the numerous practitioners who are not their members and who in many cases do not have a vested interest in training. They do not represent the client or the public interest. In particular the voice of the satisfied client has not yet really been heard. For example, the voices of the numerous people who have derived benefit from the human potential movement have yet to be heard in this debate.

As outlined in Section II, I am concerned about the threat to the integrity of human potential work posed by the statutory ambitions of the therapy bureaucracies, the more so if human potential/humanistic organizations become a part of such bodies in the absence of a clearly delineated and agreed boundary between human potential work and psychotherapy. Let us not allow human potential work to become warped in the service of categorization with labels so commonly associated with medical metaphors but also let us not allow those labels to be expropriated whilst significant ambiguity remains. I therefore urge practitioners in the human potential movement to adopt appropriate differentiating terminology as previously discussed and to eschew UKCP participant organizations. In so far as we are in a sort of 'truth business' - the promotion of personal authenticity, rather than, say, the repair and maintenance of 'false self' or persona - participation in the pursuit of professionally self-serving myths hardly makes for a very edifying 'demonstration effect'.

I urge practitioners and practitioner organizations of all persuasions not to be stampeded into participation in bodies like UKCP on the basis of fear and assumptions of the inevitability of legislation. Remember that the assumption of impending legislation is unfounded. For those who are undecided, 'sitting on the fence' or hoping to 'hedge their bets' I would say that it is difficult to remain neutral in this matter. You may be dubious about UKCP and accept the case against statutory registration, but nonetheless be tempted to 'sign up' as an 'insurance policy', just in case the law is changed at some stage. However such a move will *increase* the likelihood of that happening. If you buy into it (whatever your true opinion of its desirability) you give it more credibility - the credibility of numerical support. Through participation you support it, you make it happen, you create it. You are part of the process.

In particular, beware the seductive 'grandparent clause', a device frequently used to 'buy off' opposition from existing practitioners who might otherwise fight for their rights to practise or to use generic titles and thereby for the rights of future generations of practitioners and clients as well.

There is also the need for vigilance and opposition to *de facto* recognition of the therapy bureaucracies as 'overseers' through systems of third party payment etc., the indirect regulation discussed in Chapter 20.

For those already involved with UKCP, BAC et al. who have sympathy with the case presented here but do not wish to withdraw from such organizations, I would urge you not to support policies aimed at achieving a statutory register but rather to adopt a position of support for a voluntary register only, and to oppose the statutory aspiration.

A question of ethical action on the collective, political level is in-volved in all this. *Unless* the statutory control being sought can be justi-fied on the grounds of public benefit - and my contention is that it cannot - its pursuit by practitioners collectively is an action with regard to the public as a whole which lacks the moral integrity that most of them would aspire to in their dealings with clients individually and which statutory controls are supposed to secure. As Alberding et al. maintain: "... We hope that counselors [etc.] want to make responsible choices, not harmful choices, and that counselors are not willing to accept professionally beneficial con-sequences at the expense of the public we profess to serve" (Alberding et al., 1993:37). In the light of the arguments and evidence presented here, the onus is clearly upon those who seek these changes to prove that they would be of net public benefit, if such action is to be ethically sound.

Proposals for the statutory registration of psychotherapy in the UK had their beginnings with reactions to a 'cult' - Scientology. Let me end with a more recent parliamentary reaction to a more extreme cult. Follow-ing the Branch Davidian cult tragedy in Waco, Texas in April 1993, there were calls, both within parliament and in the media, for legislation to con-trol such cults. David Wilshire MP, of the House of Commons All Party Group on Cults, responded to such calls by arguing that new laws to re-strict cults would be inadvisable, not least because of the difficulties of defining what a 'cult' was, and of applying law in the area of belief in a democratic society ["arguably, substantial distinctions cannot be drawn between a cult and a monastery" (Trebilcock & Shaul, 1982:278)]. In-stead, Wilshire urged that existing law, in particular trading standards and consumer protection law, should be applied to this area - the law applied to the telling of the truth - to ensure that the potential consumer contem-plating involvement is not deceived.

> ... any organization that purports to be one thing, often in writing by way of its literature and in reality is something else, whatever their motives they ought to be brought within the law of having to tell the truth. [Their literature should be] honest, truthful and totally above board, so you are aware ... what you are letting yourself in for and I think we could apply that test to everybody and everything. (Wilshire, 1993)

220

Section IV

Appendices

'Case' Notes

and

Bibliography

Appendix A

Whither the Human Potential Movement?

by Juliana Brown and Richard Mowbray

We have been heartened by the recent debate in *Self and Society* (Jan. 1990) about the UKSCP and the regulation of the "profession of psychotherapy". We have been muttering to ourselves and colleagues for a good few years now about "what's happening to this movement?" and casting a jaundiced eye over the goings on at Rugby and the moves towards "regulation". Recent visits to North America and discussions with Kate Wylie (who was one of the founder members of the Open Centre) in which she bemoaned the "deadening effect" of the US licensing system on the working environment there and praised the (current) UK openness, confirmed our misgivings and inspired us to write something about our reactions. We were also thinking of proposing a special edition of this Journal [*Self and Society*] on this issue when lo and behold ...! We're glad we are not alone in having doubts.

Much of what we would have said has already been covered in the January issue, especially by John Heron, David Kalisch, Denis Postle and Jill Anderson, however we felt there were still areas where we could offer further contributions to the debate.

We feel that '1992 and all that' has become the 'bogeyman' frightening this movement into becoming a "profession" and "getting its house in order" whereas actually the main impetus seems to have been coming from a rather small nucleus of people within the movement (many with a vested interest in training)[1] rather than from actual threats of regulation from outside. Ironically it may transpire that the resulting system of internal regulation will be what precipitates legislation by making it easy for government to legislate through the *apparently* representative bodies.

The reasons put forward by Courtenay Young (1990) and others in

Self and Society to justify these moves towards regulation and licensing include: "protect the public", "definite status and legality", "official recognition", etc. Whatever the validity of these reasons, (little we feel) in our view the 'cure' is liable to prove worse than the 'disease'.

We are concerned that if these moves gain ground there will be a deterioration in the prevailing ambience of openness and choice. One of the fundamental principles of growth is choice, and introducing a system of regulation or licensing into the growth movement is liable to restrict choice. We feel that measures towards empowering the public to make more informed, responsible choices would be more in keeping with the spirit of the human potential movement.

The key thing for us is that the human potential movement is a manifestation of a *different model*, a holistic growth model. It is a 'new' field that is not medicine, not religion, not art, not even education, but something in between, which has similarities with aspects of each of these but has an essence of its own. It lies closest in principle to education, however, in practice education is often focused on the development of the intellect or the acquisition of utilitarian skills. This new field is educational in the sense of a holistic learning about oneself.

Despite areas in common with existing institutions this field should not be subsumed under any of them. It is important that it retains its autonomy and continues to establish itself in its own right. It is important that the structures we develop reflect the underlying model and that we do not 'regress' and adopt structures appropriate to other models.

In our view, the current moves towards regulation and licensing derive from an implicit association with the medical model and with the medical professions as a model for professionalization. Members of the medical professions (as well as professions such as those cited by Courtenay Young - accountants, solicitors and architects) are by and large persons who give advice or carry out actions on behalf of their clients. Their professional status assures the client of their authority and competence to act *without the client being fully involved* - not something we would hope is typical of humanistic practitioners!

Human potential work is not a medical matter. There is a danger of this holistic work becoming split: saddled with a quasi-medical framework on the one hand or going the religious route on the other.

A predisposing factor for confusion between the human potential model and the medical model derives from the ambiguous labelling so often used. The word 'therapy' is in widespread use within the movement, and is understood informally and without stigma to mean 'personal growth work'. This is in tune with its root in ancient Greek meaning 'attendance'. However, we would argue that for the general public it is a medical term referring to remedial treatment, which accords with its current dictionary definition - "the medical treatment of disease" (*Shorter Oxford English Dictionary*, 1973). The ancient Greeks may win out in the long run but they haven't done so yet!

Further, in order to distinguish this 'therapy' from other forms of therapy such as chemotherapy, radiotherapy, physiotherapy, occupational therapy, etc., the term 'psychotherapy' is resorted to. Its current dictionary definition is "the treatment of mental or psychic disease" (ibid.). We do not feel this term accurately describes the focus of the human potential movement, even with 'humanistic' tacked in front. In order to maintain the integrity of human potential movement more appropriate labelling will be necessary.

Therefore, in common with John Heron (1990:21) we feel that terminology associated with the medical model (in particular the terms 'psychotherapy' and 'therapy') should be avoided by human potential practitioners, at least officially. This has always been our practice. (Bill Swartley (1971) suggested the term 'humanologist' - a practitioner of 'humanology' - the science of becoming fully human.)

Where there is a genuine need for structures, we should develop structures that foster our values rather than betray them.

Rather than the systems of regulation currently being advanced with their approving bodies and their registers of approved practitioners etc. and eventual "official recognition", and "definite status and legality" we feel that a system based on the principle of *full disclosure*, something like that proposed by Will Schutz (1979), would be more in keeping with humanistic values than what is likely to emerge from the current endeavours. Schutz outlines a proposal whereby:

All persons offering services aimed at enhancing the human condition [in whatever way] would be required to provide potential customers with a full disclosure of all information relevant to the competence of the professional. Such information would include the practitioner's education, training, philosophy, fees, membership in professional organizations, awards, and anything else the professional feels is relevant [such as a code of ethics].... (ibid.:156)

The role of the law would be to determine the veracity and completeness of this information, and to police lying and deceit, rather than to decide who is or is not competent and thereby usurping the consumer's choice. So, rather than the client having someone else decide who is competent this decision would remain theirs, but on the basis of full and accurate information. As Schutz says :

> In the present situation [USA 1979], I rely on the state to tell me who is competent, I passively submit myself to a professional, and if I do not like what he does, I sue him for malpractice. My role is very inert and childlike. If I, as consumer, know that I am responsible for selecting a counselor, I am likely to assume a more responsible stance. In many cases, the very act of being responsible will have a therapeutic effect.
>
> Thus, choice and truth replace sham and image.... Full disclosure treats both professional and consumer as responsible adults and alters the role of the law to one of determining truth, a function it can perform well in the service of its constituents. (ibid.:157)

The US milieu provides other cautionary lessons. Over there, the medical model is dominant in licensed psychotherapy as is clearly demonstrated by the intimate relationship between the system of licensing, medical insurance, and the diagnostic labelling of the medical model.

Psychotherapists (other than psychiatrists) are licensed by the American Psychological Association[2] and are then (and only then) in a position to receive referrals from doctors, governmental organizations etc. Their 'patients' may in many cases claim their therapy against their medical insurance. One of the main incentives for practitioners to become licensed is to be able to charge higher fees and receive a steady stream of referrals financed by medical insurance payments. However no insurance company is going to fund your 'personal growth' so the reason for going to your therapist must be for the treatment of a recognized psychological disorder as specified in the *Diagnostic and Statistical Manual of Psychological Disorders Revision III*, known as DSM-III-R (verbal communication from Kate Wylie, Dec. 1989). There is therefore an 'incentive scheme' for both practitioner and client to accept a definition of the latter or of some part of the latter's experience as abnormal or pathological and needing treatment whereas from a human potential point of view the same phenomena might be viewed as signalling 'growth process at work, needing attending'. These are two very different approaches.

Not only does the US licensing system make it hard to work on the basis of a growth model, it also appears to be rather ineffective in what it sets out to achieve whilst stifling innovation:

> Licensing has not proved an effective tool for providing program quality assurance. Moreover, attempts by licensing to regulate or control program quality in general may do more harm than good by creating barriers to developing needed services. (California Assembly Permanent subcommittee on Mental Health and Developmental Disabilities, 1978:46)

> ... Licensing does not protect the public. Licensing does not exclude incompetents. Licensing does not encourage innovation. It stultifies.... (Schutz, 1979:157)

It could be said that the growth movement child is growing up and is about to come of age. It therefore faces the choices we all face at that juncture, to follow in the well-worn footsteps of Mother and Father (perhaps changing them just a little), or to risk something else - being oneself, a new individual, different, not in competition or in judgement, nor needing parental approval, but able to stand separately, in mutual respect.

[This article first appeared in *Self and Society* Vol. 18 No. 4 (July 1990) and was reprinted in *The Open Centre Programme* Autumn 1993.]

Appendix B

Registration in Australia

Then all hell broke loose. Suddenly a wide variety of persons engaged in 'therapies' of one kind or another came to realize the implications of the new Act for their practices....

(Robert A. Cummins, 1986:13)

Australia has a legal system which is derived from, and in some respects still linked to, the British one. There have been legal interventions concerning the practice of psychotherapy in Australia since 1965. In Australia, the legal framework most pertinent to the practice of psychotherapy is that concerning the practice of psychology. Unlike in the UK so far, all Australian states (but not the Australian Capital Territory (ACT) as of January 1994) now have statutory psychologist registration boards, although the legislation governing these varies from state to state and there has been little co-ordination between the boards until the *Mutual Recognition Act, 1992* was passed by the Commonwealth of Australia (i.e. national legislation) with a view to establishing mutual recognition of professional qualifications throughout all the Australian states. Access to these registers is by and large restricted to those with an academic background in psychology. In the state of Victoria, membership of the British Psycho-Analytical Society confers eligibility.

New South Wales was the last of the Australian states to make psychology a registrable profession, having enacted legislation in 1989. When I made enquires of the New South Wales Psychologists Registration Board in December 1993 as to the state of the law with regard to the practice of psychotherapy in New South Wales, I was informed by a representative of the board that: "Psychotherapists are not registered in New South Wales. Anyone can practise." And that: "There are currently no moves afoot to introduce legislation, but that there may be moves in the future to bring

psychotherapy under the control of the Psychologists Registration Board."
I was also told that the scope of the existing legislation in New South
Wales basically covered the label 'psychologist', that is it constitutes a
title act. However, close reading of the relevant Act revealed that neither
'psychology' nor 'psychologist' are defined, but the use of the title 'psychologist' is restricted to those on the register *along with*:

> ... any name, initials, word, title, addition, symbol or description
> which, having regard to the circumstances in which it is taken or
> used:
> (i) indicates; or
> (ii) is capable of being understood to indicate; or
> (iii) is calculated to lead a person to infer,
> that the person practises psychology or is qualified to practise
> psychology.... (*Psychologists Act, 1989:* Clause 4)

Although not an actual practice act, given that 'psychologist' is not defined I interpret this legislation as going well beyond a simple title act and
leaving a great deal of discretionary power with the Psychology Board.

Most of the alternative therapists in Sydney that I discussed this with
seemed to be blissfully unaware of the actual state of the law regarding
their practice. Their understanding of the situation was similar to that con-
veyed to me by the Board spokesperson and they had not realised that
their statements and public descriptions of their practice might be deemed
illegal under existing law if the Board chose to exercise its considerable
discretion and judge their descriptions of their work as "capable of being
understood to indicate" a form of psychological practice.

The fact that the New South Wales Board has not so far applied the
law beyond protecting the actual title 'psychologist' reflects perhaps a
lack of perceived economic threat from 'fringe' therapists by conventional
psychologists/psychotherapists in New South Wales. On the other hand it
may be a consequence of the fact that the therapy scandal that has eclipsed
all others in New South Wales actually involved a highly credentialled
psychiatrist whose 'Deep Sleep Therapy' resulted in the death of at least
twenty-four of his patients. It took twenty-four years to bring him to book
- three years after his death (Bromberger & Fife-Yeomans, 1991). Not a

very good advertisement for the protective efficacy of Registration.

Queensland's *Psychologists Act, 1977* is similar in form to that in New South Wales in that practice as such is not restricted (except for the practice of hypnosis), and 'psychology' is not defined (though 'hypnosis' is) but advertising and using a "description of whatsoever nature" that indicates or "could be understood to indicate" that one is a psychologist are prohibited to the unregistered (Clause 28). Although 'psychology' (or 'psychological practice') is not defined under this act, a 'psychologist' is - as someone on the register (Clause 4).

In Western Australia the *Psychologists Registration Act, 1976* has a similar 'catch-all' form of 'description protection' and goes beyond that to prohibit "any branch of psychological practice" as well, without defining the latter. A psychotherapist who trained in London was, in 1993, taking legal proceedings against the Western Australia Psychologists Registration Board because they were challenging the legality of his practising under the title 'psychotherapist'. I do not know the outcome of this case but it illustrates the fact that in Western Australia 'psychotherapy' is regarded by the board as a form of psychological practice and under its jurisdiction and that it is willing to proceed against infringers.

The *Psychological Practices Act, 1973* of South Australia is primarily a title act with some specific "prescribed psychological practices", particularly personality and intelligence testing and hypnotism. I was not able to check whether this act has been supplemented, however the Act provides for subsequent regulations to be made by the Governor "as may be necessary or convenient for the purpose of giving effect to this Act or the objects thereof, including ... the practice of psychology and the conduct of such practice ..." (Clause 41).

Victoria led the way regarding the introduction of psychology legislation in Australia with the passing of: "An Act to provide for the Registration of Psychologists, the Protection of the Public from Unqualified Persons and certain Harmful Practices and for other purposes" (*Psychological Practices Act, 1965*) . The history of the Victorian legislation has interesting parallels with the history of early attempts to introduce psychotherapy legislation in the UK in that the Scientologists were the spark there also. The Anderson Report on Scientology referred to in Chapter 5 gave rise to the legislation in Victoria and also inspired legislation to specifically prohibit

Scientology in South Australia and Western Australia in 1968 and 1969 respectively.[1] The events in Victoria also illustrate the importance of 'fringe' practitioners maintaining an awareness of how legislation sponsored by established professional groups may put their practice outside the law or under the control of such professions. It also shows that protest can be effective in this regard, though it is better to do so beforehand rather than after!

> The *Psychological Practices Act, 1965* is quite an interesting piece of legislation. One suspects that its main aim was to out-law the practice of Scientology and that the registration of psy-chologists was simply a useful device to achieve that primary goal. The wording of the Act was consistent with such a dual purpose. It made explicit the prohibition against Scientology, defined the practice of psychology and then forbade any non-registered person from engaging in that practice. (Cummins, 1986:13)

However, shortly after the Act was proclaimed the Scientologists achieved legal status as a religion with the consequence that the clauses relating directly to their prohibition were repealed. This left in place only the reg-istration of psychologists on the basis of definition of their practice.

This truncated 1965 Act is still by and large in place in Victoria and so the legal position is that a practice act applies in that state (as of January 1994). Under Clause 2 of this legislation, "Psychological practice" includes:

> 2(a) the evaluation of behaviour or cognitive processes or per-sonality or adjustment in individuals or in groups through the interpretation of tests for assessing mental abilities aptitudes in-terests attitudes emotions motivation or personality characteris-tics;
> 2(b) the use of any method or practice calculated to assist per-sons or groups with adjustment or emotional or behaviour prob-lems in the areas of work family school or personal relationships;
> 2(c) the administration of any prescribed test or the use of any prescribed technique device instrument for assessing mental abili-

ties aptitudes interests attitudes emotions motivation or personality characteristics.... (*Psychological Practices Act, 1965*)

Clearly Clause 2(b) of this definition covers what many people would
refer to as psychotherapy. Clause 2(a) was obviously aimed at the Scientologists' infamous 'personality tests' and Clause 2(c) would encompass
the 'E-Meter'.

In the early 1980s the Victorian branch of the Australian Psychological Society proposed many changes to this Act, however not including any
change to the basic restriction of 'psychological practice' to registered
psychologists. A revised form of the Act was agreed with the Minister of
Health and all went smoothly until the Act was scheduled for a second
reading in September 1984.

Then all hell broke loose. Suddenly a wide variety of persons
engaged in 'therapies' of one kind or another came to realize the
implications of the new Act for their practices. Notwithstanding
the fact that the definition of psychological practice had simply
been carried over from the old Bill, these non-psychologists came
to realize that the Act *could conceivably* be used to proscribe
against such practices as counselling, dealing with adjustment
problems, motivating football teams, etc.. Their concerns were
further exacerbated by another carry-over from the old Bill; a
proscription against anyone but a registered psychologist (with
exceptions for medical and dental practitioners) engaging in the
practice of hypnotism which was defined [in the Act] as: "'Hypnotism' includes hypnotism, mesmerism, and any similar act or
process which produces or is intended to produce in any person
any form of induced sleep or trance in which susceptibility of
the mind of that person to suggestion or direction is increased or
intended to be increased but does not include hypnotism, mesmerism or any similar act or process which is self-induced" [*Psychological Practices Act, 1965* : Clause 2].

It became widely publicised and believed that under this
clause the Act could be used to regulate the teaching of Yoga,
relaxation techniques and meditation.

232

The upshot of all this was a general clamouring from many different sections of the public for the Act to be withdrawn. Its opponents included members of our own profession [psychology], other health care professions, the Scientologists (of course) and a loosely knit group of 'Alternative Therapists' who actually held a mass demonstration on the steps of Parliament House. The reporters covering this particular event had a field day by interviewing all manner of 'natural' therapists.

Their view, however, prevailed. The Minister withdrew the Act.... (Cummins, 1986:13)

So the proposed revision of the Act was withdrawn and amendments were drafted that would meet the criticisms. However this 'revision of the revision' has not yet been enacted either, and the 1965 Act is still essentially in force (as of January 1994) - although not by and large applied other than for protection of the title 'psychologist' (Bennett, A., 1994).

Appendix C

Registration in Canada
and
the Case of the Crucial Conjunction

Transformational counsellor ... personal growth consultant ... breath
therapist ... facilitator of emotional release work ... counselling as-
trologer ... nutritional counsellor ... rebirther ... colon therapist ...
metaphysical counsellor ... transformational therapist ... process oriented counsellor ... holistic bodyworker ... counsellor ...
*(Titles used by advertisers in Vancouver resource directories
"Common Ground" and "Shared Vision" 1994)*

British Columbia (BC) lies on the Pacific rim of Canada and is something
of a centre for healing and personal growth. As the 'California' of Canada
it has a long history of involvement with the human potential movement -
Fritz Perls moved here from Esalen in 1969 and Banyen Books, Canada's
major stockist of books oriented towards human potential and spiritual
matters, was founded in Vancouver in 1970. That a vigorous scene for
personal growth still flourishes there (albeit one prone more to the 'new
age' 'wafty' end of things than the emotionally expressive 'gutsy' end of
things) may be due in no small measure to the presence of the crucial
conjunction.

When, on a visit there in September 1994, I began to enquire into the
legal framework for the practice of psychotherapy or personal growth in
BC, I formed an initial view on reading the relevant legislation that a large
percentage of the practitioners there (many of whom called themselves
'counsellors' rather than, say, 'psychotherapists'), were in fact practising
outside the law in that they were not on the psychologist's register. This
impression was reinforced by the fact that, as in Australia, none of the

practitioners I spoke to appeared to have any direct knowledge of the legislation that was relevant to them. As I had been lead to expect by what I
had previously read about the legal situation in BC (Trebilcock & Shaul,
1982:275, 288), the pertinent legislation, the *Psychologists Act, 1979* (administered by the College of Psychologists of British Columbia), appeared
to indicate that a practice act was in force and one that covered most of
what could conceivably be construed as 'psychotherapy', 'counselling' or
'personal growth'. Moreover the Act specifically referred to 'psychotherapy' and 'counselling' as being included in the practice of psychology.
    The Act defines the "practice of psychology" as including:

    (a) the provision to individuals, groups, organizations or the
    public of any service involving the application of principles,
    methods, and procedures of understanding, predicting and influ-
    encing behaviour, including the principles of learning, percep-
    tion, motivation, thinking, emotion and interpersonal relation-
    ships;
    (b) the application of methods and procedures of interviewing,
    counselling, psychotherapy, behaviour therapy, behaviour modi-
    fication, hypnosis, research; or
    (c) the construction, administration and interpretation of tests
    of mental abilities, aptitudes, interests, opinions, attitudes, emo-
    tions, personality characteristics and the assessment or diagno-
    sis of behavioural, emotional and mental disorder for fee or
    reward, monetary or otherwise.... (*Psychologists Act, 1979*, Sec-
    tion 1)

Prohibitions under the Act include:

    (1) No person shall engage in or carry on the practice of psy-
    chology and represent himself as a psychologist, unless he is
    registered under this Act.
    (2) No person shall use, assume, or employ, or advertise or
    hold himself out under the title of a "registered psychologist" or
    "psychologist" or any affix or prefix or abbreviation of the title

235

as an occupational designation relating to the practice of psychology, unless he is registered under this Act....

(7) A person represents himself as a psychologist who, for a fee or reward, monetary or otherwise, acts, represents, holds himself out or advertises as a psychologist, and uses a title or description or words incorporating the word "psychology", "psychological" or "psychologist", or other terms implying training, experience or expertise as a psychologist. (ibid., Section 16)

This seemed to me to have pretty much sewn things up and yet numerous unregistered practitioners did seem to be able to practise without incurring the attention of the psychology board. I speculated that perhaps the board was inactive in this regard because these practitioners had not yet posed a significant threat to the economic interests of registered psychologists.

The mystery began to unravel when I talked to Dr. Edwin Kramer, the Registrar of the College of Psychologists who was adamant that the Psychologists Act was only a title act. A prohibition on the unregistered practice of the wide variety of activities that the Act defines as the practice of psychology is avoided by the presence of the crucial "*and*" in Section 16(1) of the Act. This "and" apparently has the effect that unregistered practice is only prohibited if the person *also* represents himself as a 'psychologist' as defined in Section 16(7) (Kramer, 1994). Whether or not the crucial "and" represents an error in the drafting of what was intended to be a practice act I do not know.

According to Dr. Kramer, on the basis of the Act, the board regards the unregistered use of any title with 'psych-' on the front, including 'psychologist', 'psychoanalyst' and 'psychotherapist', as an infringement that it would be justified in pursuing. (Perhaps for this reason few practitioners in the personal growth field use the title 'psychotherapist'.) As is so often the case psychiatrists are exempt and consequently able to call themselves 'psychologists', 'psychotherapists' or whatever, whether or not they have any training, experience or competence in such things.[1] Since 'counsellor' does not have 'psych-' on the front, unregistered practitioners are free to use that term. Dr. Kramer agreed that the distinction between 'counselling' and 'psychotherapy' was a contentious one, though in BC the relevant distinction is more the one between 'counselling' and 'clinical psychology'. He thought that the kinds of problems worked with were rather different and that counselling tended to be more focused on normal people looking for additional growth (ibid.).

To further illustrate the niceties of these terminological matters, Dr. Kramer pointed out that whilst in the view of the College you could not call yourself a 'psychothera*pist*' without being registered, it would be possible to be unregistered and yet say that you '*do* psychothera*py*' and use 'counsellor' as your title![2]

Since access to the register now involves a minimum academic requirement of a doctorate in psychology or similar (a doctorate is a research degree that has even less relevance to basic competence in this area than a typical bachelor's or master's degree), it would seem that the current vigour of the BC personal growth movement owes much to that crucial "and" in Section 16(1).

There are however new legal challenges looming on the horizon in the form of the *Health Professions Act, 1990*. This law is intended to regulate "health professions" not so far regulated by other legislation. Under the Act a "health profession" means:

> ... a profession in which a person exercises skill or judgement or provides a service related to
> (a) the preservation or improvement of the health of individuals, or
> (b) the treatment or care of individuals who are injured, sick, disabled or infirm.... (*Health Professions Act 1990*, Section 1)

Clearly (a) and (b) above could be interpreted to cover numerous activities of a counselling or personal growth nature. Moreover like the definition of a "health profession", the legislation is of a general enabling nature rather than specific to a particular form of work and the registration of a particular "health profession" does not require going through a full parliamentary process in each case but can be decided by cabinet. Furthermore, the designation of the health profession may amount to a title act and/or a practice act as recommended by the Health Professions Council and decided by cabinet (Morrison, 1994).

This Act is now in force, though as of September 1994, no professions are yet governed by it. However, a number of occupational associations have applied for designation, including those representing acupuncturists, art therapists - and counsellors. The Canadian Professional Counsellors Association has applied for "Registered Professional Counsellors" to be recognized as a designated health profession (Counsellor Training Institute, 1994).

Regarding Canada as a whole, as of September 1994, there is no federal legislation regulating psychology, psychotherapy or counselling. Such legislation is all on a provincial basis (Canadian Psychological Association, 1994b). All the Canadian provinces and the Northwest Territories have some form of statutory regulation of psychologists. Only the Yukon does not. The legislative instruments concerned are essentially title acts rather than practice acts. Usually a doctorate will be required for admission to the psychologists' register (Canadian Psychological Association, 1994a).

In Ontario the practice of psychology is regulated by the *Psychologists Act, 1991* which protects the title 'psychologist' and the act of diagnosis. The act of diagnosis is also restricted by the *Regulated Health Professions Act, 1991*. Hence in Ontario the practice of psychotherapy is unregulated as long as you don't use a protected title or diagnose (Ontario College of Psychologists, 1994).

As regards enforcement, the sanctions for infringement of the provincial legislation vary from the trivial, (Newfoundland), to the extensive, (Ontario), to the severe, (Nova Scotia - which allows six month prison sentences for infringement) (Kramer, 1994). In BC, the response to infringements is an injunction to discontinue followed by a court order if the infringement persists.

Appendix D

Self and Peer Assessment and Accreditation

However there is a further point that it is worth bringing into the whole 'Great Accreditation Debate'. This is that there is perhaps a very legitimate stance (epitomized perhaps by Jill Hall) that *no accreditation* is also OK. That there are ways perhaps to affirm, acclaim, attest, support, check on, discipline each other which do not involve accreditation or an accreditation process....

> *(Courtenay Young, Report on the Cambridge Conference, 1992:39)*

... co-counselling or re-evaluation co-counselling are DIY approaches to psychotherapy. They actively demystify and make openly and cheaply available much of the core knowledge from psychology about human functioning and the related strategies of personal development and transformation. Where in the designs for the new psychotherapy profession do they sit? Are they represented at all? If not, why not?

> *(Denis Postle and Jill Anderson, 1990:14)*

Self and peer assessment is something that happens a great deal informally, not least in the sense that fellow practitioners do not tend to refer clients to practitioners whose work they do not respect and nor for that matter do clients tend to recommend practitioners where their experience has been unsatisfactory.

As a more formal arrangement, its history is closely associated with the co-counselling movement (Heron, 1978) and it forms the basis of the assessment procedures of the Institute for the Development of Human Potential (IDHP) which is a decentralized organization with branches in various parts of the country. IDHP has developed very much within an educational/developmental model rather than a remedial/clinical one

(Hopkinson, 1991), and has eschewed involvement with UKCP. IDHP has been using self and peer assessment and accreditation in the ongoing and final assessment and accreditation of course participants and in the selection of course facilitators since the mid 1970s and has refined these procedures to a high degree (Eales, 1991). These procedures include peer assessment both in the presence and absence of the person being assessed and various structures such as 'rattle and shake', and 'devils advocate' to focus and balance the process. The final accreditation involves a formalized process of written self-assessment which is then revised in the light of peer feedback (ibid.).

The accreditation (Hogan would say certification) procedures of AHPP are said to be based on a self and peer assessment (AHPP, 1991b) but these bear little relation to those developed by IDHP, there being little about them that is face to face: "... The AHPP accredits behind closed doors and decides in secret." (Jones, 1991b). Moreover the need to fulfil UKCP criteria for AHPP accredited psychotherapists is antithetical to genuine self and peer assessment for that category of AHPP membership. (See also Heron, 1990:23 and Chapter 23.)[1]

Another forum in which alternative forms of accreditation have been explored was that provided by 'the Cambridge Conferences' organized by the Norwich Collective - the National Conference on Accreditation for Psychotherapists and Counsellors in 1991, attended by 85 people, and the second National Conference on the Dynamics of Accreditation in 1992, attended by about 40 people (Hall, J., 1992; Cannon & Hatfield, 1992; House, 1992; Young, 1992). This conference had been preceded by various other experiments in peer accreditation (Shohet, 1990:16; Shohet et al., 1991:31; House & Hall, 1991:33).

A proposal for a network of peer groups was floated by Cal Cannon and Sue Hatfield after the second Cambridge conference (Cannon & Hatfield, 1992:34) and more recently Nick Totton proposed the creation of a self and peer accredited network, a concept conceived in conjunction with Em Edmondson (Totton, 1994a:47; 1994b). The ensuing organization, the 'Independent Therapists Network',[2] is intended to be free from hierarchy and low on bureaucracy and to: "... offer an alternative model of accountability and validation to that of the UK Council for Psychotherapy: a model which actually makes use of what we know as therapists about human interaction ..." (Independent Therapists Network, 1994). The basis of the Network is a linking of small groups of therapists who vet and accredit the members of their own group: "The unit of membership will be a *group* of at least five practitioners who *know and stand by each other's work*. In joining as a group, they take responsibility for the other members of that group: for sorting out any complaints or problems around their work - or failing that for *jointly* being removed from membership of the Network. Each group would also have cross-linkages with other groups" (ibid.).

Recognizing that competence is not founded upon the number of hours of training or numbers of essays written there would be: "no distinction of more or less qualified or 'registered' members" (ibid.).

The Network does not seek to distinguish between different types of work, "... since we see a richly pluralistic and multi-skilled ecology as the ideal ..." (ibid.). Rather than a central code of practice, each peer group can create one appropriate to its activities.

This sort of practitioner validation through membership of a small group of peers is amongst the most flexible, practical and least detrimental arrangements for monitoring 'bad work' and is in fact similar to what is already quietly practised by groups of practitioners such as the members of the Open Centre in London. The proposed Network would go beyond this through the notion of cross linking with other groups for the purposes of support, 'oversight' and as part of the complaints procedure (Totton, 1994b). An administrative group would also be necessary in order to process membership and complaints (ibid.).

The Founding Conference of the Network, attended by over 60 people, took place in London in November 1994 at the Open Centre. As a result, working parties were set up to develop an administrative structure, a newsletter, and a public face for the Network (Totton, 1995).

(For further information about the network write to: The Independent Therapists Network (ITN), 326 Burley Road, Leeds, LS4 2NZ.)

Appendix E

Psychiatry, Psychotherapy
and Personal Growth

... What is known as medical education appears to me to be an arduous and circuitous way of approaching the profession of analysis. No doubt it offers an analyst much that is indispensable to him, but it burdens him with too much else of which he can never make use, and there is the danger of its diverting his interest and his whole mode of thought from the understanding of psychical phenomena....

(Sigmund Freud, 1927:102)

... The invention of major tranquillizers [in the 1950s] strengthened the claims being made about chemotherapy facilitating the 'open door' policy in mental hospitals and enabling patients to stay in the community. This myth, since still colluded with by all but the most honest academic psychiatrists, does not tally with what is known about the changing psychiatric population. Inpatient numbers began to drop *before* the introduction of the major tranquillizers (Scull, 1977; Busfield, 1986). None the less, the authoritative claims of biological psychiatry with its chemical solutions to personal problems went, once more, into the ascendency during a post-war period.

(David Pilgrim, 1990:6)

Throughout the world, the medical profession occupies a particularly powerful position in relation to the practice of, and provision for, psychotherapy. In the UK, although psychotherapy has not been made subject to statutory controls that favour the medical profession, psychiatry has the dominant role in relation to the provision of 'mental health' services in the NHS and, through the Special Membership of the Royal College of Psychiatrists and the Institutional Membership of the Association of University Teachers of Psychiatry (AUTP), the psychiatric profession has a powerful presence on the Governing and Registration Boards of UKCP.

Psychiatrists have a background that includes a full medical degree plus subsequent specialization. There are two areas in particular where their medical background is of special relevance to matters of the psyche - the diagnosis of underlying physical disease processes which may be manifesting as emotional and psychological phenomena and the application of physical and pharmaceutical treatments. In this latter case, except where the 'symptoms' are *known* to be caused by an organic process (rather than some assumed but as yet undiscovered 'chemical imbalance') their use of drug treatments is suppressive and little different in principle from the self-prescribed use of drugs such as alcohol and heroin - to 'anaesthetize the operation of life' (Callala Beach Emporium and Off-Licence, 1994). Indeed, many of the drugs that have subsequently become street drugs were first developed for use by the medical profession. For example, heroin was originally developed as a supposedly less addictive form of morphine (Wingate, 1972:206). Moreover, all too often the drugs that have been proffered by medical practitioners to allay the troubles of the mind (for example the barbiturates or the benzodiazepines such as Valium®) have subsequently proved to be addictive or have had other deleterious side-effects. Who knows what the future holds for fluoxetine (Prozac®)? "Systematic data concerning the addiction liability of Prozac® are not available ..." (Pagliaro, 1994). Despite this chequered history, drug treatments are zealously persisted with. This reflects a psychiatric predilection for approaches that support a biodeterministic world-view, the fact that drugs do often effectively suppress psychic pain (at a price), and the fact that a large proportion of medical research funding derives from the pharmaceutical industry - 71 per cent in the UK (*Focus*, 1995b:68). A general cultural enthusiasm for drugs also ensures that new "chemical solutions" will find a ready welcome. (See also Breggin, 1991/1993; Medawar, 1992; Richman, Frank & Mandler, 1987.)

Apart from the areas mentioned above, the medical training of a psychiatrist is expensive and not particularly relevant to much of the practice of psychotherapy, and even less so to the practice of personal growth work.[1]

Moreover, medical practitioners have real social power in that through the role of diagnostician they police the gateway to the 'sick role' and therefore to the patient's ability to 'sign-off' from personal and social responsibilities with the support of the state and, usually, family. The medically qualified are also in an especially powerful position *vis-à-vis* patients regarding the diagnosis of mental illness and choice of treatment since, under certain circumstances, they have the power to detain and treat without the patient's consent (to 'section' in UK parlance). In consequence, unlike a 'lay' psychotherapist, a psychotherapist who is also medically qualified has this extra measure of socially sanctioned power in the here-and-now. However, like the police, psychiatrists are also the in the 'front line' and often have to deal with difficult behavioural and violent situations involving people who are unwilling or unable to be self-responsible.

There is in fact generally little attention paid to training in psychotherapy in the typical psychiatric training (Sinason, 1994). Moreover, the medical model that is 'absorbed' along with the information during the course of a psychiatrist's background is very hard to think 'outside of' and therefore a psychiatric background can actually be counter-productive to the practice of 'growth oriented' psychotherapy or human potential work just as an allopathic medical background does not particularly make for a good acupuncturist or homoeopath. A different world-view is involved (Scheid, 1993).[2]

In countries where there is legislation to control the practice of psychology or psychotherapy, doctors in general, or psychiatrists in particular, will frequently be exempt from such controls. Moreover, a medical qualification will often be regarded as a necessary or preferred prerequisite for training as a psychotherapist.[3] On the basis of the discussions in this book, even where psychotherapy is regarded as a remedial treatment, that is as a medical model activity, there is little reason to believe that this favouring of medical qualifications is desirable or cost-effective.

History, inertia and current political power aside, whilst any particular individual psychiatrist may well have personal attributes and an outlook appropriate to the tasks, it is by no means clear that there is a cogent argument why the profession of psychiatry - a medical specialization - should occupy the dominant position with regard to the provision of 'mental health' services, rather than occupy a collaborative or supporting role.

Appendix F

Assessing Trainers -
Some Suggested Questions
for Prospective Trainees

There follows a brief (not comprehensive) list of questions for the inquisitive prospective trainee. In general, do not *assume* competence to train - seek information. Also bear in mind the information in this book about relevant and less relevant criteria for training environments and remember the relative importance of experience in practitioner competence by contrast with, say, academic background. You are likely to be asked why you want to train when seeking admission to a course but your motivation for doing so may or may not be seriously taken into account in the decision to admit. Scrutinize it for yourself, particularly if it is not the outcome of significant positive experience of the modality in question. Also don't forget that this is a personal business. Give due weight to your personal responses to those with whom you are contemplating training.

(1)   Who will actually be doing the training on the course? What was their training? What is the relationship between those who do the training and the directors of the course, if they are not one and the same? For example did those who will be doing the training actually train with the directors of the course? How long ago?
(2)   Since completing their own training, how much experience have the trainers had in the practice of the modality in which they will be training others? (In years and hours - "10 years experience" may mean say 3 hours a week for 10 years, or ten years ago for a year and then for the last 3 years or, 50 hours a week for the last 10 years).
(3)   Do all those who train on this course continue to practise (and if so how much) or do they just train?
(4)   How much experience of practice did those who set up this training organization have at the time of doing so?
(5)   Are prospective trainees required to have significant *prior* experi-

ence of the work in which they will be training or are people admitted to the course who have little or no direct personal experience of the work before undertaking the course?

(6)   During the course, are trainees required to be in therapy with someone approved by the trainers? Does this have to be with someone 'in house'? If so, how much experience have they had since being trained by the programme, assuming that they were? Also to what degree is the content of such sessions directly or indirectly a factor that may influence assessment by the trainers? For example, do the 'in house' practitioners also participate in any way in the running of the course?

(7)   If the choice of practitioner is not restricted to someone who is 'in-house', are there any other restrictions placed on the trainee's freedom of choice as to which practitioner to work with?

(8)   Do the trainers reserve the right to assess how such personal work is proceeding? If so, what actions may they take if dissatisfied?

(9)   What proportion of the course duration is devoted to:

(a) experiential work,

(b) the practical development of skills and

(c) work which is neither of these, such as theoretical presentation, study of appropriate literature, essay writing, etc.?

What degree of significance is allotted to academic work, as in (c), in the assessment of trainees?

(10)   What is the 'failure rate' of those who undertake this course? That is, what proportion of trainees fail to graduate and for what proportion of those is this a refusal on the part of the trainers to graduate them? What criteria have led/will lead to such a refusal?

(11)   What sort of support is available to graduates of this training programme? For example, is there a graduate practitioner organization and if so what sort of relationship is there between it and the training organization? What degree of autonomy does it have, if any? Does it have a say in any accreditation (i. e. certification) procedures?

(12)   How long does the training take, including accreditation, and what is the total cost, including the cost of all the required activities such as personal therapy and supervision of work with clients? Does the training organization take a percentage of any income derived from work with clients prior to accreditation? If so under what circumstances and how much?

Appendix G

Supervision - Who's in Charge?

Supervisor - overseer, foreman, manager, controller, superintendent, superior, director, chief, head, administrator; invigilator; *colloq.* boss, super, *Brit. colloq.* gaffer, *sl.* governor....
("The Readers Digest Oxford Complete Wordfinder", 1993)

Unfortunately, it has become the habit amongst psychotherapists to call this process of seeking to enlarge one's range and depth of understanding by the rather inappropriate term 'supervision'. This term is easily misunderstood as belonging to student days, and is often queried by tax inspectors. In other professions it is recognised that any practitioner needs to seek the opinion of another practitioner about some cases - not necessarily difficult ones, nor must the help be sought from a more senior practitioner. Two heads are better than one. Seeking an opinion is normal in all walks of life....
(Fanning, Pokorny & Hargaden, 1994:358)

The term 'supervision', from the medieval Latin: 'supervidere', meaning to: "over-see" or "see from above", is yet another word with general and common-sense understanding that has been taken up by psychotherapists and counsellors and redefined in a way that may have a modicum of 'etymological correctness' but which conflicts with everyday meanings (and other associated terms e.g. 'superior'). In everyday understanding its use indicates a hierarchical relationship in which the 'supervisor' has authority and responsibility for overseeing the work of the supervisee. As used in the 'therapy' world, 'supervision' is usually supposed to indicate a non-hierarchical relationship with a "benevolent and experienced other" (Ziehl, 1994c) which provides an external perspective, feedback and support for the practitioner's work with the client, can be "an enormously helpful gift" (ibid.) and in which the supervisor is not usually seen as being responsible *for* the practitioner's work with the client.

BAC has recognized the drawbacks arising from ambiguous use of the term 'supervision', particularly in terms of confusion between supervision and accountability to management and has attempted to promote 'consultative support' as an alternative term. However, according to Tim Bond its use is falling out of fashion because: "... although it avoids confusion arising from the use of 'supervision', it too generates potential confusion over the term 'consultant', which to many people is associated with expertise and status rather than independence ..." (Bond, 1993:154).

Kadushin (1976) proposed a distinction between 'supervision', where the supervisor carries some responsibility for the work of the supervisee and 'consultancy' where the responsibility for the work remains with the consultee (Hawkins, 1985:74). Retaining the term 'supervision', Peter Hawkins offers a distinction between 'consultancy supervision' and 'training supervision' (ibid.:75; Hawkins & Shohet, 1989).

UKCP has also recognized the problematic nature of the term 'supervision' and at one time suggested "continuing professional development" (Pokorny, 1990:5). However, the term 'supervision' is what is currently used in UKCP documents. A 'supervisor's report' is required prior to the accreditation of a psychotherapist by organizations such as AHPP in the Humanistic and Integrative Psychotherapy Section (AHPP, 1994b). In this case the supervisor clearly has an overseeing function.

The everyday understanding that 'supervision' involves a hierarchical relationship seems likely to hold sway in the US courts (see Chapter 21), and I doubt that the 'therapeutic' revision of meaning will make much headway against the inertia of public common-sense understanding of the term, especially when the 'therapists' themselves use it ambiguously.

Compulsory supervision of therapists is held out to the public as part of the 'protection of the public through registration' argument. As a consequence of the confusion discussed above, unless they are particularly 'savvy', members of the public may be mislead into assuming that an overseeing role is involved, whereas in practice the supervisor will rarely have had a direct experience of the practitioner's work and usually it is the practitioner who 'supervises' what is presented to the supervisor.

The basic notion of available sources of feedback, confrontation and support is one thing. However, if a requirement for supervision goes beyond that to specifying the *form* it should take, one should not discount the possibility that motivation for such a requirement may stem from the drive for professionalization and the business aspects of supervision and training since significant income potential is involved (see also Chapter 18).

'Case' Notes

Introduction: The Emperor's Wardrobe

1. *Self & Society* Vol. 18 No. 1 (Jan. 1990).
2. Courtenay Young for example sought to "correct some of the misapprehensions that are still floating about", complained about being "lambasted" through the pages of *Self & Society,* called for an end to the "bullshit", reassured us that UKCP is: "resisting strongly any enforced academic bias" and urged people not to get: "too paranoid about the process of change that is happening" (Young, 1991).

   John Rowan sought to correct some of the "misinformation", opined that: "I don't want anyone slagging it off [what UKCP stands for]", cited the "virulent form" of the criticism and sought to reassure people that UKCP is not a very formal and hierarchical set-up by referring to the fact that: "... Michael Pokorny habitually wears a rugby shirt when chairing the formal sessions of the conference" (Rowan, 1991).

   These reactions had an air about them reminiscent of the hurt and shock of someone in receipt of angry ingratitude from an elderly person they have helped across a road which he or she had no wish to traverse. [See also Jill Hall's response to John Rowan (Hall, 1991).]

Notes to Section I

Chapter 1: The Terminology of Regulation
1. As stated in the Preface, emphasis in quotations is in *italics* if present in the original and in ***bold italics*** if added by myself.

Chapter 2: Some Stated Justifications for a Psychotherapy Register - and Some Refutations

1. If we really want to remedy disorder in the field, something like the proposals in Chapter 26 is more 'in order'.

2.   See also the discussion between Martin Jelfs and David Jones: "Are Therapists Dentists?" *(Self & Society,* 1992:46-47).

Chapter 3: The European Bogeyman

1.   The European Economic Community (EEC) officially became the European Community (EC) when the Treaty of European Union (the Maastricht Treaty signed in February 1992) came into force in November 1993. Only since then has it been legally correct to refer to the European Community (Cuthbert, 1994:89-91). Unlike the European Community which has a legal personality created by the Treaty of Rome (Article 210 EC) and merely underwent the aforementioned official change of name under Maastricht (Article G(1) TEU), the European Union (EU) is not a legal entity and only operates through the institutions of the Community (ibid.). "The European Union is an umbrella term which covers three separate areas or 'pillars': the existing European Communities' structures and laws; intergovernmental co-ordination in matters of foreign policy and common external defence; and political intergovernmental co-operation in internal affairs such as criminal justice and policing, immigration and rights of asylum" (O'Neill & Coppel, 1994:6). Confusingly however, since Maastricht, the media and politicians have taken to referring to the European Union (EU) as though it were the legal 'European entity', rather than merely *including* the legal entity, just as they referred to the EEC as the EC before it became so. Furthermore, 'EC' has also sometimes been used as an abbreviation for the European Commission. For the sake of clarity in this 'transitional phase' (in the understanding of many of us, that is) I will in the main refer to the European Community/Union - combining both official and commonly used titles for the 'European entity'.

2.   SEPLIS - Société Européene des Professions Libérales Indépendantes et Sociales - is an organization which the European Association for Psychotherapy (EAP) is considering joining and which has: "considerable leverage with the European Commission" (UKCP, 1994). A representative of the Commission informed me that they have had discussions with various professional associations (including EAP). The Commission is happy to exchange views with all of them. Some are more representative than others, but none have any particular legal recognition or privileged status at the Commission (European Commission, DG 15/E/2, 1995).

3.   EC Directives are binding on Member States as to the result to be achieved,

'Case' Notes

but leave the choice of form and methods to the national authority. EC Regulations do not leave such discretion to the national authorities and are directly applicable without national legislative mediation.

4. The Maastricht Treaty does not materially affect the existing rights of economically active citizens such as the right of establishment in member countries and the right to offer a service or practise a profession (Cuthbert, 1994:92). The fact that the Treaty has the official title Treaty of European Union and was signed in 1992, the same year by which the European 'common market' was intended to be established under the Single European Act, may go some way to account for the 'paranoia' regarding '1992' amongst those not familiar with the Maastricht Treaty's provisions. That is, most of us.

5. See Notes 1 and 4 above.

6. "The Directive [89/48/EEC] also covers cases of 'indirect' regulation by a professional body which enjoys a special form of recognition by the State, which has responsibilities for upholding standards of professional conduct, and which confers on its members a professional title, designatory letters or other form of status. This definition refers in particular to the chartered professional bodies in the UK [this includes the British Psychological Society] and their equivalent in the Republic of Ireland. These bodies will be obliged to accept as full members, professionals from other Member States who meet the requirements of the Directive" (Commission of the European Communities document, 3.90). Directive 89/48/EEC is complemented by Directive 92/51/EEC which entered into force in June 1994 and covers all other levels of occupational diplomas, that is, those not at a university level (European Commission, DG15/E/2, 1995). For more on indirect regulation, see Chapter 20.

7. Regarding the area of concern for the Commission, that is the facilitation of migration, if the psychotherapist is also a doctor, the clear sectoral directive for medical practitioners dating from 1976 applies. If the psychotherapist is also a psychologist the Mutual Recognition Directive 89/48/EEC applies (European Commission, DG15/E/2, 1993)

8. Note the parallel with the situation *within* the UK - unwarranted fears of governmental legislative initiatives served as a recruiting officer for UKCP, and the more 'united' the 'profession' appears to be in consequence, the more likely is it that the government might eventually respond to its calls for legislation (see Chapter 2).

9. For more on EAP, see Note 2 above and Note 4, Chapter 8.

251

10. The Maastricht Treaty holds that the Community: "is to conduct its activities on the basis of 'an open market economy with free competition' (Cuthbert, 1994:91).

11. However, a new law is under consideration that would once again reverse this trend if enacted (Ziehl, 1994b). See also Note 2 Chapter 8.

12. As will be evident from the discussion in Chapter 6, the training criteria that UKCP is promoting appear to be designed to be compatible with the European Commission's requirements for recognition of diplomas incorporated in the Mutual Recognition Directive 89/48/EEC.

Chapter 4: The Hidden Agenda of Professions

1. Not to be outdone, the Institute of Plumbers has long campaigned for statutory registration of plumbers in the UK (Warne, 1993:14).

2. See Chapter 5 regarding the American Medical Association and the 'threat' from Scientology. See also Peter Breggin's comments on the 'psychopharmaceutical complex' (Breggin, 1991/1993). For historical background on the rise to power of the medical profession see Clark & Pinchuck (1984), Inglis (1980) and Kett (1968).

Chapter 6: The Nature of UKCP

1. In the Australian State of Victoria, the *Psychological Practices Act, 1965* specifically refers to membership of the British Psycho-Analytic Society (a prime mover behind the Sieghart Report) as grounds for admission to the register of psychologists - apparently without the need for a psychology degree. Victoria was the first Australian state to introduce psychology legislation in response to the Scientology scare. See Appendix B for further information about the Australian legislation and Pilgrim (1990) and Heron (1990) for more about the history and politics of the UK scene.

2. Charlatans deliberately dupe, whereas quacks misguidedly believe that they are suitably qualified to offer the service in question (Hogan, Vol. 1, 1979:262; Jameson, 1961).

3. According to Whiz Collis, on retiring from the Chair of UKCP at the 1995 UKCP conference, Emmy van Deurzen-Smith: "... urged a more democratic way of operating within UKCP. Our new Chair is Digby Tantam from the PPS [Psychoanalytic & Psychodynamic Psychotherapy Section], who was elected in preference to Ken Evans from HIPS who

also stood. Digby [a Fellow of the Royal College of Psychiatrists] then spoke of the unlikelihood of the conference being as involved in the detailed running of UKCP as previously, which immediately filled me with fear for Emmy's wish for more democracy!" (Collis, 1995b:45).

4. In 1984, with approximately 2,800 on the register, each registrant paid £25 so about £70,000 was derived from that source. This was in addition the income from fees paid by the 67 Member Organizations (approximately £26,800 per year at 1994 rates) and from other sources such as sales of publications (including the register) and from charitable donations and grants (UKCP, 1994:4-5). At the 1995 AGM, the fee for inclusion on the register was raised to £40 per registrant per year: "... mainly to pay for the lobbying for a statutory status, and to fund the external relations with the media, where work is going on to change the image of psychotherapy ..." (Collis, 1995b:45).

Chapter 8: Comparisons with Other Countries

1. Actually, Switzerland has twenty cantons and six half-cantons.
2. The situation regarding statutory regulation in the European Community/Union is complex and the difficulties of getting accurate and complete information about all the Member States are formidable. Even DG15/E/2, the relevant unit of the European Commission, has not yet been able to obtain exact information for the whole Community. Note that the whole debate in the UK about 'European pressure' has occurred in a state of widespread ignorance, about both the role of the Commission and EC law and the actual status of psychotherapy in European countries.

    According to a 1993 study for the European Parliament: "In most Member States [that is the twelve countries that constituted the Community at that time] there is no recognition of psychotherapy as a distinct profession, but [only as] a form of therapy" (European Parliament, 1993). In January 1995, Austria, Finland and Sweden joined the Community, making a total of fifteen Member States. As it happens, all three of these new Member States have some form of legal recognition of psychotherapy as a profession but it is still the case that Member States which have legal recognition of psychotherapy as a distinct profession are in the minority.

    The information which follows is based on the study for the European Parliament mentioned above, along with information supplied by the European Commission (DG15/E/2) which was derived from a February 1995 meeting of the committee of national representatives that assists the Commission with the management of Directives 89/48/EEC and 92/51/EEC. Information is also from other sources where cited. All this information is by way of illustration only. It illustrates the ambiguous status of psychotherapy in Europe (and the ambiguous nature of the activity itself) and should not be relied upon in particular cases without confirmation in the state concerned. The representative of DG15/E/2 was at particular pains to impress upon me that the accuracy and completeness of their information could not assured. In what follows, it is often not clear whether title or practice acts apply in those countries where statutory regulation of psychotherapy does appear to exist. Moreover, even where psychotherapy does not appear to be directly regulated, indirect regulation via access to third party payments may well occur.

Austria - Psychotherapy is a quite heavily regulated profession. Only registered psychotherapists can practise psychotherapy [i.e. a practice act applies?]. Doctors are exempt and may practise psychotherapy without registration. Registration requires a qualification in psychology or medicine and subsequent specific training in psychotherapy. (DG15/E/2, 1995). According to David Boadella (1991:38), the Austrian legislation, which came into force in 1990 [or 1991? (Evans, 1994)], superseded an older medical law which restricted the practice of psychotherapy to doctors (see Chapter 26). The new law allows members of ten professions (albeit limited to a few chosen specialities) access to psychotherapy training (duration approximately 3,200 hours). Boadella indicates that the law may be a title act rather than a practice act (ibid.:40).

Belgium - Until 1992, only psychiatrists could practise. Since then, psychologists and psychoanalysts also practise (European Parliament, 1993). The profession of psychotherapy is not regulated. The profession of psychology (or clinical psychology) is regulated. (DG15/E/2, 1995).

Denmark - DG15/E/2 (1995) understands that psychotherapy is regulated and requires specific training. However, the 1993 study for the European Parliament concluded that psychotherapy is not regulated by statute, a view confirmed by the Danish Ministry of Health (1995).

Finland - Psychotherapy became a regulated profession very recently. A psychotherapist must be a psychologist and have had further specific training. Doctors may or may not be exempt. (DG15/E/2, 1995).

France - The practice of psychotherapy is totally unregulated (European Parliament, 1993); (DG15/E/2, 1995).

Germany - It is illegal to practise psychotherapy unless you are a psychiatrist, medically qualified with a specialized training in psychotherapy, a clinical psychologist, a Diplom psychologist with a Heilpraktiker licence, or a 'Heilpraktiker' (health practitioner). Licensing as a Heilpraktiker provides an alternative to the conventional academic routes. Traditionally, Heilpraktiker had to learn enough medical knowledge to be able to detect certain conditions and and refer the case to a doctor. The Heilpraktiker system has recently been liberalized due to a January 1993 court case which successfully challenged the need for medical knowledge as a prerequisite to practise as a psychotherapeutic health practitioner - consequently there is now a special category of psychotherapeutischer heilpraktiker, who is exempt from the medical knowledge part of the examination before licensing. However, there are variations between the sixteen different Länder (federal counties) in Germany and only the rules for payment by health insurance, both private and public, are nationwide so far. A new law under consideration would standardize legal requirements nationwide and increase restrictions if passed (Ziehl, 1994b).

Greece - There are no legal provisions concerning psychotherapy (European Parliament, 1993). A recognized profession does not exist. Generally, it is doctors who practise psychotherapy (DG15/E/2, 1995).

Ireland - As in the UK psychotherapy is unregulated. There is no register and anyone can advertise himself/herself as a psychotherapist (European Parliament, 1993); (DG15/E/2, 1995).

Italy - A 1989 law stipulates that the practice of psychotherapy is limited to those with a degree in medicine or psychology plus at least four years training at an approved institution (European Parliament, 1993). The legislation constitutes a title act. Only people with the above background can use the title 'psychotherapist' (DG15/E/2, 1995).

Luxembourg - Psychotherapy is unregulated and there is no national register of psychotherapists. The information is ambiguous as to what happens in practice: psychiatrists are regarded as psychotherapists but psychologists also practise as psychotherapists (European Parliament, 1993). Only doctors (psychiatrists or otherwise) can do psychotherapy. Not even psychologists can do psychotherapy (DG15/E/2, 1995).

Netherlands - A 1986 law established a register of psychotherapists. Access to the register is restricted to those with a medical degree or a recognized doctoral degree in psychology or social sciences or a doctoral degree in another subject if the first degree was in a recognized social science discipline. In addition a least 50 hours specific training is required and an interview by a panel. Registration is *not* (yet) mandatory, but only registered psychotherapists are eligible for health insurance reimbursement and referral by medical practitioners (European Parliament, 1993). Registration will become mandatory in a year or so and will require basic training as a doctor or psychologist followed by specific training of two and a half years. Psychiatrists and clinical psychologists are exempt from this latter requirement (DG15/E/2, 1995).

Portugal - There are no legal provisions concerning psychotherapy (European Parliament, 1993). Psychotherapy is unregulated. Usually clinical psychologists will be the ones who practise psychotherapy though doctors probably do so also. In Portugal, clinical psychologists and psychologists are two separate professions rather than one being a specialization of the other as in the UK (DG15/E/2, 1995).

Spain - Psychotherapy is not recognized as a separate profession and is normally carried out by psychiatrists and psychologists who undergo six years of study, followed by four years of practice to gain their qualifications. However, anyone with a diploma from a correspondence course can set up a private practice (European Parliament, 1993). Psychotherapy is not regulated in any way (DG15/E/2, 1995).

Sweden - A profession of psychotherapy exists and is regulated at the level of title. A 'psychotherapist' must be a doctor with a psychiatric qualification or a psychologist and have had an additional three years specific training in psychotherapy (DG15/E/2, 1995).

United Kingdom - There is no statutory registration of psychotherapists. Anyone, even without specific training, may set him/herself up as a psychotherapist (European Parliament, 1993); (DG15/E/2, 1995).

3. According to the study for the European Parliament cited above, as of November 1993, eligibility for reimbursement of fees for psychotherapy under health insurance schemes in European Community/Union countries was as follows (cautions as in Note 1 above apply here also):

Belgium - Psychiatrists only (partial reimbursement).

Denmark - Psychiatrists are reimbursable.

France - Psychiatrists (partial reimbursement).

Germany - Psychiatrists, psychologists, and doctors with training in psychotherapy are eligible. [A Heilpraktiker is also eligible (Ziehl, 1994b).]

Greece - No reimbursement (needs verification).

Ireland - No reimbursement (needs verification). [Reimbursement is available if the psychotherapist is a clinical psychologist in the public sector (DG15/E/2, 1995).]

Italy - Reimbursement is available if the psychotherapy is provided by a medical practitioner (needs verification).

Luxembourg - Psychiatrists (partial reimbursement).

Netherlands - Registered practitioners are reimbursable.

Portugal - No reimbursement (needs verification).

Spain - No reimbursement.

United Kingdom - [Psychotherapy is to some extent available under the NHS - by psychiatrist or clinical psychologist - or from others under medical patronage. Since 1990, GPs have been eligible for reimbursement for the fees of counsellors etc. employed in their practices (Harris, 1994). See Chapter 20.]

4.   Regarding European countries outside the EC/EU, in *Norway* it appears that psychotherapy is not a recognized profession and the use of the title 'psychotherapist' is unrestricted (DG15/E/2, 1995). However, Sharaf (1983), claims that Norwegian therapists are still bedevilled by a licensing requirement stemming from a royal decree issued when Wilhelm Reich was there. *Iceland* is an interesting case since psychotherapy is unregulated but *no one* can use the title 'psychotherapist' (DG15/E/2, 1995).

    Practitioners from European countries outside the EC, such as Austria (which joined the EC in January 1995), Switzerland and Hungary were amongst the prime movers behind the European Association for Psychotherapy (EAP) which was founded in 1990 to promote the development of psychotherapy as a discipline independent of psychiatry and psychology. UKCP has joined this body (Evans, 1994).

5.   The legal systems in much of continental Europe are derived from statute based, 19th-century civil law. The main influence on this has been the Napoleonic code, the French civil code enacted in 1804. By contrast, common law, also known as Anglo-American law, is a body of customary law that has evolved on the basis of judicial decisions and precedents.

6.   For another example of this effect, see Note 2, Chapter 28.

Chapter 12: Licensing and Psychotherapy - Definitions and Boundaries

1.   Freud was, of course, himself medically qualified and practised psychoanalysis from his doctor's surgery. He believed that psychoanalytic theory

(though not the practice) should be regarded as a part of medicine and that despite the importance of early childhood experience in psychoanalytic theory, he believed that most neurotic and psychotic disorders would ultimately be found to have organic causes (Hogan, Vol. 1, 1979:15). The association between psychoanalysis and medicine allowed the former to attain prestige it would not otherwise have gained: "It is generally agreed that the introduction and entrenchment of the concept of mental health as part of the general health-disease model is due to Freud" (Macklin, 1973:53).

2. According to the President Elect of the European Association for Counselling (EAC), counselling and psychotherapy are not differentiated in many European countries (Collis, 1994b). This has inspired Whiz Collis to wonder whether there needs to be an EAC if counselling doesn't exist as a separate entity in Europe as a whole (Collis, 1994a).

Chapter 13: Licensing and Psychotherapy - Protecting the Public from Harm

1. For example, the survey of research into individual psychotherapy by Barkham (1990) refers to the 'no-treatment control' group, the 'placebo' group, 'spontaneous remission', the 'dose-effect curve'and the 'dysfunctional' group (i.e. clients as opposed to the 'normal population').

2. The MMPI is the Minnesota Multiphasic Personality Inventory.

3. An example is the case of the hypnotherapist whose sexual assault on a woman patient in London in 1993 led to calls for regulation. The *Time Out* article mentioned (Pepinster, 1993) cited it as just the latest headline example of the sexual abuse of clients by therapists thus demonstrating the need for more regulation. Many newspapers made similar calls for registration. What tended to get lost in the uproar was the fact that this man was actually to be prosecuted under existing law for the sexual assault (which took place without consent under hypnosis) and for falsely claiming to be a 'doctor'. (*Guardian, Times, Daily Mail*, 10 Apr. 1993). It is worth mentioning, as a corrective to the media stereotype of the sexually predatory therapist, that apparently the more common situation is that of patients pursuing the therapist/psychiatrist for sexual contact (Holmes & Lindley, 1989:157).

4. It seems that some of these relationships have prospered despite the context of their initial meeting. Eight per cent of those psychologists who

had engaged in sexual relations with a patient were now married to or in a committed relationship with the patient (Garrett, 1994:445). Peter Rutter has also indicated that it is not beyond the realms of possibility for a healthy intimate relationship to develop between people who have met in this type of professional context (Gale, 1990:10).

Chapter 14: Licensing and Psychotherapy - Qualifications, Standards and the Requirements of Entry to the Occupation

1. Access to the British Psychological Society's register of 'Chartered Psychologists' requires an approved Honours Degree plus a further three years of approved training and supervised experience. (BPS, 1993a). Junior clinical psychologists in the NHS would therefore have had the above background and would require a further two years professional experience before becoming a senior clinical psychologists. For clinical psychologists to become specialists in psychotherapy, that is: "fully independent practitioners within a specified model of psychotherapy" (Kosviner, 1994:297) requires a minimum of three to four years further training in the psychotherapy concerned, bringing the grand total to: "a minimum of twelve years of professional training, including a minimum of eight to nine years of psychotherapy training" (ibid.).

2. For an idea of the costs of pursuing 'higher' standards with no proven relationship to public benefit and safety, see Note 9, Chapter 23.

Chapter 17: Practitioner Selection and the Perils of Transference

1. See for example, Hogan (1979), Holmes & Lindley (1989), Russell (1981/1993), Smith, (1993), Feltham & Dryden (1993:150).

2. The notion of a 'fear of freedom', was explored by Wilhelm Reich in the 1930s during the rise of Fascism in Europe (Reich, 1950, 1972) and borrowed, in part, by Erich Fromm for his book of the same name (1942). Reich stated that: "in those with neurotic character structures [i.e. most people] there is at the same time *fear of freedom* and *fear of responsibility (pleasure anxiety)*" (Reich, 1950:255).

   David Boadella explains Reich's position as follows: "... conflicting with the urge for change, the longing for improved conditions and the hunger for freedom, was a positive *fear of freedom*, which led people to identify in an emotionally dependent way on a movement which promised freedom on their behalf in a paternalistic way. For Fascism to succeed it required, therefore, to appeal precisely to the irrational, mystical and emotionally infantile elements in people, and to reinforce their need to cling to the authority-figures who promised a 'new life' " (Boadella, 1973:89).

Elizabeth Tilden, a psychiatrist, has made a study of cults which involve apocalyptic beliefs that have led to mass suicides/killings (as at Jonestown, Guyana, and Waco, Texas). In her view such events were the outcome of people searching for a powerful mother and father who will take charge of their life, and take away the need for individual decision-making, enabling them thereby to escape from the pains of the world and attain eternal bliss by so doing. She regarded them as forms of mass delusion (Tilden, 1994).

Chapter 18: The Training Business and the Business of Training

1. Aveline cites Auerbach and Johnson (1977) as a reference for this.
2. See Note 9, Chapter 23 for details of the inflating costs of training in the humanistic area.

Chapter 19: Carving up the Field and Doing the NVQs

1. The NVQ in counselling is due to be published in 1995 (Davis, 1995:49).

Chapter 20: Third Party Payments and 'de facto' Regulation

1. See Note 1, Chapter 14 on the professional background of clinical psychologists and Note 1, Appendix E on that of psychiatrists and consultant psychotherapists.
2. See Note 3, Chapter 8.

Chapter 21: The Codes of Practice of 'Defensive Psychotherapy'

1. "Lieberman (1978, 1970) believes that most professional codes are actually designed to protect the profession more than the public....." (Hogan Vol. 1, 1979:332).
2. Compare this situation with Austria, for example, where diagnosis has to be confirmed by a doctor and lay psychotherapists are at risk of being sued if they practise without medical supervision (Collis, 1994b:6-7).

Notes to Section II

Chapter 23: Humanistic Psychology Joins in - the Humanistic and Integrative Psychotherapy Section of UKCP

1. In *Ordinary Ecstasy,* first published in 1976 (with second edition in 1988), John Rowan describes humanistic psychology as: "interested in personal growth, existential choice and the fulfilment of human potential" and as: "... not just a new brand of psychology to set side by side on the shelves with all the old brands. It is a whole different way of looking at psychological science. It is a way of doing science which includes love, involvement and spontaneity, instead of systematically excluding them. And the object of this science is not the prediction and control of people's behaviour, but the liberation of people from the bonds of neurotic control, whether this comes from outside (in the structure of our society) or from inside" (Rowan, 1988:xii-3). If this is what the 'mainstream' is like now, I've obviously been out of it too long!

2. Many human potential modalities had roots in previous psychotherapies, however the point is that derivations from those approaches were, in the human potential movement, refocused on potential rather than remedial action and on 'ordinary people' rather than those classified as 'unwell' (see Chapter 25).

3. In other countries, for example Australia and Canada, terms such as 'humanistic psychology' or 'humanistic psychotherapy' are rarities in the growth movement. (See Chapter 26 and Appendices B and C.)

4. In 1994, the member organizations of the Humanistic and Integrative Psychotherapy Section were: Association of Humanistic Psychology Practitioners (AHPP); Bath Counselling & Psychotherapy Courses; The Boyesen Training Centre; British Psychodrama Association (BPA); Centre for Counselling & Psychotherapy Education; Chiron Centre for Holistic Psychotherapy; Creative Counselling Centre; The Gestalt Centre; Gestalt Psychotherapy Training Institute; Institute of Psychosynthesis; Institute of Transactional Analysis; Karuna Institute; metanoia Psychotherapy Training Institute; The Minster Centre; Psychosynthesis & Education Trust; Regent's College School of Psychotherapy & Counselling; Re-Vision; Sherwood Psychotherapy Training Institute; Stockton Psychotherapy Training Institute (Pokorny, 1994:518).

5. 'Clinical' means: "of or pertaining to the sick bed", and is derived from

261

the ancient Greek, 'kline' meaning "bed, sick-bed" (*Shorter Oxford English Dictionary*, 1973). Clinical language is also creeping into and becoming more commonplace in humanistic circles generally. Publicity for the 1994 AHP(B)/AHPP conference for example featured a workshop on working with "obsessive/compulsive disorder".

6. Total AHPP membership for 1995 numbers 157. Of these, 100 are full members (73 of whom are UKCP registered). The remainder consist of 5 affiliates and 52 associates (Collis, 1995a:45). Associates are people working towards qualification for full membership (for example trainees) and thus, if current ratios are sustained, most of these will eventually become UKCP registered also.

7. In 1991, AHPP was said to favour legal protection of the title 'registered psychotherapist' rather than 'psychotherapist' (AHPP, 1991a:37).

8. See Note 4, above.

9. In 1994, AHPP increased its criteria for accrediting a psychotherapy training to include 900 hours of 'tutor' contact time (Forrester, 1994) as required by the criteria for membership of the Humanistic and Integrative Psychotherapy Section (HIPS) of UKCP (UKCP, 1993j:3). Logging the accreditation requirements of HIPS gives an idea of just how expensive humanistic training is becoming under the auspices of UKCP. Training must be with a "recognised and approved course" and last for a *minimum* of three years part-time including the 900 hours of tutor contact referred to above. This 900 hours excludes any prerequisites for entry to the course, personal therapy, personal study time or peer group work. In addition to the three years of training, two years of supervised practice with clients is required, including approximately 450 hours of client contact with a recommended initial supervision ratio of 1:6 (ibid.). Adding the cost of training, personal therapy (a training requirement), and supervision, the cost of a typical UKCP humanistic psychotherapy training may now total in the order of £10-20,000, not counting the academic prerequisites. Whilst some income may be derived from clients during the two years of supervised practice, the training organization may well take a percentage of this, especially if they have been the source of client referral.

10. Other titles that come to mind include, 'Association for Human Potential' (AHP), 'Association for Human Potential Practitioners and Clients' (AHPPC); 'Human Potential Practitioners and Clients Forum or Fellowship' (HPPCF); 'Human Potential Practitioners and Clients Network' (HPPCN); 'Human Potential Network' (HPN). Although not focused on

human potential work specifically, the Independent Therapists Network (ITN), which was formed in 1994, looks set fair to have the makings of a more humanistic alternative. See Appendix D. See also Chapter 26 on 'humanistic psychology' and 'humanology'.

It makes sense to me to try to include clients as well as practitioners in such organizations and to harness the support of the numerous clients who have found value in humanistic psychology and the human potential movement. At the very least their voices could lend numerical support to defend those activities in the event of antipathetic political moves. Let us hear from the satisfied customers! Much emphasis has been placed on the need for complaints procedures etc. but satisfaction, appreciation and acknowledgement deserve a platform too. (See also Chapter 29.)

Chapter 24: Human Potential Work and Psychotherapy - Ambiguous Terminology and the Right to Practise

1. The therapeutes were the attendants of the cult of Asklepios and served the god Asklepios by carrying out the prescribed ritual in the Asklepieion or sanctuary (Meir, 1967).
2. A further example is the term 'psychosis'. For the ancient Greeks 'psychosis' meant the 'principle of life', 'animation', 'to give soul or life to' - rather than 'derangement' (*Shorter Oxford English Dictionary,* 1973)
3. See also Chapter 26, especially the discussion of the term 'therapy'.
4. Bill Swartley suggested the term 'humanology' - the science of becoming fully human (Swartley, 1971). Other more cumbersome terms that are used include: 'human potential work', 'personal growth work', and the practise of 'personal development', 'self-development' or 'self-realization'. Oswald Schwarz suggested 'psychogogy' meaning 'education of the psyche' (Schwarz, 1951) and Bugental suggested 'ontogogy' meaning 'education for being' (Bugental, 1965) [both cited by Maslow, (1971:53; 1968:38)]. Can any would-be copywriter dream up something better? I myself favour 'human potential work' or 'humanology' for reasons explained in Chapter 26.
5. I am grateful to Juliana Brown for coming up with this imagery.
6. An interesting historical aside is that Wilhelm Reich was prompted to redefine his work as 'Vegeto-Therapy' when banned from practising psychoanalysis by the king of Norway (Boadella, 1991:34).

Chapter 25: Human Potential Work and Psychotherapy - a Subtle but Important Boundary

1. As Ken Wilber has commented on the gullibility of some of those who became involved with new age trends: "The New Age folks try to come straight from the heart, thus bypassing the obstruction known as their brains" (quoted in Ingram, 1987:49). However, "in pursuit of personal growth there is no need to lose your mind" (McGrath, 1984:75).

   I am convinced that such people are in fact suffering from an as yet undocumented psychiatric condition - 'gulliboia' which is related to 'paranoia' but the inverse thereof and of undiscovered aetiology. Unquestioning acceptance of the medical model and indeed of the claims of psychotherapy registration aficionados can be take as other tell-tale signs, albeit of the subacute condition - 'gulliboid personality disorder'.

2. The different 'models' (or paradigms) referred to involve different worldviews, different ways of looking at and interpreting the world. Thus the medical model is not medicine as such, that is medicine as a discipline, but rather the world-view, the axioms, the assumptions implicit in medicine which may be applied elsewhere as a metaphor. The perennial pitfall is to confuse the model with reality rather than approach it as a viewpoint on, or representation of, reality. The less conscious you are of the metaphors that you are using, the more likely you are to confuse the 'map' with the 'territory', to use Korzybski's metaphors (Korzybski, 1933). See Chapter 13 and Appleyard (1992), Capra (1975), Grof (1985) and Lonie (1991b) for more on the Newtonian-Cartesian world-view.

3. Psychiatry's dominance in this area was in part the result of early successes in the application of the medical model to the treatment of some mental disturbances that *did* have organic aetiology, such as general paralysis of the insane (GPI) due to tertiary syphilis. However despite these early successes: "the medical approach to psychiatry has failed to find specific organic aetiology for problems vexing the absolute majority of its clients" (Grof, 1985:317) and: "For major mental illness classifications, none of the components of the medical model has been demonstrated: cause, lesion, uniform and invariate symptoms, course, and treatment of choice" (Scheff, 1974). The medical model of diagnosis simply does not work for most of the conditions that psychiatry addresses.

4. Many such 'disorders' are cited in the *Diagnostic and Statistical Manual of Mental Disorders* (DSM) which is modelled on the *International Clas-*

sification of Diseases (ICD) (see also Chapter 20). A useful test for medical terminology and diagnostic categorization is the 'grandmother test': Does the diagnosis and labelling tell you any more about it than your grandmother would have known? If not, obfuscation and inappropriate medicalizing may be involved - rather than clarification (see Note 1 above).

5. See Note 1, Chapter 12.
6. 'SAFAA' draws inspiration, in part, from Eric Berne's delineation of the 'Adult ego state', or 'Adult' for short (Berne, 1961, 1968; Whitton, 1993). However the notion of 'adult' used in SAFAA is broader than Berne's conception of the 'Adult' which is seen as: "a data processor which takes in information and decides what is probably the best course of action and when to act" (Whitton, 1993:14). The term 'adult', as I have used it, is more in line with the usage adopted by both Bill Swartley (1977) and Frank Lake (1980) and is intended to mean all that a person has of themselves present in the 'here-and-now', including feelings and empathy. That is, their ability to be 'in touch' with the present both perceptually and emotionally. Moreover it is 'adult *autonomy*' that is referred to, so it is a question of sufficient ability to be in touch with the present *and* to be self-responsible and self-directing that is involved.

    Note also that it is '*sufficient available functioning* adult autonomy' that is cited. SAFAA is not a pejorative diagnostic label but rather a functional criterion to allow for 'safer' working through appropriate discrimination. The requirement is minimal and not fixed. Someone's availability of sufficient autonomous adult functioning may vary with time and circumstances and what constitutes 'sufficient' may vary depending upon the particular type of growth work being contemplated. So, sufficient for *what* is the pertinent question. SAFAA has parallels with the notion of 'ego strength'. However, I think SAFAA is more refined, more understandable, more usable (by both practitioners *and* clients), less prone to confusion with vanity or 'willpower' than the notion of 'ego strength' - and a lot nicer!
7. The words 'heal' and 'whole' derive from the same roots in Old English (e.g. 'hǣlan'), as does 'health' (*Concise Oxford Dictionary*, 8th edn.) however I draw a distinction here between the terms 'healing' and 'wholing'. In Stanislav Grof's terms both processes are 'holotropic' ('towards wholeness') (Grof, 1985). I make the distinction merely to illustrate the difference in emphasis between human potential work and other growth work where the person concerned is *not* capable of self-regulating and

remaining responsible for their process of growth on the outer as well as the inner levels. In either case however, the activation of intrinsic, healing/wholing 'growth forces' (Kent, 1969) is involved. As far as I know 'wholing' does not exist as a word, if not, it deserves to as a useful description of the growth process, at and beyond the SAFAA level.

8. The medical model referred to is primarily an allopathic medical model based on counteracting germs, disease, or symptoms since this is the prevailing orthodoxy in the west. Disease processes can also be approached in the light of an alternative more holistic, 'homoeopathic', medical model that is less based on counteracting and suppression and rather more parallel to the growth model described here (Scheid, 1993; West, 1993). However the SAFAA criterion is not relevant to that sort of work either - it is still a 'medical model' in that sense. 'Healing' and 'wholing' can be differentiated by the SAFAA requirement in *this* area - where a growth model is applied to the realm of the psyche, but under a medical model, whether allopathic or homeopathic, SAFAA is not relevant. The 'client' is a patient in the care of the practitioner.

9. From the practitioner's point of view, indications of sufficient available functioning adult autonomy on the part of the potential client would include: an ability to function 'in the world' such as to be self-supporting, cope with a job and generally 'have a life', of some sort, 'out there' including relationships and other means of personal support; the ability to sustain strong feelings without acting them out against self or others in violent or other destructive ways; and the ability to make a commitment and to adhere to agreements, including those contracts and safety rules involved in undertaking the form of human potential work in question. In the case of some forms of work, an interview of some sort may be necessary to be sure, as best one can, that the SAFAA criterion is met.

10. 'Healer' and 'healing' are used here in a sense that corresponds more to the medical model (and also, in a sense, to some models of 'spiritual healing') whereby the healer is active and is the source of the healing (whether as a 'channel' or not) and the client is a passive recipient of the healing, rather than to the intrinsic growth forces referred to above.

11. Winnicott coined the terms 'good-enough mother' and 'not a good-enough mother' (cf. 'good mother') (Winnicott, 1960).

12. Compare the emphasis on a contractual basis for the relationship here with the status basis for the relationship engendered by officially recognized professions (see Chapter 4).

13. There is a parallel here with the 'clinical' versus 'non-clinical' distinction under a medical model, such as clinically versus non-clinically depressed. Here however the focus is on looking for the *presence* of sufficient adult functioning and autonomy rather than the *presence* of specific 'symptoms' however 'strong' or 'severe' they may be.

Chapter 26: What's in a Name?

1. Perhaps the label for a practitioner of such work could be 'transformational crisis facilitator' or 'spiritual emergency facilitator'?
2. See also Note 1, Chapter 24.
3. One also has to bear in mind the linguistic associations in other languages. For example the Italian for 'counsellor' - 'consigliere', is closely linked to its Latin root, 'consiliarius', meaning advisor. Then there is also the use of the term 'Counsel' to refer to legal advisor ...
4. Historically, the American Psychoanalytic Society was opposed to analysts without medical training. This was a position with which Freud disagreed, even though he was a doctor himself (Freud, 1926/7; Fine, 1979). As a result, psychoanalysts are more likely to be medically qualified in the US than in the UK and hence 'psychotherapist' and 'psychiatrist' are more often equated. However, there is also a considerable overlap between psychoanalysis and psychiatry in the UK (see Chapter 7).
5. In British Columbia, Canada, 'counselling' is used by the 'fringe' - 'psychologist' and 'psychotherapist' being protected titles. In New South Wales, Australia, 'therapist' is used by the fringe, whilst 'psychologist' is a protected title and 'psychotherapist' is on the whole avoided except in medical contexts. The term 'counseling' is increasingly becoming unavailable to the fringe in the USA - by 1993 over half the states had introduced statutory regulation of 'counseling' (Alberding et al., 1993:33). See also Note 2, Chapter 12 regarding counselling in Europe.
6. See Note 7, Chapter 25.
7. There are some organizations that use the term human potential as part of their title, for example IDHP (see Appendix D).
8. AHPP has a bewildering array of practitioner categories, 22 at the last count and of these, 12 are listed as 'therapist' categories and 5 as 'psychotherapist' categories (AHPP, 1993). However, there were 62 AHPP members listed on the 1993 UKCP register (UKCP, 1993g) - a majority of AHPP full members (AHPP, 1991b, 1994) and by January 1995, 73

per cent of AHPP full members were UKCP registered psychotherapists (Collis. 1995a:45). So, the 'psychotherapist' category is by far the strongest numerically. I doubt that the wide range of other categories will remain meaningful in the longer term if current trends persist.

9.   See Note 10, Chapter 23.

Chapter 27: Preserving the Fringe

1.   Psychoanalysis was at one time, especially during the 1920s and 1930s, regarded by many analysts as a social movement designed to change the world situation and applicable to all human beings: "not just neurotics" (Fine, 1979:103). "... there was broad agreement with the proposition that psychoanalysis had all of mankind as its patient" (ibid.:104).
2.   Lloyd deMause argues that a degree of splitting is mankind's common legacy of the experience of birth and prenatal existence (deMause, 1981).
3.   "The individual afflicted with the emotional plague does not content himself with a passive attitude; he is distinguished from the neurotic character by a more or less life-destructive *social activity* ..." (Reich, 1950:255).
4.   See also David Kalisch's spirited discussion of bureaucratization and professionalization (Kalisch, 1990:24).

Notes to Section III

Chapter 28: Disclosing the Alternatives

1.   'F.R.C.Psych.' - Fellow of the Royal College of Psychiatrists; 'Mb.H.R.' - Member of the Human Race.
2.   In 1994, the UK government proposed to eliminate the current exemption from licensing for herbal remedies under the UK *Medicines Act, 1968* (Steward, 1995). Once again, the finger was pointed at Europe. It was claimed that this change was necessary to 'harmonize' UK law with European law. However, this was refuted by the European Commission, which revealed that in no other country in the Community had the pertinent EC Directive been interpreted as was being done in the UK (ibid.). Thanks to a vigorous campaign, the government backed down and, for now, most herbal remedies have escaped since they are not "industrially produced" and therefore not subject to the EC Directive (Department of

Health, 1994). The origin of this pressure on herbal remedies is not clear, however the medical profession and pharmaceutical interests must be prime candidates (see also Parsons, 1994; Fulder and Monro, 1981 and Walker, 1994). At root [*sic*] the question is one of borderline distinctions between medicines and foods, the intention with which they are taken and the 'side-effects' of either. A notice in a Finchley chemist's shop asserts: "Medicines are poisons with some beneficial side-effects."

Chapter 29: Politics, Politics

1. The revision of the *Architects (Registration) Acts, 1931-1969* will provide for more public representation on the governing board and a more efficient disciplinary process (ARCUK, 1995).
2. I understand that the rule of thumb applied in government circles is that for every person who bothers to write to their MP or to a government department there are ten others who share that view.

Notes to Appendices

Appendix A: Whither the Human Potential Movement?

1. See also Postle & Anderson, 1990:13.
2. Actually, licensing is normally the function of a state psychology board, though in practice these are, more often than not, closely associated with, or influenced by, the American Psychological Association.

Appendix B: Registration in Australia

1. The *Scientology (Prohibition) Act, 1968* in South Australia was repealed in 1974 in conjunction with the introduction of the *Psychological Practices Act, 1973*. A similar scenario may apply in Western Australia.

**Appendix C: Registration in Canada
and the Case of the Crucial Conjunction**

1. There are also exemptions for those who practise in governmental, academic or school settings.

2. Compare the titular precision of the BC working environment with the broad 'catch-all' definitions common in Australian legislation that leave more discretionary power with the psychology board (see Appendix B). A related example of these legal niceties: A practitioner of Reiki (a healing art from Japan that involves work with the body) explained to me that since the practice of Reiki did not involve movement of the hands *along* the body, it was not subject to British Columbia's *Physiotherapists Act, 1979* (a practice act which also covers massage practitioners) - or so her lawyer says. Presumably the same applies to myotherapy, shiatsu, Jin Shin Do and other hands-on approaches that do not necessarily involve the: "kneading, rubbing or massaging" referred to by the Act.

Appendix D: Self and Peer Assessment

1. AHPP has now introduced the requirement of a face-to-face meeting with two members of the Membership Committee before membership is finalized (Collis, 1995a:45).
2. To broaden the appeal of the Network, particularly for those who do not refer to their work as 'therapy', proposals have been made to change its name to something more inclusive (Brown, 1994b; Fee, 1995;).

Appendix E: Psychiatry, Psychotherapy and Personal Growth

1. In the UK, a junior psychiatrist will be fully qualified to practise as a doctor (five years training plus one years internship) but is unlikely to have had any training in, or experience of, psychotherapy prior to starting to practise as a psychiatrist. A senior registrar in psychiatry will have had at least eight or nine years of professional training, including the *possibility* of some training in psychotherapy during the two to three years of 'in service' training as a psychiatrist subsequent to becoming medically qualified. A consultant psychotherapist will have had a further training in a particular psychotherapy for at least four years and hence a professional training totalling at least twelve years (Kosviner, 1994:296).
2. As mentioned in Chapter 25, many of the early promoters of the human potential movement came to it through a study of religion rather than medicine. (Swartley, 1971:2).
3. See, for example, Note 2, Chapter 8.

Bibliography

Access to Health Records Act, 1990. London: HMSO.

Alberding, Beverly; Lauver, Philip and Patnoe, Jerry. "Counselor Awareness of the Consequences of Certification and Licensure." *Journal of Counseling & Development,* Vol. 72 (Sept. 1993): pp. 33-38.

American Psychiatric Association. *Quick Reference to the Diagnostic Criteria from DSM-IV.* Washington DC.: American Psychiatric Association, 1994.

'Anderson Report'. *The Report of the Board of Inquiry into Scientology.* chaired by Kevin Victor Anderson, QC for the Legislative Council of the Australian State of Victoria, 1965. [Quoted in Foster, 1971.]

Appleyard, Bryan. *Understanding the Present.* London: Pan, 1992.

[ARCUK] Architects Registration Council of the United Kingdom, personal communication, Feb. 1995.

[AHP(B)] Association for Humanistic Psychology in Britain. The AHPP Position. statement, 1989.

_____ . "Constitution." Apr. 1992.

_____ . "Membership List No. 1." 1994.

[AHPP] Association of Humanistic Psychology Practitioners. "The AHPP Page: Registration and Training." *Self and Society,* Vol. 19 No. 2 (Mar. 1991a).

_____ . "Membership Directory." 1991b.

_____ . "Category Guide and Psychotherapist Category Note." Dec. 1993.

_____ . "Additions & Amendments to AHPP Membership Directory." leaflet, Mar. 1994.

_____ . "Application for AHPP Full Membership." 1994b.

[ASPPB] The Association of State and Provincial Psychology Boards. *Handbook of Licensing and Certification Requirements for Psychologists in North America.* Montgomery, Alabama, Jan. 1994a.

_____ . "Entry Requirements for Professional Practice of Psychology." leaflet, Montgomery, Alabama, 1994b.

Auerbach, A. A. and Johnson, M. "Research on the Therapist's Level of Experience." in Gurman, A. S. and Razin, A. M. (eds.) *Effective Psychotherapy.* Oxford: Pergamon Press, 1977.

Austin, Kenneth M.; Moline, Mary E. and Williams, George T. *Confronting Malpractice: Legal and Ethical Dilemmas in Psychotherapy.* Newbury Park, California: Sage Publications, 1990.

Aveline, Mark. "The Training and Supervision of Individual Therapists." in Dryden, 1990.

Barkham, Michael. "Research in Individual Therapy." in Dryden, 1990.

Baron, Judith. "In the Manager's Chair." *Counselling: The Journal of the British Association for Counselling*, Vol. 5 No. 1 (Feb. 1994).

Benne, Kenneth D. [Foreword to Hogan, Vol. 1, 1979.]

Bennett, Adrianne, Executive Director of the Australian Psychological Society, personal communication, 14 Jan. 1994.

Bennett, Catherine. "Lend Me Your Ears." *Guardian*, 5 May 1994.

Berke, Joseph H. *I Haven't Had to Go Mad Here*. Harmondsworth: Penguin, 1979.

Berman, Jeffrey S. and Norton, Nicholas C. "Does Professional Training Make a Therapist More Effective?" *Psychological Bulletin*, Vol. 94 No. 2 (1985).

Berne, Eric. *Transactional Analysis in Psychotherapy*. New York: Grove Press, 1961.

____ . *Games People Play*. Harmondsworth: Penguin, 1968. (Original 1964.)

Boadella, David. *Wilhelm Reich - The Evolution of his Work*. London: Vision Press, 1973.

____ . "Organism and Organisation: The Place of Somatic Psychotherapy in Society." *Energy and Character* (Special Edition), Vol. 22 (Aug. 1991).

Bond, Tim. *Standards and Ethics for Counselling in Action*. London: Sage Publications, 1993.

Bordin, E. S. "The Generalizability of the Psychoanalytic Concept of the Working Alliance." *Psychotherapy, Theory, Research and Practice*. Vol. 16 No. 3 (1979): pp. 252-260. [Cited in Russell, 1981/1993.]

Brammer, Laurence M. and Shostrum, Everatt L. *Therapeutic Psychology - Fundamentals of Counselling and Psychotherapy*. New Jersey: Prentice Hall, 1982. [Cited in Bond, 1993.]

Breggin, Peter. *Toxic Psychiatry*. New York: St. Martin's Press, 1991. (The U.K. edition published by Fontana, 1993, includes an introduction and additional notes on the British context by Dorothy Rowe.)

[BAC] British Association for Counselling. "Code of Ethics and Practice for Counsellors." Rugby, 1992.

BBC Radio 4. *The World This Weekend*, 28 Feb. 1993a.

____ . *The Food Programme*. EC legal commentator, 26 Apr. 1993b.

____ . news bulletin, Feb. 1994a.

____ . *File on Four*, 28 June 1994b.

____ . *Science Now*. discussion on 'scientific heretics', 4 July 1994c.

____ . *File on Four*, 5 July 1994d.

____ . *The World this Weekend*, 14 Aug. 1994e.

[BCP] British Confederation of Psychotherapists. "Response from the BCP." (Letter to the Editor.) *British Journal of Psychotherapy*, Vol. 10 No. 1 (1994).

British Medical Association. *Medical Ethics Today*. London, 1993.

Bibliography

[BPS] British Psychological Society. *Bulletin of the British Psychological Society.* Jan. 1984.
_____ . "Summary of the BPS November 1990 Policy Statement on Psychological Therapy Services." [Reprinted in *Self and Society*, Vol. 19 No. 2 (Mar. 1991).
_____ . "Guide and Index to the Directory of Chartered Psychologists." Leicester, Nov. 1993a.
_____ . "Chartered Psychologists." leaflet, Leicester, Nov. 1993b.
_____ . general information leaflet, Leicester, Nov. 1993c.
_____ . "Broad Areas in which Chartered Psychologists Offer Services." Leicester, Feb. 1995.
Bromberger, Brian and Fife-Yeomans, Jane. *Deep Sleep - Harry Bailey and the Scandal of Chelmsford.* East Roseville, N S W: Simon & Schuster, 1991.
Brown, Juliana, personal communication, 1994a.
_____ . Letter to the Independent Therapists Network, 18 Dec. 1994b.
Brown, Juliana and Mowbray, Richard. "Whither the Human Potential Movement?" *Self and Society*, Vol. 18 No. 4 (Jul. 1990). [Included as Appendix A.]
_____ . review article of Grof, Stanislav and Grof, Christina. *The Stormy Search for the Self.* in *Self and Society*, Vol. 19 No. 5 (Sept. 1991).
_____ . "Primal Integration." in Jones, David (ed.) *Innovative Therapy - A Handbook.* Buckingham: Open University Press, 1994a.
_____ . "NVQs, UKCP and the XYZ of ABC." *Self and Society*, Vol. 22 No. 5 (Nov. 1994b). [Appears as: "No They Don't!"]
Bugental, J. F. *The Search for Authenticity.* New York: Holt, Rinehart & Winston, 1965. [Cited in Maslow, 1971.]
Bundesverwaltungsgericht. Urteil vom 21, Januar 1993; Az.: 3 C34/90 = NJW 1993, S.2395.
Burgess, Marolyn. "Proposed Changes to the Structure of the Association for Humanistic Psychology in Britain." letter to AHP(B) members, 1 Feb. 1994.
Busfield, J. *Managing Madness.* London: Hutchinson, 1986. [Cited in Pilgrim, 1990.]
Bynum, W. F. "Rationales for Therapy in British Psychiatry." *Medical History.* Vol. 18 (1974): pp. 39-45. [Cited in Pilgrim, 1990.]
California Assembly Permanent Subcommittee on Mental Health and Developmental Disabilities *Improving California's Mental Health System: Policy Findings and Reccommendations.* Jan. 1979. [Quoted in Schutz, 1979.]
Callala Beach Emporium and Off-Licence, notice outside, Jan. 1994.
Canadian Psychological Association. *Provincial Registration Requirements for the Practice of Psychology in Canada*, Ottawa, Mar. 1994a.
_____ . personal communication, 13 Sept 1994b.
Cannon, Cal and Hatfield, Sue. "Some Thoughts after the 2nd National Confer-

273

ence on the Dynamics of Accreditation, Cambridge, June 1992." *Self and Society*, Vol. 20 No. 4 (July-Dec. 1992): pp. 28-34.

Capra, Fritjof. *The Tao of Physics*. London: Wildwood House, 1975.

Carlin, J. E. *Lawyers' Ethics: A Survey of the New York City Bar*. New York: Russell Sage Foundation, 1966. [Quoted in Hogan, Vol. 1, 1979.]

Carlson, Rick J. *The End of Medicine*. New York: Wiley, 1975.

'Centipede'. *Guardian*, 18 Mar. 1993.

Charity Commissioners for England and Wales. *Political Activities and Campaigning by Charities: Revised Guidelines by the Charity Commission*. CC9. Charity Commission, Mar. 1994

Church of Scientology. *Kangaroo Court - An Investigation into the Conduct of the Board of Inquiry into Scientology*. Victoria, Australia, 1967. [Quoted in Foster, 1971.]

Clark, Richard and Pinchuck, Tony. *Medicine for Beginners*. London: Writers and Readers Publishing Cooperative, 1984.

Clarkson, Petruska. "The Nature and Range of Psychotherapy." in Clarkson and Pokorny, 1994.

Clarkson, Petruska and Pokorny, Michael (eds.) *The Handbook of Psychotherapy*. London: Routledge, 1994.

Cohen, Kenneth. "Some Legal Issues in Counselling and Psychotherapy." *British Journal of Guidance and Counselling*, Vol. 20 No. 1 (Jan. 1992).

Collins, R. *The Credential Society*. New York: Academic Press, 1979.

Collis, Whiz. "AHPP Page." *Self and Society*, Vol. 22 No. 4 (Sept. 1994a).

____ . "European Conference: A Peaceful Revolution for Health Care in Europe." report for AHPP, 1994b.

____ . "The AHPP Page." *Self and Society*, Vol. 22 No. 6 (Jan. 1995a).

____ . "The AHPP Page." *Self and Society*, Vol. 23 No. 1 (Mar. 1995b).

Combs, A. W. "Problems and Definitions in Legislation." *American Psychologist*, Vol. 8 (1953): pp. 554-63. [Quoted in Hogan, Vol. 1, 1979.]

Commission of the European Communities. *Mutual Recognition of Professional Qualifications in the European Community*. document 111/D/2 NP/3.90.

Consortium for the Advancement of Diversified Programs in Psychology [CADPP], 1989. [Quoted in O'Hara, 1989.]

Consultants at Work. "Report on Psychotherapy Feasibility Study." London, Jul. 1993.

Cooper, C. L. "Coping with Life Stress After Sensitivity Training." *Psychological Reports*, Vol. 31 (1972): p. 602. [Quoted in Hogan, Vol. 1, 1979.]

Cottingham, H. F. "Some Broader Perspectives on Credentialling Counseling Psychologists." *The Counseling Psychologist*, Vol. 9 (1980): pp. 19-21.

Counsellor Training Institute, Vancouver, Canada, personal communication from the director of the Institute, 13 Sept. 1994.

Cummins, R. A. "The Victorian Psychologists Bill 1984." *Bulletin of the Australian Psychological Society*, Mar. 1986: p. 13.

Cuthbert, M. *E.C. Law*. London: Sweet & Maxwell, 1994.

Daily Mail. "Comment: The Vulnerable." 10 Apr. 1993.

Danish Ministry of Health, personal communication, 20 Apr. 1995.

Danish, S. J. and Smyer, M. A. "The Unintended Consequences of Requiring a License to Help." *American Psychologist*. Vol. 36 (1981): pp. 13-21.

Davis, J. W. "Counselor Licensure: Overkill?" *The Personnel and Guidance* Journal, Vol. 60 (1981): pp. 83-85.

Davis, Margaret. review of Whyld, Janie. *NVQs and the Assessment of Interpersonal Skills*. in *Self and Society*, Vol. 23 No. 1 (Mar. 1995).

deMause, Lloyd. "Fetal Origins of History." *The Journal of Psychohistory*, Vol. 9 No. 1 (Summer 1981). [Reprinted in deMause. *Foundations of Psychohistory*. New York: Creative Roots Inc., 1982.]

Department of Health. "Position of Herbal Medicines Safeguarded Confirms Tom Sackville." press release, 11 Nov. 1994.

Deurzen-Smith, Emmy van, UKCP chair 1993-5. [Quoted in Pepinster, 1993.]

Dewees, Donald N. (ed.) *The Regulation of Quality: Products, Services, Workplaces, and the Environment*. Toronto: Butterworths, 1982.

Dobson, Roger. "Increase in 'False Memory' Insurance." *Independent on Sunday*, 12 Feb. 1995.

Dror, Miriam, "Letter to the Editor." *Self and Society*, Vol. 18 No. 1 (Jan. 1990).

Drury, Nevill. *The Elements of Human Potential*. Shaftsbury: Element Books, 1989.

Dryden, Windy (ed.) *Individual Therapy: A Handbook*. Buckingham: Open University Press, 1990.

Dryden, Windy. "Approaches to Individual Therapy: Some Comparative Reflections." in Dryden, 1990.

Dryden, Windy and Feltham, Colin (eds.) *Psychotherapy and its Discontents*. Buckingham: Open University Press, 1992.

Eales, Mike. "Self and Peer Assessment and Accreditation." *Self and Society*, Vol. 19 No. 4 (Jul. 1991).

Easton R. H.; Carr, R. J.; and Whitely, J. M. "Issues in the Encounter Group Movement." *Counseling Psychologist*, Vol. 3 No. 2 (1972): pp. 89-120. [Quoted in Hogan, Vol. 1, 1979.]

Eisenhammer, John. "Germany's East Wind of Change." *Independent on Sunday*, 25 Apr. 1993.

Ekstein, Rudolph and Wallerstein, Robert S. *The Teaching and Learning of Psychotherapy*. New York: Basic Books, 1958. [Quoted in Masson, 1988.]

Eliade, Mircea. *Shamanism: Archaic Techniques of Ecstasy.* New York: Pantheon, 1964. (Original, Paris, 1951.)

European Commission, DG 15/E/2 personal communication, Nov. 1993.

____ . personal communication, Feb. 1995.

European File. "The European Community and Recognition of Diplomas for Professional Purposes." Brussels: Commission of the European Communities, Directorate-General for Information, Communication and Culture, Oct. 1989.

European Parliament. "Psychotherapy in the European Communities (Outline)." document, 26 Nov. 1993.

Evans, Ken. "My Cynicism Took Quite a Knock." interview with the President of the European Association for Psychotherapy. *UKCP Newsletter* No. 2, Apr. 1994.

Fanning, Alexandra; Pokorny, Michael and Hargaden Helena. "Psychotherapy in Private Practice." in Clarkson and Pokorny, 1994.

Fee, Mary. "The Independent Therapists Network." article in press, to appear in *Self and Society* in 1995.

Feltham, Colin and Dryden, Windy. *Dictionary of Counselling.* London: Whurr Publishers, 1993.

Fine, Reuben. *A History of Psychoanalysis.* New York: Columbia University Press, 1979.

Focus: The Magazine of Discovery. "The Far-out World of Cults." London, Feb. 1995a.

____ . "One Small Secret of the Universe." London, Feb. 1995b.

Forrester, Andrew, letter, 22 Nov. 1994.

Foster, John G. *Enquiry into the Practice and Effects of Scientology.* House of Commons Report 52, London: HMSO, Dec. 1971.

Freely, Maureen. "Mysterious Power of the Age of Unreason." *Guardian*, 6 Oct. 1994.

Freidson, Eliot. *Profession of Medicine: A Study of the Sociology of Applied Knowledge.* New York: Dodd Mead & Co., 1972: p. 382. [Quoted in Masson, 1988.]

Fretz, B. R. and Mills, D. H. "Professional Certification in Counseling Psychology." *The Counseling Psychologist.* Vol. 9 (1980): pp. 2-17.

Freud, Sigmund. *The Ego and the Id.* Standard Edition, Vol. 19. London: Hogarth Press. (Original 1923.) [Cited in Kline, 1992.]

____ . *The Question of Lay Analysis.* Standard Edition, Vol. 19. London: Hogarth Press. (Original 1926, postscript 1927. page numbers from the Norton edition, New York, 1950.)

____ . *New Introductory Lectures on Psychoanalysis,* Standard Edition, Vol. 22, London: Hogarth Press. (Original 1933. page numbers from the Pelican edition, London, 1973.)

___ . *Analysis Terminable and Interminable.* Standard Edition, Vol. 23. London: Hogarth Press. (Original 1937.)

___ . "The Psychotherapy of Hysteria." in Freud, Sigmund and Breuer, Josef. *Studies on Hysteria.* Standard Edition, Vol 2. London: Hogarth Press. (Original 1893-1895. page numbers from the Pelican edition, London,1974.)

Fromm, Erich. *The Fear of Freedom.* London: Kegan Paul, 1942.

Fulder, Stephen and Monro, Robin. *The Status of Complimentary Medicine in the United Kingdom.* London: The Threshold Foundation, 1981. See also: Fulder, Stephen. *A Handbook of Complimentary Medicine.* Wellingborough: Thorsons, 1983.

Gale, Derek. *What is Psychotherapy? - A Personal and Practical Guide.* Loughton, Essex: Gale Centre Publications, 1989.

___ . "Derek Gale Interviews Peter Rutter." *Self and Society,* Vol. 18 No. 3 (May 1990).

Garrett, Tanya. "Sexual Contact between Psychotherapists and their Patients." in Clarkson and Pokorny, 1994.

General Medical Council. *Professional Conduct and Discipline: Fitness to Practice.* pamphlet ['Blue Book']. London: General Medical Council, 1991.

Gerty, F. J.; Holloway, J. W. and MacKay, R. P. "Licensure or Certification of Clinical Psychologists." *Journal of the American Medical Association,* Vol. 148, 1952: pp. 271-73. [Quoted in Hogan, Vol. 1, 1979.]

Gill, S. J. "Professional Disclosure and Consumer Protection in Counseling." *The Personnel and Guidance Journal,* Vol. 60 (1982): pp. 443-446.

Gladstone, Guy. "Conference Afterthoughts." *Self and Society,* Vol. 22 No. 6 (Jan. 1995).

Goode, W. J. "Encroachment, Charlatanism, and the Emerging Profession: Psychology, Sociology and Medicine." *American Sociological Review,* Vol. 25 (1960): pp. 902-914. [Quoted in Hogan, Vol. 1, 1979: p. 231.]

'A Government Source'. "The EEC Directive on Higher Education Diplomas: Effect on The Alternative Professions and Complementary Therapies." *Self and Society,* Vol. 18 No. 1 (Jan. 1990).

Grant, J. A. C. "The Guild Returns to America: Part 1." *Journal of Politics,* Vol. 4 (1942): pp. 303-336. [Quoted in Hogan, Vol. 1, 1979.]

Grof, Stanislav. *Beyond the Brain.* Albany, New York: State University of New York Press, 1985.

___ . *The Adventure of Self Discovery.* New York: State University of New York Press, 1988a.

___ . response to personal question, 1988b.

Grof, Stanislav and Grof, Christina. *Spiritual Emergency.* Los Angeles: Jeremy P. Tarcher/Perigee, 1989.

____ . *The Stormy Search for the Self.* London: Mandala, 1991.

Gross, S. J. "Professional Disclosure: Alternative to Licensing." *The Personnel and Guidance Journal,* Vol. 55 (1977): pp. 586-588.

____ . "The Myth of Professional Licensing." *American Psychologist,* Vol. 33 (1978): pp. 1009-1016.

Guardian. "Profession Lacks Control." 10 Apr. 1993.

Gwyther, Matthew. "Doctors in Disgrace." *Observer,* 11 Oct. 1992.

Hall, Celia. "Therapists Seek Laws on Sex with Patients." *Independent,* 5 Apr. 1993.

Hall, Jill. "Letter to the Editor: Jill Hall replies to John Rowan *(Self and Society,* May/June 1991)." *Self and Society,* Vol. 19 No. 5 (Sept. 1991).

____ . "Conference on Accreditation at the Cambridge Graduate Centre, September 27th, 1991." *Self and Society,* Vol. 20 No. 4 (May 1992).

Ham & High. "Government Refuses to Act on Register of Psychotherapists." London, 28 May 1993.

Hampden-Turner, Charles. *Radical Man.* USA: Schenkman, 1970.

Harnad, Stevan. "The Warp Factor." *Guardian* , 23 Feb. 1995.

Harner, Michael. *The Way of the Shaman.* New York: Harper & Row, 1980.

Harris, Myles. *Magic in the Surgery.* Research Report 20. London: The Social Affairs Unit, 1994.

Hawkins, Peter. "Humanistic Psychotherapy Supervision: A Conceptual Framework." *Self and Society,* Vol. 13 No. 2 (Mar. 1985).

____ . "Registration of Psychotherapists - Whither, Why and How." *Self and Society,* Vol. 18 No. 1 (Jan. 1990).

____ . "A Response to John Heron, David Kalisch and Roger Horrocks." *Self and Society,* Vol. 18. No. 4 (Jul. 1990).

Hawkins, Peter and Shohet, Robin. *Supervision in the Helping Professions.* Buckingham: Open University Press, 1989.

Health Professions Act, 1990. SBC1990, c. 50. Victoria, BC: Crown Publications, 15 Nov. 1990. (British Columbia, Canada).

Heron, John. *Co-Counselling Teachers' Manual.* London: British Postgraduate Medical Federation,1978.

____ . "The Politics of Transference." *Self and Society,* Vol. 18 No. 1 (Jan. 1990).

Hogan, Daniel B. *The Regulation of Psychotherapists,* 4 Vols. Cambridge, Massachusetts: Ballinger, 1979.

____ . "A Position Statement on Licensing Counsellors and Psychotherapists." Cambridge, Massachusetts: Department of Psychology and Social Relations, Harvard University. Published in *American Psychological Association Division of Community Psychology Newsletter,* (Special Issue) Vol. 12 No. 3 (Summer 1979): pp. 9&11-12.

____ . "The Impact of Professional Certification on Counseling Psychology." *The Counseling Psychologist*. Vol. 9 (1980): pp. 29-43.

Holmes, Jeremy and Lindley, Richard. *The Values of Psychotherapy*. Oxford: Oxford University Press, 1989.

Hopkinson, Kate. "The Origins and Birth of the IDHP." *Self and Society*, Vol. 19 No. 4 (Jul. 1991).

Horrocks, Roger. "Letter to the Editor." *Self and Society*, Vol. 18 No. 2 (Mar. 1990).

House, Richard. "Conference Reports - A Tale of Two Conferences." *Self and Society*, Vol. 20 No. 4 (July-Dec. 1992).

House, Richard and Hall, Jill. "Peer Accreditation ... Within a Humanistic Framework?" *Self and Society*, Vol. 19 No. 2 (Mar. 1991).

Hubbard, L. Ron. *Dianetics: the Modern Science of Mental Health*. Los Angeles: The Church of Scientology, 1950.

____ . "Attacks on Scientology (Continued)." Hubbard Communications Office Policy Letter of 18 February 1966. [Quoted in Foster, 1971: p. 139.]

Illich, Ivan. *Deschooling Society*. London: Calder & Boyars, 1971.

Illman, John. "Catching Up with the Charlatans of the Couch." *Guardian*, 25 May 1993.

Independent. "Therapy That Women Can Do Without." leading article, 6 Apr. 1993.

Independent Therapists Network. "Founding Conference of the Independent Therapists Network." publicity leaflet, Apr. 1994.

Inglis, Brian. *Natural Medicine*. London: Fontana, 1980.

Ingram, Catherine. "The Pundit of Transpersonal Psychology." *Yoga Journal*, Berkeley, California, Issue 76 (Sept. 1987): p. 49.

Jackins, H. *The Human Side of Human Beings*. Seattle, Washington: Rational Island, 1965.

Jameson, E. *The Natural History of Quackery*. London: Michael Joseph, 1961.

Jelfs, Martin. "The AHPP Page." *Self and Society*, Vol. 20 No. 1 (Jan. 1992).

Jervey, H. E., Jr. "A Survey of Medical Discipline." *Federation Bulletin,* Vol. 48 (1961): pp. 83-95.

Jones, David. "Editorial: The Registration of Psychotherapists." *Self and Society*, Vol. 18 No. 1 (Jan. 1990).

____ . "Registration of Psychotherapists." *Self and Society*, Vol. 19 No. 1 (Jan. 1991a).

____ . "Editorial." *Self and Society*, Vol. 19 No. 4 (Jul. 1991b).

____ . "Editorial: European Parliament 1992." *Self and Society*, Vol. 20 No. 1 (Jan. 1992).

____ . "Editorial." *Self and Society*, Vol. 22 No. 1 (Mar. 1994).

Kadushin, A. *Supervision in Social Work*. New York: Columbia University Press, 1976.

Kalisch, David. "Professionalization - A Rebel View." *Self and Society*, Vol. 18 No. 1 (Jan. 1990).

Kardener, S. H.; Fuller, M.; and Mensh, I. N. "A Survey of Physicians' Attitudes and Practices Regarding Erotic and Nonerotic Contact with Patients." *American Journal of Psychiatry*, Vol. 130 (1973): pp. 1077-81. [Quoted in Hogan, Vol. 1, 1979.]

Kelley, Charles. *The Radix Teaching Profession and the Law*. The Radix Institute, 1985. [Available from the author at 13715 SE 36th St., Steamboat Landing, Vancouver, WA 98684 USA.]

____ . "Radix and Psychotherapy." *Chuck Kelley's Radix Newsletter*, Issue No. 3 (August 1989). [Available from the author - see above.]

____ . *Personal Growth and Psychotherapy in Radix Work*. booklet, 1991a. [Available from the author - see above.]

____ . "Personal Growth and Psychotherapy in Radix Work." *Chuck Kelley's Radix Newsletter*, Issue No. 8 (Spring 1991b). [Available from the author - see above.]

Kent, Caron. *The Puzzled Body*. London: Vision Press, 1969.

Kett, J. F. *The Formation of the American Medical Profession, 1780-1860*. New Haven, Connecticut: Yale University Press, 1968.

Kline, Paul. "Problems of Methodology in Studies of Psychotherapy." in Dryden and Feltham, 1992.

Koocher, G. "Credentialling in Psychology: Close Encounters with Competence?" *American Psychologist*, Vol. 34 (1979): pp. 696-702.

Korzybski, A. *Science and Sanity: An Introduction to Non-Aristotelian Systems and General Semantics*. Lakeville, Connecticut: The International Non- Aristotelian Library Publishing Company, 1933.

Kosviner, Adele. "Psychotherapists within the NHS." in Clarkson and Pokorny, 1994.

Kramer, Dr. Edwin, Registrar of the College of Psychologists of British Columbia, personal communication, 14 Sept. 1994.

Lake, Frank, personal communication, 1980.

Lawson, Max. "Growing Up Lightly: Rascal-Gurus and American Educational Thought." *Educational Philosophy and Theory*, Vol. 20 No. 1 (1988).

Leifer, R. *In the Name of Mental Health: Social Functions of Psychiatry*. New York: Science House, 1969. [Quoted in Hogan, Vol. 1, 1979.]

Lieberman, J. K. *The Tyranny of the Experts: How Professionals are Closing the Open Society*. New York: Walker, 1970. [Quoted in Hogan, Vol. 1, 1979.]

____ . *Crisis at the Bar: Lawyers' Unethical Ethics and What to do About It*. New

York: W. W. Norton, 1978. [Cited by Hogan, Vol. 1, 1979.]

Lindner, Robert. "The Problem of Medical and Lay Psychotherapy: Who Shall Practice Psychotherapy?" *American Journal of Psychotherapy*, Vol. 4 (1950): pp. 432-42. [Quoted in Hogan, Vol. 1, 1979.]

Lippitt, R. L.; Benne, K. D.; Bradford, L. and Gibb, J. "The Professionalization of Laboratory Practice." 1975. In Benne, K. D.; Bradford, L.; Gibb, J. and Lippitt R. L. (eds.) *The Laboratory Method of Changing and Learning: Theory and Applications*. Palo Alto, California: Science and Behaviour Books, 1975: pp. 471-90. [Quoted in Hogan, Vol. 1, 1979.]

Lister-Ford, Christine and Pokorny, Michael. "Individual Adult Psychotherapy." in Clarkson and Pokorny, 1994.

Lonie, Isla. "The Burning Fiery Furnace: Psychotherapy Research - Scientific Method or Scientific Trial?" *Australian Journal of Psychotherapy*, Vol. 10 No. 2 (1991a).

_____ . "Chaos Theory: A New Paradigm for Psychotherapy?" *Australian and New Zealand Journal of Psychiatry*, Vol. 25 (1991b): pp. 548-560.

Macklin, R. "The Medical Model in Psychoanalysis and Psychotherapy." *Comprehensive Psychiatry*, Vol. 14, 1973: pp. 49-69 [Quoted in Hogan, Vol. 1, 1979: p. 15.]

Maclean Matheson, Sheena and Sylvester, Richard. "Letter to the Editor." *Self and Society*, Vol. 21 No. 6 (Jan. 1994).

_____ . "The Training and Accreditation of Psychotherapists and Counsellors." *Self and Society*, Vol. 20 No. 3 (May 1992).

Malan, David H. *Individual Psychotherapy and the Science of Psychodynamics*. London: Butterworths, 1979. [Quoted in Rowan, 1983: p. 12.]

Maslow, Abraham H. *Toward a Psychology of Being*. New York: Litton Educational Publishing - Van Nostrand Reinhold Company, 1968.

_____ . *The Further Reaches of Human Nature*. New York: The Viking Press, 1971.

Masson, Jeffrey. *The Assault on Truth: Freud and Child Sexual Abuse*. New York: Farrar, Straus and Giroux, Inc., 1984.

_____ . *Against Therapy*. USA: Atheneum, 1988: p. 294.

_____ . *Final Analysis*. USA: Addison-Wesley, 1990.

_____ . "The Tyranny of Psychotherapy." in Dryden and Feltham, 1992.

McGrath, Susan. "Gurus or Self-Help?" *Nature and Health*, Australia, Vol. 5 No. 5 (1984).

Medawar, Charles. *Power and Dependence*. London: Social Audit, 1992. [Cited in Breggin, 1991/1993.]

Meir, C. A. *Ancient Incubation and Modern Psychotherapy*. Evanston, USA: Northwestern University Press, 1967. (Original 1949.)

Meltzer, M. L. "Insurance Reimbursement: A Mixed Blessing?" *American Psy-*

chologist, Vol. 62 (1975): pp. 1150-1156.

Morrison, Helen, Director, Health Professions Council, Victoria, British Columbia, Canada, personal communication, 14 Sept. 1994.

Morstyn, R. "Quantum Metaphors in Deep Psychotherapy." *Australian and New
Zealand Journal of Psychiatry*, Vol. 23 (1989): pp. 483-490. [Quoted in Lonie,
1991b.]

Mowbray, Richard. "Primal Integration at the Open Centre." *Self and Society*, Vol.
18 No. 3 (May 1990).

____ . "The Death of the Human Potential Movement?" (Letter to the Editor.) *Self
and Society*, Vol. 22 No. 2 (May 1994).

[NCC] National Consumer Council. Letter to the Department of the Environment
from NCC Chairperson Lady Wilcox, 13 Sept. 1994.

Official Journal of the European Communities. "Council Directive 89/48/EEC."
L19 Vol. 32 (24 Jan. 1989): p. 17.

O'Hara, Maureen. "Alert! Alert! Alert! American Psychological Association Seeks
to Control Practice of Psychology." *Journal of Humanistic Psychology*, 1989.

O'Neill, Aidan and Coppel, Jason. *EC Law for UK Lawyers: The Domestic Impact of EC Law within the UK*. London: Butterworths, 1994.

Ontario College of Psychologists, personal communication, 13 Sept 1994.

O'Sullivan, Jack. "Scalpel to Blunt an Axe." *Independent on Sunday*, 10 July 1994.

Pagliaro, Louis A. "Better Living Through Drugs." *Psynopsis*, Ottawa: Canadian
Psychological Association, Summer 1994: p. 14.

Palmer, Caroline. "Cult of the Personality Test." *Observer*, 9 Oct. 1994.

Parloff, M. B. "Group Therapy and the Small-Group Field - An Encounter." *International Journal of Group Psychotherapy*, Vol. 20 (1970): pp. 267-304.
[Quoted in Hogan, Vol. 1, 1979.]

Parsons, Talcott. "Professions." in D. L. Sills (ed.) *International Encyclopedia of
the Social Sciences*, Vol. 12. New York: Macmillan, 1968: pp. 536-47. [Quoted
in Hogan, Vol. 1, 1979.]

____ . "Illness and the Role of the Physician." In Kluckhorn, C. and Murray, H.
(eds.) *Personality in Nature, Society and Culture*. New York: Knopf, 1953.

Parsons, Tony. "Letter from the Editors." *London & South East Connection*. Issue
No. 10 (Dec. 1994):2.

Pedder, Dr. Jonathan. [Quoted by Sinason, 1994.]

Pepinster, Catherine. "Presence of Mind." *Time Out*, 19-26 May, 1993.

Percy, Margaret. "Ruthless Adventure: The Lives of L. Ron Hubbard." BBC Radio 4, 30 Nov. 1987.

Perry, John Weir. *The Far Side of Madness*. Englewood Cliffs, New Jersey: Prentice-
Hall, 1974.

Pfeffer, Jeffrey. "Administrative Regulation and Licensing: Social Problem or

Solution?" *Social Problems*, Vol. 21 (1974): pp. 468-79. [Quoted in Hogan, Vol. 1, 1979.]

Phillips, Andrew. *Charitable Status: A Practical Handbook*. London: Inter-Action, 1979: p. 46.

Physiotherapists Act, 1979. RS1979 c. 327. Victoria, BC: Crown Publications, 15 Nov. 1990. (British Columbia, Canada).

Pilgrim, David. "Psychologists and Psychopathy." *Bulletin of the British Psychological Society*. Vol. 40, (1987): pp. 168-71. [Cited in Pilgrim, 1990.]

___ . "British Psychotherapy in Context." in Dryden, 1990.

Podvoll, Edward M. *The Seduction of Madness*. New York: HarperCollins, 1990.

Pokorny, Michael R. "United Kingdom Standing Conference for Psychotherapy: A Proposal to Establish a Register of Psychotherapists." paper on behalf of the Council of UKSCP, 10 July 1990.

___ . "The United Kingdom Standing Conference for Psychotherapy (UKSCP) - The Psychotherapy Register." *Self and Society*, Vol. 20 No. 4 (July-Dec. 1992).

___ . "Structure of the United Kingdom Council for Psychotherapy and List of its Member Organizations." in Clarkson and Pokorny, 1994.

Pope, Kenneth. S. and Bouhoutsos, Jacqueline. C. *Sexual Intimacy between Therapists and Patients*. New York: Praeger, 1986.

Postle, Denis and Anderson, Jill. "Stealing the Flame." *Self and Society*, Vol. 18 No. 1 (Jan. 1990).

Prince Charles. [Reported in Sinason, 1994.]

Psychological Practices Act, 1965. No. 7355. (Victoria, Australia).

Psychological Practices Act, 1973. No. 37. (South Australia).

Psychologists Act, 1977. No. 15. (Queensland, Australia).

Psychologists Act, 1979. RS1979, c. 342. Victoria, BC: Crown Publications, 10 Nov. 1992. (British Columbia, Canada).

Psychologists Act, 1989 No. 51. (New South Wales, Australia).

Psychologists Registration Act, 1976. (Western Australia).

Psychology Today, New York: Sussex Publishers Inc., Nov/Dec 1993: p. 17.

The Psychotherapy Centre. "A Statutory Register of Psychotherapists? Factors for and Against and the Position Now." 4th edn., London, 1992.

Raimy, V. C. (ed.) *Training in Clinical Psychology*. New York: Prentice Hall, 1950. [Quoted in Hogan, Vol. 2, 1979: p. 2.]

Rawson, P., in *Counselling: Journal of the British Association for Counselling*, May 1993. [Referred to by Rowan, 26 Nov. 1993a.]

Rayack, E. *Professional Power and American Medicine: The Economics of the American Medical Association*. Cleveland, Ohio: World Publishing Co., 1967. [Quoted in Hogan, Vol. 1, 1979: p. 330.]

___ . *An Economic Analysis of Occupational Licensure*. unpublished manuscript,

US Department of Labour, Manpower Administration, 1975. [Cited by Hogan, Vol. 1, 1979: p. 263.]

Reeves, Phil. "Did Someone Play Tricks on Holly's Mind?" *Independent*, 22 April 1994.

Reich, Wilhelm. *Character Analysis*. 3rd edn., London: Vision Press, 1950. (1st edn. 1933.)

____ . *The Mass Psychology of Fascism*. 4th edn., London: Souvenir Press, 1972. (1st edn.1933.)

Reiff, R. "The Control of Knowledge: The Power of the Helping Professions." *The Journal of Applied Behavioural Science*, Vol. 10 (1974): pp. 451-461.

Richards, Joscelyn, Chair of the Council of Institutions of the British Confederation of Psychotherapists. "Update. February, 1994."

Richman, David; Frank, Leonard and Mandler, Art. *Dr. Cagliari's Psychiatric Drugs*. 3rd edn. Berkeley: Network Against Psychiatric Assault, 1987.

Rogers, Carl R. "Some New Challenges." *American Psychologist*, Vol. 28 (May 1973): pp. 379-387. [Quoted in Russell, 1981/1993.]

Rose, Steven. "Mean Gene Streak." *Guardian*, 2 June 1994.

Rottenberg, S. (ed.) Introduction. *Occupational Licensure and Regulation*. Washington, DC: American Enterprise Institute for Public Policy Research, 1980.

Rowan, John. *The Reality Game: A Guide to Humanistic Counselling and Therapy*. London: Routledge & Kegan Paul, 1983.

____ . *Ordinary Ecstasy*. 2nd edn. London: Routledge, 1988. (1st edn. 1976.)

____ . "Accreditation." *Self and Society*, Vol. 19 No. 3 (May 1991).

____ . "What is Humanistic Psychotherapy?" *British Journal of Psychotherapy*, Vol. 9 No. 1 (1992a): pp. 74-83.

____ . "Response [to Katharine Mair]." in Dryden and Feltham, 1992b: pp. 160-166.

____ . "BAC 1993." 26 Nov. 1993a.

____ . "Note on Competence Statements by Lead Body." 26 Nov. 1993b.

____ . "The UKCP 1993." 26 Nov. 1993c.

____ . personal note, 17 Mar. 1994.

[RCP] Royal College of Psychiatrists. supplement to the *British Journal of Psychiatry*, Jul. 1972. [Quoted in the Sieghart Report, 1978.]

____ . personal communcation, 3 April 1995.

Russell, Roberta. *Report on Effective Psychotherapy: Legislative Testimony*. Lake Placid, New York: Hilgarth Press, 1981 (with 1993 update).

____ . "Laing & Me: Lessons in Love." *Human Potential*, Vol. 2000 minus 27 (Summer 1993).

____ . "Alliances Extend Life." *London & South East Connection*. Issue No. 9 (Aug. 1994):26.

Rutter, Peter. *Sex In The Forbidden Zone*. USA: Jeremy P. Tarcher, 1989.
Sarbin, T. R. "The Scientific Status of the Mental Illness Metaphor." in S. C. Plog and R. B. Edgerton (eds.) *Changing Perspectives in Mental Illness*. New York: Holt, Rinehart and Winston, 1969: pp. 9-31. [Quoted in Hogan, Vol. 1, 1979.]
Sarson, Richard. "Great Paper Chase." *Guardian*, 3 Mar. 1994.
Scheff, Thomas J. "The Labelling Theory of Mental Illness." *American Sociological Review*, Vol. 39 (1974): p. 444.
Scheid, Volker. "Orientalism Revisited: Reflections on Scholarship, Research, and Professionalization." *European Journal of Oriental Medicine*, Vol. 1 No. 2 (Autumn 1993).
Schutz, B. M. *Legal Liability in Psychotherapy*. San Francisco, California: Jossey-Bass, 1982. [Cited in Austin et al., 1990.]
Schutz, Will. *Profound Simplicity*. USA: Joy Press, 1979.
Schwarz, Oswald. *The Psychology of Sex*. London: Pelican, 1951. [Cited in Maslow, 1968 & 1971.]
Scull, A. *Decarceration*. Englewood Cliffs, New Jersey: Prentice-Hall, 1977. [Cited in Pilgrim, 1990.]
____ . *Museums of Madness*. London: Allen Lane, 1979. [Cited in Pilgrim, 1990.]
Self and Society. "Accreditation." Vol. 18 No. 4 (Jul. 1990).
____ . Foreword to "Summary of the BPS November 1990 Policy Statement on Psychological Therapy Services." Vol. 19 No. 2 (Mar. 1991).
____ . "Are Therapists Dentists?" Vol. 20 No. 4 (July-Dec. 1992): pp. 46-47.
____ . "The AHPP Page - News from the UKCP Conference." Vol. 22 No. 1 (Mar. 1994): p. 42.
Sharaf, Myron R. *Fury on Earth: A Biography of Wilhelm Reich*. London: Andre Deutsch, 1983.
Shohet, Robin. "A Group Begins to Tackle Accreditation." *Self and Society*, Vol. 18 No. 1 (Jan. 1990).
Shohet, Robin; Wilmot, Joan; Adeline, Elizabeth; Hall, Jill; Page, Steve. "Peer Group Accreditation of Psychotherapists." *Self and Society*, Vol. 19 No. 2 (Mar. 1991).
Sieghart, Paul. *Statutory Registration of Psychotherapists: The Report of a Profession's Joint Working Party*. London: Copyright Paul Sieghart in trust for the professional bodies that composed the working party, 1978.
Sinason, Valerie. "A Standard Practice." *Guardian*, 12 Mar. 1994.
Slovenko, Ralph. [Series foreword to Hogan, 1979: p. xvii.]
____ . "Legal Issues in Psychotherapy Supervision." in Hess, A. K. (ed.) *Psychotherapy Supervision*. New York: John Wiley, 1980. [Cited in Austin et al., 1990.]

Smail, David. "Psychotherapy and Psychology" in Pilgrim, David (ed.) *Psychology and Psychotherapy: Current Trends and Issues*. London: Routledge and Kegan Paul, 1983.

_____ . *Illusion and Reality*. London: Dent, 1984. [Cited in Kline, 1992.]

_____ . *Taking Care: an Alternative to Therapy*. London: Dent, 1987.

Smith, Deborah. "Does Therapy Work?" *Sydney Morning Herald*, 1 June 1993: p. 12.

Stevens, John O. and Stevens, Barry. Introduction to Stevens, John O. (ed.) *Gestalt Is*. Moab, Utah: Real People Press, 1975.

Steward, Christine. "A Pinch of Herbs." *Kindred Spirit*, Vol. 3 No. 6 (Spring 1995).

Striano, Judi. *Can Psychotherapists Hurt You?* Santa Barbara, California: Professional Press, 1988.

Swartley, William. "Defining the Status of a Patient." transcript of a presentation given at Hahnemann Medical College and Hospital Symposium: The Encounter Movement and Psychiatry, 16 June 1971.

_____ . "Primal Integration." Philadelphia: Centre for the Whole Person, 1975. [Reprinted in *Self and Society* Vol. 15 No. 4 (Jul. 1987).]

_____ . personal communication, 1977.

_____ . Introduction to *The Undivided Self*. Rowan, John and Holme, Ken (eds.) London: The Churchill Centre, 1978.

Swiss Embassy, London, personal communication, 5 Apr. 1995.

Szasz, Thomas S. *The Myth of Mental Illness: Foundations of a Theory of Personal Conduct*. New York: Dell Publishing Co., 1961.

_____ . *The Ethics of Psychoanalysis*. London: Routledge & Kegan Paul, 1974. (Original: USA, 1965.)

Taft, Jesse. *The Dynamics of Therapy in a Controlled Relationship*. New York: Dover Publications, 1962. (Original 1933.)

Tantam, Digby and Rickard, Ian. "The Boundary between Counselling and Psychotherapy: Comments on the 1992 Annual Conference of the British Association of Counselling and on the plans for an Advice, Guidance, and Counselling Lead Body." paper, 5 Sept. 1992.

Taylor, Noel Leigh. *Doctors and the Law*. London: The Law Society with Oyez Publishing, 1976.

Thompson, Andrew. *Guide to Ethical Practice in Psychotherapy*. New York: John Wiley & Sons, 1990.

Thorne, Brian. "Person-Centred Therapy." in Dryden, 1990.

_____ . "The Accountable Therapist: Standards, Experts and Poisoning the Well." paper consisting of extracts from a lecture delivered at the annual general meeting of the Ashby Trust, 1991.

_____ . "Psychotherapy and Counselling: The Quest for Differences." *Counselling:*

Bibliography

Journal of the British Association for Counselling, Vol. 3 No. 4, (1992). [Cited in Bond, 1993.]
Tilden, Elizabeth. interviewed in *All in the Mind*, BBC Radio 4, 26 Oct. 1994.
Times. "Reassuring the Patient." leading article, 10 Apr. 1993.
Totton, Nick. "Therapists on the Couch." *i to i*, July-Sept. 1992.
____ . "Letter to the Editor." *Self and Society*, Vol. 21 No. 6 (Jan. 1994a): p. 47.
____ . "A Proposed Structure for the ITN." paper distributed at the Founding Conference of the Independent Therapists' Network in London, Nov. 1994b.
____ . "Independent Therapists Network Founding Conference: A Personal View." *Self and Society*, Vol. 22 No. 6 (Jan 1995).
Townsend, C., in *Counselling: Journal of the British Association for Counselling*, Nov. 1993. [Referred to by Rowan, 26 Nov. 1993a.]
Trebilcock, Michael J. "Regulating Service Quality in Professional Markets." in Dewees, 1982.
Trebilcock, Michael J. and Shaul, Jeffrey. "Regulating the Quality of Psychotherapeutic Services." in Dewees, 1982.
[UKCP] United Kingdom Council for Psychotherapy. "Constitution." Jan. 1993a.
____ . explanatory leaflet and list of member organisations, Jan. 1993b.
____ . Training Standards Committee. "Entry Requirements, Curriculum Contents and Requirements of Training Courses." 4 Mar. 1993c.
____ . "Ethical Guidelines." 5 Mar. 1993d.
____ . "Ethical Guidelines." revised, 27 Mar. 1993e.
____ . *Directory of Member Organisations: General Information and Training Courses.* London, May 1993f.
____ . *National Register of Psychotherapists.* London, Jul. 1993g.
____ . *Newsletter*, No. 1, Jul. 1993h.
____ . "Mid-Year Report." 20 Sept. 1993i.
____ . "Criteria and Guidelines for Membership of the Humanistic and Integrative Section of the United Kingdom Council for Psychotherapy." 25 Oct. 1993j.
____ . *Newsletter*, No. 2, Apr. 1994.
[UKSCP] United Kingdom Standing Conference for Psychotherapy. letter, Nov. 1990.
____ . preface to *Directory of Member Organisations: General Information and Training Courses.* Rugby, Sept. 1992.
Wade, Shirley. "Psychotherapy as a Profession." *Self and Society*, Vol. 18 No. 5 (Sept. 1990).
Walker, Martin. *Dirty Medicine.* London: Slingshot Publications, 1994.
Warne E.J.D. *Review of the Architects (Registration) Acts 1931-1969.* London: HMSO, Feb. 1993.
Wasdell, David. "In the Shadow of Accreditation." *Self and Society*, Vol. 20 No. 1 (Jan. 1992).

287

West, Ruth. "What is Alternative Medicine?" in *The A-Z of Alternative Medicine*. London: Abercorn Hill Associates, 1993.

Whitton, Eric. *What is Transactional Analysis - A Personal and Practical Guide*. Loughton, Essex: Gale Centre Publications, 1993.

Wibberley, Michael, personal communication, April 1994a.

_____ . "Marathon Groups Then and Now." *Self and Society*, Vol. 22 No. 2 (May 1994b). Reprinted in *Human Potential*, Vol. 2000 minus 21 (Winter 1994). [An earlier version of the article appeared in *The Open Centre Programme*, Winter/Spring 1994.]

Wilshire, David, MP, interview on *The World at One*. BBC Radio 4, 20 Apr. 1993.

Wilson, Jenifer Elton and Barkham, Michael. in Clarkson and Pokorny, 1994.

Winborn, B. B. "Honest Labelling and Other Procedures for the Protection of Consumers of Counseling." *The Personnel and Guidance Journal*, Vol. 56 (1978): pp. 206-209.

Wingate, Peter. *The Penguin Medical Encyclopedia*. Harmondsworth: Penguin, 1972.

Winnicott, D.W. "Ego Distortion in Terms of True and False Self." (1960) in Winnicott, D.W. *The Maturational Process and the Facilitating Environment*. London: The Hogarth Press, 1965.

Witmer, J. M. "Professional Disclosure in Licensure." *Counselor Education and Supervision*, Vol. 18 (1978): 71-78.

Wood, G. *The Myth of Neurosis*. London: Macmillan, 1983.

Wylie, Kate, personal communication, 11 Oct. 1993.

_____ . letter, May 1994.

Yeo, Tim. Speech for PS(C) - 20 May 1993 - United Kingdom Council for Psychotherapy. Department of Health, CM01719.05.

Young, Courtenay. "1992 And All That!" *Self and Society*, Vol. 18 No. 1 (Jan. 1990).

_____ . "Don't Cry Wolf." *Self and Society*, Vol. 19 No. 1 (Jan. 1991).

_____ . "Report of the Cambridge Conference." *Self and Society*, Vol. 20 No. 4 (July-Dec. 1992).

Ziehl, Silke, personal communication, 22 Apr. 1994a.

_____ . personal communication, May 1994b.

_____ . "In Praise of Supervision." *Bodymind World News and Research Report*, Vol. 5 No. 1 (Fall1994c) [published by the International Centre for Release and Integration, 450 Hillside Avenue, Mill Valley, California, USA 94941.]

Index

Index

European Community/Union (EC/EU)
Document 3.90. 25, 251
European Community/Union (EC/EU) 3,
20, 21, 25, 26, 73, 76, 250, 253. *See
also* European Commission
Directives 76, 250, 268
indirect regulation in 146, 251, 256–
257
Mutual Recognition Directive 89/48/
EEC 22, 23, 24, 251, 253
diplomas and 24, 116, 252
Regulations 251
sectoral directives 23, 24, 251
criteria for 25
European File 24
European internal market 20, 24, 27, 251
European legislation 72, 73
as 'stalking horse' 26
herbal remedies and 268
European Parliament 26, 146, 253, 254,
255
evaluation forms 209
Evans, Ken 252, 254, 257
exploitation. *See* abuse. *See* harm

F

facilitation/facilitator. *See* human potential
work/practice; personal growth
work/facilitation
titles & meanings 190, 191
false memory implantation/syndrome 1,
114, 131, 148, 153, 154
false self 219
family therapy 15
'family values' policy 63
Fanning, Alexandra 247
Fascism 200, 259, 260
fear of freedom 130, 214, 259
Fee, Mary 270
Feltham, Colin 94, 96, 259
Fife-Yeomans, Janet 229
Fine, Reuben 267, 268
Finland 253, 254

Florida 112
Focus 130, 243
Forbidden Science 199
Forrester, Andrew 262
Foster Report 14, 17, 35, 36, 38, 39, 41,
42, 43, 44, 47, 58, 69, 83, 93, 106,
126, 128, 129, 194
and lay membership 58
Foster, Sir John. *See* Foster Report
France 254, 256
Frank, Jerome 123
Frank, Leonard 243
Franks, Cyril M. 107
Freidson, Eliot 28
Freud, Sigmund 11, 93, 102, 128, 131,
153, 180, 185, 203, 242, 257, 267
Fromm, Erich 259
Fulder, Stephen 269
full disclosure 2, 165, 203, 205–209, 216,
218, 225–226. *See also* consumer
and practitioner organizations 208

G

Gale, Derek 50, 51, 259
Garrett, Tanya 112, 204, 259
General Medical Council (UK) 30, 80–
81, 82, 83
Germany 27, 66, 255, 256
Gerty, F. J. et al. 97
Gestalt Centre 161, 261
gestalt therapy/therapist 66, 128, 161
Gladstone, Guy 135
good-enough adult 184, 211
Goode, W. J. 31
grandfather/parent clause 43, 219
Grant, J. A. C. 33
Grawe, Klaus 122
Greece 255, 256
grievance procedures. *See* complaints &
disciplinary procedures
Grof, Christina 187, 189, 212
Grof, Stanislav 102, 128, 144, 178, 179,
180, 183, 187, 189, 212, 264, 265
Gross, S. J. 78, 88, 206